The 10 Key Campaigns of the American Revolution

THE 10 KEY CAMPAIGNS

of the

AMERICAN REVOLUTION

Edited by

EDWARD G. LENGEL

REGNERY
HISTORY

Regnery History™ is a trademark of Salem Communications Holding Corporation
Regnery® is a registered trademark of Salem Communications Holding Corporation

ISBN: 978-1-68451-125-9
eISBN: 978-1-68451-126-6
Library of Congress Control Number: 2020935845

Published in the United States by
Regnery History, an imprint of
Regnery Publishing
A Division of Salem Media Group
300 New Jersey Ave NW
Washington, DC 20001
www.RegneryHistory.com

Manufactured in the United States of America

10 9 8 7 6 5 4 3 2 1

Books are available in quantity for promotional or premium use. For information on discounts and terms, please visit our website: www.Regnery.com.

To our ancestors

Contents

Editorial Note

BY EDWARD G. LENGEL

It's hard to believe that just a couple of generations ago the best single treatment of the Revolutionary War was Christopher Ward's two-volume treatise, *The War of the Revolution*, published in 1952. We have come a long way since then. Over the past twenty years several broad studies of the war have appeared in print; at the time of this writing, Pulitzer Prize–winning historian Rick Atkinson has finished the first volume in his new trilogy about the Revolutionary War and is well into the research for his second—relying in part upon expert assistance from the authors of some of the essays in the book you now hold in your hands.

The American War for Independence remains—now, nearly 250 years since its onset—a relatively new field of study. Historians are exploring parts of it for the first time. Shocking as it may seem, many of the war's campaigns and battles have become the subjects of book-length treatments only over the past several years. Some, incredibly, remain largely ignored to this very day. Fortunately, this generation is blessed by the emergence of a new phalanx of dedicated and talented Revolutionary War historians determined to fill the outstanding gaps in our understanding of the war that created the United States of America.

This book, *The 10 Key Campaigns of the American Revolution*, represents some of the best new work and keenest insights on the Revolutionary War. In it, the war's leading historians look closely at the campaigns that paved the way to victory in the quest for American independence. This is history in the truest sense—carefully researched, clearly described, and best of all told with a storyteller's instinct for high drama and excitement. For the story of America's founding is dramatic, indeed—one of the most dramatic stories ever told.

Glenn Williams, one of America's leading military historians and the author of books on Lord Dunmore's War and General John Sullivan's 1777 campaign against the Iroquois, leads off with the story of the shots that echoed 'round the world in April 1775 at Lexington and Concord, Massachusetts. What began as a parade for British redcoats against what they assumed would be negligible opposition became a humiliating rout at the hands of American minutemen, inspiring confidence in thousands of their countrymen that they held the power to determine their own destiny.

Mark Anderson, the author of several books on Canada's crucial role in the Revolutionary War, follows up with one of the conflict's most exciting campaigns: Benedict Arnold's campaign to Quebec in the fall and winter of 1775–1776. Never, perhaps, has there been a more thoroughly quixotic military campaign in the annals of North American history; and yet, Arnold and his fellow adventurers very nearly pulled it off. The adventure ended in disaster, however; and as historian Todd Braisted describes in his gripping account of the struggle for Long Island and Manhattan in the summer of 1776, it was followed by an equally devastating series of defeats that lost New York City to British occupation and nearly ended the Revolution before it even began in earnest. And yet it was here, in these dark times, that the Declaration of Independence marked the birth of a new nation.

And the turnaround was not long in coming. William L. "Larry" Kidder, author of the new book *Ten Crucial Days*, takes us along with George Washington's half-frozen soldiers as they leave bloody footprints in the snow on the way to their world-shaking victories at Trenton and

Princeton in the winter of 1776–1777. Never in military history, perhaps, have such numerically small engagements had such wide-ranging implications. On a much larger scale, as Professor James Kirby Martin explains to us in his exciting study of General John Burgoyne's campaign into Upstate New York in the fall of 1777, the British defeat and surrender at Saratoga marked a strategic victory of epic proportions, wrecking British hopes of occupying the Hudson River corridor and inciting France to intervene in the war on behalf of American independence.

Still, victory was not to be easily won, as George Washington and his soldiers learned to their sorrow in the brutal Philadelphia campaign of August–December 1777. Michael C. Harris, the author of important new books on the under-studied battles of Brandywine and Germantown, tells the story of how the American commander in chief nearly lost everything—including his own position—in a series of defeats that culminated in the British occupation of Philadelphia and the Delaware River corridor and led to the traumatic winter encampment at Valley Forge. Incredibly, though, Washington's magnificent leadership ensured that the Continental Army would emerge from these horrendous trials even stronger than before.

Until very recently, no serious study of the June 1778 Battle of Monmouth had ever been written. Professor Mark Lender and Garry Wheeler Stone put that to rights with their seminal 2017 work *Fatal Sunday*, demonstrating—as Lender does again here in his essay for this volume—that the battle's impact, following on the British evacuation of Philadelphia thanks to French intervention in the war, was magnified by Washington's ability to "spin" it as a victory that confirmed his own leadership and inspired hope for ultimate victory. Washington, a man who famously lost more battles than he won but eventually achieved victory in the Revolutionary War, understood that the conflict was above all a contest for American hearts and minds.

Nowhere was this truer than in the war in the South, which is the subject of the final three essays in this volume. John "Jack" Buchanan, author of the first—and what remain the best—full studies of the southern campaigns, shows how American fortunes in this theater swung from what seemed total defeat at the surrender of Charleston, South Carolina, in May 1780, to smashing victory at the Battle of Kings Mountain in October of that same year. Historian John Maass, author of several important books on the culminating battles of the southern campaigns, continues the story with his stirring account of the Battle of Cowpens in January 1781 and the Battle of Guilford Courthouse two months later. Together, these two battles sealed the fate of British general Charles Lord Cornwallis's southern army and led directly to the war's final dramatic campaign.

Robert Selig concludes this survey of the Revolutionary War's ten key campaigns with his account of the long, grueling, and ultimately bloody land–sea campaign that concluded with the siege and surrender of Yorktown, Virginia, in October 1781. The story is one of inspired leadership characterized by vital strategic decision-making, careful logistical preparation, collaboration between unlikely allies, bravery in battle on land and at sea, and, finally, plain good luck—as Napoleon Bonaparte quipped, the most important ally of all great generals. In many ways, though, Washington and Rochambeau's victory at Yorktown marked the culmination of all that had gone before—of ten key campaigns that ultimately put the seal on American independence.

Taken as a whole, *The 10 Key Campaigns of the American Revolution* encompasses a human drama of epic proportions. At different points in time, at locations separated by hundreds and often thousands of miles, individuals—often the unlikeliest imaginable—took destiny in their hands and accomplished astonishing things that profoundly changed the course of human history. Their deeds should be—and thanks to this book, they are—unforgettable.

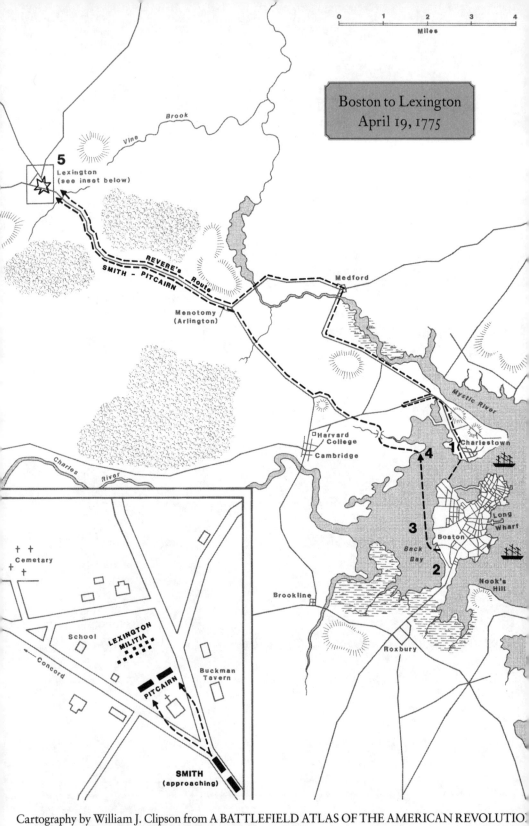

Boston to Lexington
April 19, 1775

Cartography by William J. Clipson from A BATTLEFIELD ATLAS OF THE AMERICAN REVOLUTIO
published by Savas Beatie, www.savasbeatie.com

Let It Begin Here

BY GLENN F. WILLIAMS, PH.D.

On April 19, 1775, few on either side of the Atlantic realized that Great Britain and its American colonies stood on the brink of a war that would lead to the establishment of a free and independent American republic. American colonists had been petitioning King George III and the Parliament for redress of grievances without satisfaction. As the king's American subjects resisted each new law they perceived as arbitrary and a threat to the liberties guaranteed by the constitution of Great Britain, the government in London reacted by imposing ever harsher measures. Resistance to unjust laws became open rebellion when six companies of British light infantry marched into Lexington, Massachusetts, and formed a line of battle on the village green facing members of the local militia company. According to tradition, Captain John Parker told the men of his company, "Stand your ground. Don't fire unless fired upon, but if they mean to have a war, let it begin here." Within minutes, shots were fired, and Americans were killed.

The several colonies, in sympathy with Massachusetts Bay, convened the First Continental Congress to coordinate their mutual support and collective resistance to the Coercive Acts, and they formed the Continental Association to implement its resolutions. When Lieutenant General

Thomas Gage, commander in chief of His Majesty's forces in North America as well as royal governor of Massachusetts, dissolved the Massachusetts House of Representatives, the members met in Concord to establish the extralegal Provincial Congress, a shadow government that effectively exercised actual authority outside of Boston. It ordered the towns to stop collecting taxes for the royal government and to forward those funds to the Provincial Congress instead. The shadow government developed a new plan for the militia and ordered the gathering of munitions and military supplies for an "Army of Observation" as it began preparing for a potential armed conflict with the "ministerial forces." Among its significant acts was the establishment of a select militia.

All free males in the colony between the ages of sixteen and sixty were required to perform military training as members of the militia and mustered for training at least once annually, or more often under certain circumstances. The colony encouraged all the militia units to "obtain the skill of complete soldiers" by training more often. With political tensions in the colony rising, the congress formed a select militia directly under the authority of its executive Committee of Safety, leaving the regular militia under the counties. Consisting of one quarter of the total force, this select militia recruited younger, physically fit, preferably single, and enthusiastic Whigs. They were armed and accoutered and paid to attend frequent and rigorous training assemblies, at public expense. Organized into companies, battalions, and regiments, they were required to assemble and deploy anywhere in the colony at a minute's notice, and hence were called "minutemen."

After the British government declared the Massachusetts Bay Colony in a state of rebellion, General Gage had to act. He developed a plan to send a column of his best troops on a swift march to Concord to seize the gunpowder, military stores, and fourteen cannon that his informants reported to be stored there for use against the Crown's forces. Having already ordered his regiments occupying Boston to increase their training activities, he hoped the Americans would assume the expedition to be another in a series of such exercises. As it was not unusual for officers to ride horses into the surrounding country for pleasure and physical exercise, Gage instructed them to use the excursions for gathering intelligence. The seizure of the military stores gathered at Concord had become a military necessity as well as a legal requirement. The general wanted the people of other colonies to view his move as a preemptive strike at troublemaking radicals who had broken the law, not an act of aggression against the king's American subjects. He ardently hoped that the judicious use of military force sent to strike the head of the rebellion in Concord might suppress patriots with a single, hopefully bloodless, stroke.

On April 15, of the thirteen infantry regiments in Boston, Gage ordered the commanders of the Fourth, Fifth, Tenth, Eighteenth, Twenty-Third, Thirty-Eighth, Forty-Third, Forty-Seventh, Fifty-Second, and Fifty-Ninth Regiments of Foot to detach their grenadier and light infantry companies and Major John Pitcairn, the commander of the attached First Battalion, British Marines, to provide one company of marines as well. The twenty-one companies, about seven hundred men total, were relieved from routine camp duties purportedly to participate in special training exercises from the new drill manual. Gage selected the senior regimental commander, Lieutenant Colonel Francis Smith of the Tenth Regiment of Foot, to command the expedition, with Pitcairn, the most senior officer of that rank in Boston, as his second-in-command.

The general presented Smith with written orders "to seize and destroy all Artillery, Ammunition, Provisions, Tents, Small Arms, and all Military Stores whatever" found collected at Concord "for the Avowed Purpose of raising and supporting a Rebellion against His Majesty." To accomplish his mission, Smith's expedition was to march "with the utmost expedition and Secrecy" from Boston to Concord, a distance of about twenty miles. The soldiers were to be under the strictest discipline and expressly forbidden to "plunder the Inhabitants, or hurt private property." Gage provided Smith with a map that showed the "Houses, Barns, &c." where the military supplies were placed. The soldiers were to spike and knock a trunnion off each gun they found and destroy the carriages. All barrels of gunpowder and flour were to be emptied into the river, all tents burned, pork and beef destroyed. The soldiers were to put as many musket balls into their pockets as they could, throwing all they could not carry into "Ponds, Ditches &c.," but scattered so as not to be easily recovered.[1]

As the preparations progressed, Gage sent "a small party on Horseback," consisting of ten officers and ten sergeants, with orders to prevent any patriot express riders leaving Boston from alerting the militia along the way or patriot leaders in Concord before Smith's men got there. The general requested his Royal Navy counterpart, Vice Admiral Samuel Graves, commanding the North American Station, to provide sailors and ships' boats from the warships moored in the harbor to move the troops from the city to Lechmere Point, on the north bank of Back Bay of the Charles River. From there they could march into the interior without parading through Boston and alerting the patriot informants. Despite the attempted secrecy, the patriot Sons of Liberty in Boston soon guessed what was afoot and sent a message of warning to Concord, where the Provincial Congress was then meeting. The congress immediately adjourned on April 15.

On the evening of April 18, the light infantry, grenadiers, and marines were ordered out of their barracks, which were at several locations in the city, and marched to an assembly area at the common near the bank of the Charles River. At about 9:30 p.m., they began boarding the boats. When it was discovered that the navy had not allocated enough boats, only about half of the troops and supplies embarked. The rest waited idle for about two hours while the boats made the round trip to Lechmere Point. The second half of the troops did not disembark on the far shore until midnight. The British wasted more time in arranging the order of march, getting the light infantry companies to the head of the column, trudging through the marshy ground, and waiting for the provisions to be brought ashore. When Smith finally gave the order to march, high tide flooded the marsh. The troops had to wade through water that in some places had risen to a depth of three feet for about a quarter-mile before they reached the bridge over Willis Creek and a good dry road. Preceded by an advance party of several mounted officers and a Loyalist civilian guide, who acted as scouts and detained colonists found on the road who might spread the alarm and alert the militia, the column was finally marching toward Lexington by 1:30 a.m.

At dusk, while the British troops were still at the common, a member of Lexington's militia company observed one of Gage's mounted patrols and informed Orderly Sergeant William Munroe, who was also the proprietor of Munroe's Tavern. Believing the patrol had come to arrest patriot leaders John Hancock and John Adams, who were staying at the nearby home of Reverend Jonas Clarke, Munroe mounted a nine-man guard at the parsonage. The sergeant also sent a messenger to alert Captain Parker and ordered three men to follow the patrol when it continued toward Concord. The captain immediately ordered the company to muster. The meeting house bell rang the alarm and within about thirty minutes, or at about 1:00 a.m., 130 men of Lexington's militia company stood in ranks on the green, a two-acre triangle of public land in the center of town. After a short deliberation with the other officers, Parker determined that they should not provoke the regulars if they approached, "even should they insult us." After they fired a volley to clear their weapons, Parker dismissed the men. Some of the men returned to their homes, but others went into Buckman's Tavern just across the road.[2]

Gage's plan had become an open secret; only the details of the operation were unknown. Doctor Joseph Warren, leader of the Sons of Liberty, activated the patriots' warning system and alerted express riders Paul Revere and William Dawes to spread the alarm with the assistance of fellow "Liberty Boys" in Boston, Cambridge, and Charlestown. Two compatriots rowed Revere across to Charlestown, carefully avoiding the British ship of the line *Somerset* moored near the ferry way. Provided with a strong horse, he waited for the signal on the steeple of Christ Church, also called Old North Church, that was to tell him the British were being ferried across Back Bay, not marching out via the Boston Neck. Although aware that the British were watching to intercept alarm riders, Warren also sent Dawes to Lexington by the alternate route, by land across Boston Neck. Other riders stood ready to fan out should Revere and Dawes be stopped, to make sure Adams and Hancock were warned. Dawes passed the guard post on the Neck without incident, and both riders arrived at Reverend Clarke's before Smith's troops had left Lechmere Point. After speaking with Adams and Hancock, Revere and Dawes remounted their horses and were soon riding toward Concord.

When they had only two more miles to go, one of the British mounted patrols surprised and captured Revere and Dawes as well as Doctor Samuel Prescott, an ardent patriot who met them as he returned home from visiting his fiancée in Concord. Their captors forced them into a nearby pasture for questioning. Prescott agreed to help Revere and Dawes spread the alarm. On a signal, Prescott and Revere spurred the horses, riding in opposite directions, while Dawes turned and galloped back toward Lexington. Prescott and Dawes managed to outrun their pursuers, but Revere was recaptured. When threatened with summary execution unless he divulged the patriots' plans, he told them he had alarmed the country and five hundred militiamen now stood between them and Boston. He added that the boats transporting Smith's men had run aground, and they should not expect any help. The patrol retreated, but when they heard musketry, unaware it was Parker's men clearing unspent cartridges, the officers thought it inadvisable to pass around Lexington. After commandeering Revere's horse to replace the tired mount of a sergeant, they released Revere and the three militiamen Munroe sent to shadow them whom they had captured. Revere immediately returned to Clarke's parsonage to inform Hancock and Adams of what had transpired.

In the meantime, the column of British troops continued toward Lexington as church bells and muskets shots sounded the alarm in their various towns. They had lost the element of surprise. The advance party encountered more traffic on the road than they expected to find in the predawn hours. Farmers heading to market in Boston were detained, and three militiamen Captain Parker had sent to scout the road to Boston were captured and sent back to Pitcairn and Smith for questioning.

It was now 3:00 a.m., and the column had not yet reached Lexington, nor had the militia been alerted. Smith sent Pitcairn marching ahead with the six leading companies of light infantry to get into Lexington quickly. As the detachment drew closer to town and the officers observed armed men watching from the high ground, Pitcairn ordered out flankers as a precaution against ambush. He gave the command for the troops to load their muskets, but cautioned them not to fire unless ordered to do so.

The Lexington Company of militia had reassembled after scouts reported the British were only a few miles away and approaching fast. Parker ordered the company drummer, sixteen-year-old William Diamond, to beat "To Arms," and the company began to assemble near the northwest corner of the two-acre triangular common, facing the fork in the road from Boston. About seventy men were standing in the ranks when the first British company appeared, with the sound of drums and fifes, at about 5:00 a.m. Other militiamen were still on their way, and several spectators stood along the boundaries of the green or watched from their homes.

The light infantry formed into line of battle facing the militia as Major Pitcairn approached, accompanied by the officers of the advance party. Waving his sword as his horse cantered toward them, Pitcairn ordered the militiamen, "Lay down your arms." Other officers shouted, "Disperse, ye rebels!" and "Surrender!" Parker faced about and "immediately ordered our Militia to disperse and not to fire." As they broke ranks and slowly started heading home carrying their weapons, Pitcairn ordered his men "not to fire, but to surround and disarm them!" As the light infantrymen advanced a shot was fired by an unknown gunman. Regardless of who fired, the shot confirmed the suspicions men on either side had about their opponents. With a shout, the regulars "rushed furiously, fired upon and killed eight of our party with out receiving any provocation therefor from us," according to Parker.

The British soldiers then went about their work with the bayonet while their officers desperately attempted to bring them under discipline. The company officers were just restoring order when Lieutenant Colonel Smith rode into the chaotic scene. He ordered a drummer to beat "To Arms," at which the soldiers ceased firing and formed back into their ranks. The lieutenant colonel rebuked them for their lack of discipline and ignoring their officers' commands. After about ten minutes, the rest of the British column arrived. After giving three cheers and firing a volley to signal their "victory," the march to Concord resumed at about 5:30 a.m. One British soldier had been wounded in the leg, and Major Pitcairn's horse had been hit by two musket balls. Four Lexington militia soldiers lay dead or mortally wounded on the green, with another four dead nearby. Ten more wounded militiamen limped or staggered to safety.[3]

With the British marching toward their town, the people of Concoord, although unaware of the deadly encounter at Lexington, worked feverishly to hide the ammunition, ordnance, and other military stores that had been gathered in the neighborhood. Around dawn, Colonel James Barrett, who commanded the local militia regiment, alerted the two companies each of militia and minutemen to muster at the Wright Tavern in the center of town. The minuteman company from Lincoln soon arrived, bringing the news of a confrontation in Lexington. Shortly thereafter, a scout returned to report that the regulars had fired on Parker's company and were heading in their direction. Barrett ordered Captain David Brown and his minuteman company to advance along to the road junction at Meriam's Corner and for Captains Nathan Barrett and George Minot to advance theirs along the ridge parallel to the road to guard his flank. The colonel ordered the remaining companies to the crest of the high ground above the town's burial ground, which was on the same ridge, vainly hoping the British were under orders not to engage if opposed by militia.

When the British advance guard saw the minutemen in the road ahead at Meriam's Corner and the companies on the ridge, Smith had the light infantry deploy to the flank on the high ground. As ordered, the outnumbered minutemen on the ridge retreated. When the grenadiers and marines resumed marching, Captain Brown's minutemen faced about smartly and marched off in good military order in front of them, remaining so close that they fell into step with the cadence of the British drums. When the three companies had returned, Colonel Barrett ordered his men to withdraw to high ground four hundred yards to the north of town.

The first British troops entered Concord at about 7:00 a.m. As the light infantry descended from the ridge to join their comrades in town, they cut down Concord's "Liberty Pole." Lieutenant Colonel Smith was pleased that his expedition had reached Concord without further incident and ordered his men to find and destroy all the military supplies and equipment hidden in Concord. He sent one light infantry company to secure the South Bridge over the Sudbury River, and ordered Captain Lawrence Parsons of the Tenth Regiment to lead seven light infantry companies to the North Bridge. From there he would detach three companies to secure his line of retreat in the event of trouble and with the other four advance two miles to the Barrett farm, where spies reported some cannons and military supplies were stored.

Since the British outnumbered his 250 men, at about 8:00 a.m. Barrett ordered his men to retreat across the bridge to Punkatasset Hill, the high ground a mile west of town on the west side of the Concord River, to wait for reinforcements. The colonel placed Major John Buttrick of the minuteman battalion in temporary command and then raced to make certain the weapons and supplies at his farm were well concealed before Parsons arrived. Major Buttrick divided the troops into two battalions, with the minuteman companies on the right and militia companies on the left. As more arrived, they would fall in with their respective battalions. He also appointed Lieutenant Joseph Hosmer to serve as the acting adjutant to assist in forming the ad hoc brigade. Buttrick then commanded the troops to advance to a lower hill closer to the west bank of the river that served as the local muster field.

Meanwhile, Smith and Pitcairn stayed in the center of town to maintain control as the grenadiers and marines went about the task they had been sent to accomplish, ensuring that they took no untoward liberties with private property or local citizens. The soldiers succeeded in finding and disabling some cannons. Artillery carriages, tents, cartridge paper, and entrenching tools were collected into piles and set on fire. Barrels of musket balls and flour were thrown into the millpond—but much of it was later recovered by the patriots. Other sacks of flour and the chest that contained the treasury of the Provincial Congress went unmolested when the colonists convinced the soldiers they were private property. When sparks from the burning military items ignited a fire on the roofs of the townhouse (courthouse) and other nearby buildings, Mrs. Martha Moulton demanded that British officers order their men to extinguish the flames before they caused any destruction.

Back at the North Bridge, Captain Walter S. Laurie of the Forty-Third Regiment, the officer in charge of the light infantry companies detached to secure the span, watched nervously as more companies joined the American force on the hill above him, only about four hundred yards away. The captains of the other two companies saw them as well and thought it prudent to leave their forward positions and rejoin Laurie's men at the bridge. After conferring with his fellow officers there, Laurie sent a subordinate to inform Lieutenant Colonel Smith of the developing situation and request reinforcements. That officer returned with the news that reinforcements were on their way. Laurie then had the three companies take a defensive stance on the east bank of the river, where they could still guard the bridge and allow Parsons's men to cross.

Colonel Barrett returned at about 9:00 a.m. to learn his force had been reinforced to six minuteman and five militia companies, or about five hundred men. Having now learned of the bloodshed at Lexington, the militiamen were looking to avenge their neighbors. Barrett conferred with Major

Buttrick and Lieutenant Colonel John Robinson, second-in-command of a minuteman regiment that was still marching to Concord, to decide their next move. Tradition holds that when he saw the smoke rising from the burning wood, canvas, and paper items, Lieutenant Hosmer asked, "Will you let them burn the town down?"

Colonel Barrett gave the order for the men to load their muskets and prepare to march into Concord. Officers took their posts with their units and informed them of the mission and Colonel Barrett's order not to fire their weapons unless the regulars at the bridge fired first. Major Buttrick ordered his battalion of minutemen to face to the right in a column of two files. When he commanded the companies forward, they stepped off with the Acton company of Captain Isaac Davis first. As the mounted Colonel Barrett watched them pass, he kept repeating his order not to fire first.

With drums beating the cadence and fifers playing "White Cockade," Barrett's troops marched down the hill to the river bank, then left onto a causeway that carried the road through the marsh, which was inundated when the river overflowed its banks with the recent spring freshets. Robinson, Buttrick, and Davis marched near the head of the column as it approached the bridge. The British officers were impressed by the regularity with which the colonial militia advanced. Laurie ordered all his men to the east bank and directed one company into the adjacent fields to the left and right of the road and and the other two companies to form for "street fighting" and to prepare to fire by divisions. In this manner, the men in the front rank would fire a volley, then retire to the rear of the formation to reload as the second rank stepped forward to fire and the process repeated through the entire formation. While the tactic maintained continuous firing, the fire was directed on a narrow front. As they waited for the Americans to draw closer, Laurie ordered some men to remove the planks from the bridge, which might slow the Americans but would also strand Parsons's detachment on the far side. They did not accomplish their task.

The Americans quickened their pace as some British soldiers fired a few harmless random, possibly warning, shots—or blank cartridges. At about 9:30 a.m., as the leading minutemen approached to within about fifty yards of the bridge, the light infantry fired a volley. A musket ball struck and killed Captain Davis instantly. After a split-second hesitation, Major Buttrick realized that the British were using ball ammunition, and shouted, "Fire, fellow soldiers, for God's sake fire!" The command was repeated along the column as the men of the Acton company returned the fire to their front and along the riverbank.

Four of the eight British officers present, a sergeant, and four privates were wounded in the initial return fire. In another instant, one redcoat fell dead, and another was mortally wounded. Having believed they faced untrained amateurs who would flee rather than fight, the British regulars were stunned by the tenacity of the American militia. In contrast, many of the redcoats fired too high, ironically a characteristic common to less-than-well-trained soldiers. The volume of fire directed against them caused the light infantrymen to begin to break and run down the road toward Concord despite the valiant but vain efforts of their officers to rally them. At the same time, Lieutenant Colonel Smith rode toward the bridge leading two grenadier companies, the reinforcements he had promised Laurie. Buttrick ordered the minutemen who had crossed to the east side of the bridge to take cover behind the stone wall on the high ground a few hundred yards from the road.

Smith restored order and reformed Laurie's three light infantry companies. Looking at the numbers of provincials on either side of the bridge, he assessed the situation. Worried about the four companies with Parsons, he was prepared to go to fight his way to their relief with the entire expeditionary force if necessary. Smith sent runners to tell Major Pitcairn to cease the search and assemble all the companies near the Wright Tavern as he led the five companies back from the bridge to join them. At about 10:00 a.m., Smith and Pitcairn climbed to the hill above the burial ground to survey the surrounding terrain with their spyglasses.

They saw groups of Americans advancing toward the South Bridge, as well as Parsons's men on the north bank marching at the double-quick on the road to the North Bridge. With Americans positioned on the hills, the four companies trotted across the bridge, unnerved by the sight of dead and dying comrades. Remarkably, Barrett's and Buttrick's men allowed them to pass unmolested to rejoin the rest of the British in Concord.

With the Americans closing in and the entire command reunited, Smith knew it was time to leave. After thanking local doctors for their help, he left the severely wounded in their care. Except for one soldier interred without ceremony, the dead were left behind for the towns-people to bury. Wounded officers were loaded aboard impressed chaises, but the ambulatory enlisted casualties had to walk. American militia and minuteman companies throughout the region had mustered and were marching to the scene of the action. Smith and his officers knew marching seven hundred tired soldiers twenty miles through a country infested with hostile irregulars was to be no easy task. He ordered the light infantry companies to send skirmishers out for flank security, and the half-mile-long column began the sad retreat to Boston at about noon, marching silently without the accompanying sound of drums and fifes.

The Americans allowed the British to march unmolested along the road toward Lexington for about one mile, with the troops from Concord in pursuit. When the British column reached the junction of the Lexington and Bedford roads called Meriam's Corner, militia and minuteman companies numbering between five hundred and six hundred men took them under heavy fire from positions around the house, barn, outbuildings, and stone walls of the farm of Nathan and Abigail Meriam, about one hundred yards from the road. As the column trudged along, climbing and descending hills and crossing streams, light infantry flankers did their valiant best to keep the American skirmishers from approaching the road to get in position for better shots.

The British column moved as quickly as possible. The militia and minuteman officers led their companies through the brush and along the fields bordering the road, with the men frequently changing positions, and kept the redcoats under almost constant fire in a running gun battle. When the road turned left, or north, at Hardy's Hill, the British were subject to deadly fire from about two hundred to three hundred Americans firing from behind cover. The number of casualties mounted as places along the road became deadly, with names like the "Bloody Angle." The fight was not all one-sided, though. At times, the regulars were able to deliver effective volleys that took a toll on attacking Americans, while flankers achieved some success when they surprised and killed groups of Americans waiting in concealed positions.

When the front of the marching column made the turn and crossed into the town limits of Lexington, the men of Parker's company were waiting in ambush to exact a measure of revenge for the unprovoked killing of their townsmen that morning. They opened fire into the staggering column. About a dozen redcoats went down in the volley, including Lieutenant Colonel Smith, who fell from his horse with a painful thigh wound. Pitcairn road to the front of the column and sent grenadiers and light infantrymen to attack the flanks of Parker's ambuscade. The Lexington men withdrew after engaging in some bitter fighting.

When the column halted, Americans pursuing from the Bloody Angle continued to torment the rear and center companies. Moving again, as the British approached a hill the local residents called "the Bluff," Pitcairn sent the company of marines to hold it and prevent the swarming Americans from taking positions there as the column limped past. Not long after that ordeal, the British were taken by another blast of withering musket fire at an elevation called Fiske Hill. Pitcairn was thrown from his horse, which then deserted its rider. As the British troops ascended the last hill before entering Lexington, the companies lost cohesion until the heroic efforts of their officers reformed their ranks.

Tired, hungry, dispirited, limping along, dragging their wounded, with ammunition nearly exhausted, Smith's expedition reached the Lexington Green. Suddenly, the men in the rear heard cheers from the front of the column. On a hill east of the common, near Munroe's Tavern, stood a fresh brigade of about one thousand British infantry in full array, supported by two pieces of artillery. Gage had sent the reinforcements in response to Smith's request earlier in the day when he first suspected there could be trouble. Brigadier General Hugh Lord Percy had arrived to save Smith's shattered command. The men of the expedition staggered and stumbled to the area behind Percy's brigade and collapsed in exhaustion as the British field guns kept the pursuing Americans at bay. The provincials regrouped as Brigadier General William Heath and Doctor Joseph Warren arrived to assume control of the Massachusetts forces in the field.

Unfortunately for the redcoats, the battle was not yet over. They still had to march eleven miles back to the safety of Boston. Percy planned the retreat and placed Smith's battered companies in the lead, not expecting more trouble. The wounded Lieutenant Colonel Smith was helped aboard a chaise for the trip. Flankers were ordered out and the combined British force marched toward the town of Menotomy (present-day Arlington), where they experienced another vicious firefight. As the Americans maintained the pressure, the redcoats now took advantage of natural cover and stone walls—skirmishing not unlike their enemies—as they withdrew. Unfortunately, some of the British troops also engaged in looting and plunder of private property and abused civilians.

As Lord Percy's column entered Cambridge, the general saw a regiment of Americans positioned to block the road toward Boston in an attempt to force the British against the Charles River, where militiamen had removed the planks of the bridge at Watertown. Instead, he had his men drive forward to Charlestown with his two artillery pieces in front, and the Americans withdrew, leaving the way open to Charlestown and the ferry to Boston. Percy posted a rear guard on Bunker Hill to cover their retreat. Although reinforcements continued to arrive, American zeal had tapered off, and no further aggressive moves were made. Percy evacuated the casualties and Smith's exhausted soldiers to Boston first. The battle was over. It had cost the British 65 dead, 180 wounded, and 27 missing. The Americans suffered 50 dead, 39 wounded, and 5 missing.

After the exchanges of musketry at Lexington and Concord, the British Army retreated into Boston, which became even more of an armed camp than it had been the day before. The Provincial Congress of the Massachusetts Bay Colony began forming a standing army in earnest and called on its neighbors, Rhode Island, Connecticut, and New Hampshire, to join in the struggle. As their militia soldiers responded to the alarm, a state of war now existed between the four colonies and the British government. The Army of Observation surrounded Boston and placed the British troops who occupied it under siege, but they needed help. They appealed to delegates who represented all thirteen colonies to join them in the struggle for American liberty that should involve not only New England, but the entire continent.

When the Second Continental Congress convened in Philadelphia on May 10, the delegates soon learned that armed men commanded by Ethan Allen and Benedict Arnold had captured the British forts at Ticonderoga and Crown Point on Lake Champlain. The constitutional crisis, in which Americans sought a redress of grievances from the British king and Parliament, had transitioned into open hostilities. The delegates realized that even though many in the colonies desired reconciliation with the mother country, they would now have to address the new military situation. Congress took the next step that eventually transformed a local rebellion into a war for independence by establishing the Continental Army.

On June 14, 1775, Congress "Resolved, That six companies of expert riflemen, be immediately raised in Pennsylvania, two in Maryland, and two in Virginia ... [and] as soon as completed, shall march and join the army near Boston, to be there employed as light infantry, under the command of the chief Officer in that army." The delegates then prescribed an oath of enlistment that required the soldiers to swear:

> I have, this day, voluntarily enlisted myself, as a soldier, in the American continental army, for one year, unless sooner discharged: And I do bind myself to conform, in all instances, to such rules and regulations, as are, or shall be, established for the government of the said Army.

The next day Congress voted to appoint George Washington "to command all the Continental forces" and began laying the foundation for "the American army." On June 17, "The delegates of the United Colonies…reposing special trust and confidence in the patriotism, valor, conduct, and fidelity" of George Washington, issued its first commission by appointing him "General and Commander in chief of the Army of the United Colonies, and of all the forces now raised, or to be raised by them, and of all others who shall voluntarily offer their services, and join the Defense of American liberty, and for repelling every hostile invasion."[4] The Revolutionary War had begun.

Further Reading

Bell, J. L. *The Road to Concord: How Four Stolen Cannon Ignited the Revolutionary War*. Yardley, Pennsylvania: Westholem, 2016.

Borneman, Walter R. *American Spring: Lexington, Concord, and the Road to Revolution*. New York: St. Little Brown, 2014.

Fischer, David Hackett. *Paul Revere's Ride*. New York: Oxford University Press, 1995.

Greenwalt, Phillip, and Robert Orrison. *A Single Blow: The Battles of Lexington and Concord and the Beginning of the American Revolution, April 19, 1775*. El Dorado Hills, California: Savas Beatie, 2018.

Philbrick, Nathaniel. *Bunker Hill: A City, a Siege, a Revolution*. New York: Viking, 2013.

About the Author

Glenn F. Williams is a historian at the U.S. Army Center of Military History, Fort McNair, Washington, D.C. He has served as the historian of the National Museum of the U.S. Army Project, the Army Lewis and Clark Bicentennial Commemoration, and the National Park Service's American Battlefield Protection Program. He is the author of a number of books and articles, including the award-winning *Year of the Hangman: George Washington's Campaign against the Iroquois* and *Dunmore's War: The Last Conflict of America's Colonial Era*. He holds a Ph.D. in history from the University of Maryland.

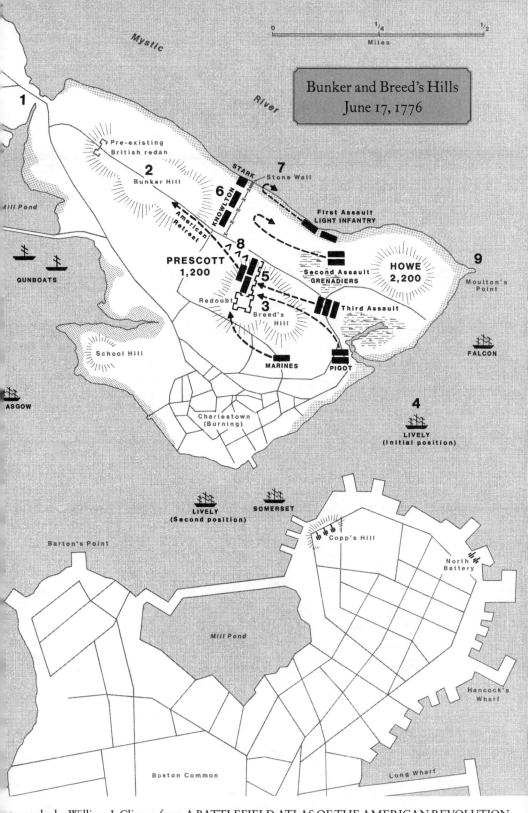

Bunker and Breed's Hills
June 17, 1776

Mystic River

1

Pre-existing
British redan

2
Bunker Hill

STARK **7**
Stone Wall

6
KNOWLTON

American Retreat

First Assault
LIGHT INFANTRY

8

PRESCOTT
1,200

Second Assault
GRENADIERS

9
Moulton's
Point

HOWE
2,200

Mill Pond

GUNBOATS

5

Redoubt

3
Breed's
Hill

Third Assault

School Hill

ASGOW

MARINES

PIGOT

FALCON

Charlestown
(Burning)

4
LIVELY
(Initial position)

LIVELY
(Second position)

SOMERSET

Barton's Point

Copp's Hill

North
Battery

Mill Pond

Hancock's
Wharf

Boston Common

Long Wharf

:tography by William J. Clipson from A BATTLEFIELD ATLAS OF THE AMERICAN REVOLUTION,
lished by Savas Beatie, www.savasbeatie.com

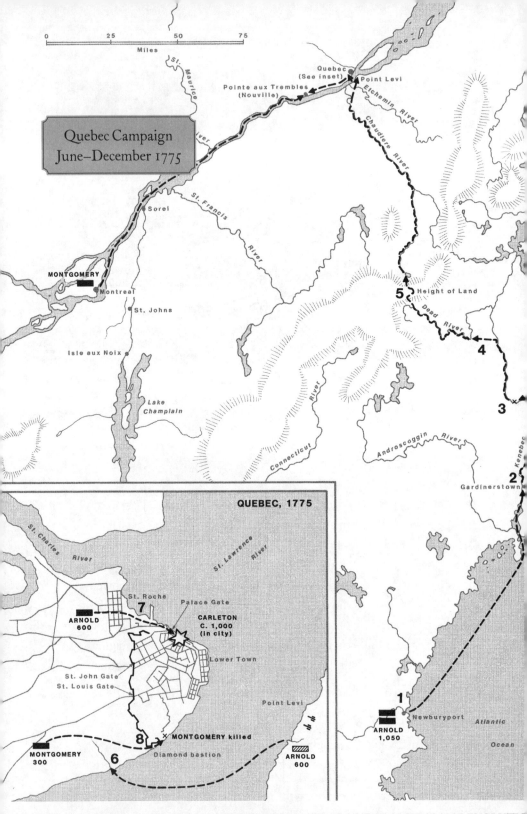

Quebec Campaign
June–December 1775

QUEBEC, 1775

Cartography by William J. Clipson from A BATTLEFIELD ATLAS OF THE AMERICAN REVOLUTION
published by Savas Beatie, www.savasbeatie.com

The Fourteenth Colony:
The Quebec Campaign

BY MARK ANDERSON

It took less than one month for the opening shots at Lexington and Concord to reverberate three hundred miles away in Canada. Both history and geography suggested that the northern province would eventually become involved in the brewing imperial conflict. Until 1760 it had been a French possession and, as such, the wartime bane of the "old" English North American colonies. It had since become the British Province of Quebec after its French and Indian War conquest. Now, at the dawn of the Revolutionary War, London saw similar opportunities there—as a strategic North American base and source of manpower.

The rebel colonies, however, saw a different prospect—to bring the Canadians into their Continental cause in their struggle with the ministry. Yet despite Quebec's apparent proximity, it was both foreign and remote. Its nearly one hundred thousand inhabitants were predominantly French-speaking Catholics living along the colony's defining geographic feature, the St. Lawrence River. Since the St. Lawrence entered the Atlantic so far north, Quebec City was a thousand sea miles from Boston, and the northern Appalachian highlands partitioned Canada from New York and New England. Only the Lake Champlain–Richelieu River corridor readily connected them—the region's traditional route for trade and war.

In early 1775, a small British garrison held the key military post on this path, Fort Ticonderoga. After Lexington and Concord, both Connecticut and Massachusetts recognized Ticonderoga's importance and launched separate, covert efforts to seize it. Under Connecticut's authority, Ethan Allen ventured forward with about one hundred rough-and-tumble Green Mountain Boys and a few dozen western Massachusetts and Connecticut volunteers, while Massachusetts-commissioned Benedict Arnold scouted the area as his men were being recruited. The two parties encountered each other near their common target, and after some debate, Allen agreed to let Arnold join the imminent attack. On May 10, the Green Mountain Boys surprised the British garrison and took the fort and its valuable artillery without a fight. The next day they secured nearby Crown Point and additional cannon there.

Arnold's orders gave him an additional objective—a British government sloop, based one hundred miles away, across the Quebec border at Fort Saint Johns. The ship was key to naval control of Lake Champlain. So, five days after taking Ticonderoga, Arnold led about fifty men north by boat. On May 18, his troops swept in on the fort, seized the ship, and departed with supplies, guns, and eleven prisoners before the British in Montreal could react.

Not to be outdone, Allen led about ninety Green Mountain Boys to occupy Fort Saint Johns. They approached Canada in small boats later that same day, even after Arnold discouraged their mission in an open lake meeting. When a British redcoat detachment came from Montreal that evening in a belated response to Arnold's raid, the Green Mountain Boys prudently re-embarked before there was a serious engagement and sailed back to Ticonderoga.

On May 20, word of the rebels' Fort Saint Johns raids and the loss of Ticonderoga reached British governor Guy Carleton in Quebec City. As the province's military commander in chief, he would need to draw on military experience garnered in Great Britain's last two major wars. He was challenged to defend Quebec with scant forces—one regular regiment was committed to four distant and remote Great Lakes forts, leaving just two other regiments to defend the three-hundred-mile colonized St. Lawrence Valley expanse. Since any substantial rebel attack would undoubtedly come along the Champlain corridor, Carleton concentrated his troops to protect the border at Fort Saint Johns. Small detachments guarded Montreal, Quebec City, and Fort Chambly, eleven miles north of Saint Johns.

Internally, Carleton placed little confidence in Quebec province's tenant farmer *habitants*, but liberal British policy changes had recently secured support from the Catholic Church and French Canadian elite. To buttress Canada against the spread of rebellion, the governor declared martial law on June 9 and attempted to reinstate the long-disbanded militia. He was disappointed but unsurprised when many rural parishes blatantly resisted mobilization and city musters were half-hearted. About fifty French- and Anglo-Canadian Loyalists augmented the redcoats at Fort Saint Johns that summer.

Carleton had another potential source of military power—the Indian Seven Nations of Canada. Living in Catholic mission villages at strategic points along the St. Lawrence Valley, these Indians frequently allied with their French colonial neighbors in wartime and had terrified English frontier colonists over a century of episodic raiding. However, despite Carleton's repeated efforts to draw these village-nations into alliance in the coming war, they considered themselves independent and pursued a loose, general neutrality. Individual warriors were free to fight as they wished, though, and a few joined the British at Fort Saint Johns while others cooperated with the Americans.

When the Congress established its Continental Army in June 1775, it carved out a Northern Department to protect the New York and New England frontiers even though the army was concentrated in Cambridge, Massachusetts. That summer, intelligence from Quebec accurately reflected British military weakness and Canadian sentiments, but reports on Seven Nations Indians' intentions remained confusing and contradictory. On June 27, a seemingly authoritative report warned that the Canadian Indians had taken up the hatchet with Carleton, and the

Continental Congress interpreted that as an indication that the British were preparing to attack from the north. So that day, Congress gave Major General Philip Schuyler authority to lead the Northern Army into Quebec as necessary "for the peace and security" of the colonies. There was a key constraint though—he should only invade if it would "not be disagreeable to the Canadians."[1] British forces were the enemy, not the province's inhabitants.

As a commander, Major General Schuyler's skills favored strategic organization and civil-military coordination. He was accustomed to leading through family position and elite connections as a landed New York patrician, but he also had vital logistics experience from the French and Indian War. His deputy, Brigadier General Richard Montgomery, brought field combat experience as a former British Army captain. Montgomery had moved to America just a few years earlier and married into another prominent New York family, the Livingstons, prompting his quick rise in patriot politics and military rank. When Schuyler arrived to command his army at Fort Ticonderoga on July 18, he found just two regiments, and he lacked the intelligence, supplies, and watercraft necessary to venture into Canada. While waiting for logistics to flow north and additional Connecticut and New York regiments to arrive, he sent scout parties into Quebec, relying heavily on Massachusetts major John Brown.

Friendly Canadians and Seven Nations Indian factions actively encouraged an American intervention in their homeland, while Northern Army soldiers and key colonial leaders itched to launch the invasion. Yet even as Schuyler's army grew to two thousand men in August, he waited. Finally, on August 27, General George Washington asked Schuyler to confirm that the invasion would happen because he was planning an expedition to march men from the main Cambridge army through the Maine wilderness to attack Quebec City. Schuyler, in Albany for an important Indian conference, committed positively, unaware that his deputy had already set the operation in motion.

With Schuyler away from headquarters, Montgomery had received alarming intelligence two days earlier. The British were ready to launch two armed ships at Fort Saint Johns, putting Continental naval superiority and any invasion of Canada at immediate risk. To preempt this threat, Montgomery assembled 1,200 Connecticut and New York men at Crown Point and, on August 30, sailed north for Quebec. Schuyler rushed to rejoin them, reaching the small Continental invasion fleet just before it crossed the provincial border.

The Siege of Fort St. Johns and the Richelieu Valley

Over the summer, General Carleton was able to supplement his paltry military force. Colonel Allan Maclean recruited a new provincial Royal Highland Emigrants Regiment, and hundreds of its men augmented British regulars around the province. On July 26, Carleton and Indian Superintendent Guy Johnson hosted a massive Indian conference for visiting Six Nations Iroquois and Great Lakes Indians, with Seven Nations of Canada representation, too. At British bidding, several hundred warriors had taken up the hatchet. Johnson wanted these men to take the war to the rebels, but Carleton insisted they be used in a purely defensive role. Keeping Native allies concentrated on the Island of Montreal, Johnson rotated small parties of warriors to scout north of the provincial border from Fort Saint Johns.

British major Charles Preston used the summer months to transform that long-neglected post into a substantial defensive work amidst the swampy, mosquito- and snake-ridden forests on the Richelieu River's west bank. By the end of August, sod-covered ramparts and a ditch encompassed the old barracks and a neighboring house. Soldiers cleared landward fields of fire and mounted cannon to control the river. The rebels would now have to fight their way into Canada.

On September 5, the American Northern Army finally reached Canada and established a base camp on Ile aux Noix, an island ten miles south of Fort Saint Johns. There, Schuyler composed a manifesto declaring his army's purpose—not to wage war on Canadians or Indians, but to free them from British oppression. Major John Brown and Ethan Allen—now a volunteer officer—delivered translated copies to local allies who distributed them throughout the region.

The next day, General Montgomery landed on the mainland with five hundred men to scout near Fort Saint Johns. British major Preston sent about eighty warriors to meet them. They encountered Americans in a break in the marshy woods, about a mile and a half from the fort. Each side lost about twenty men in a short firefight, and both parties withdrew. The next morning, Schuyler brought his men back to Ile aux Noix, awaiting more substantial signs of Canadian support. The Indians returned to Fort Saint Johns, complaining that the British had failed to join the battle; many warriors left in disgust. On September 10, the Americans made another landing with similar outcomes—each side incurred casualties in a brief fight near the same ground, the Continentals withdraw back to the island, and more disgruntled Indians departed Saint Johns.

Meanwhile, Anglo-Canadian James Livingston gathered supplies and rallied Richelieu Valley volunteers to support the invaders. Within a week, hundreds gathered in armed camps to assert control over the region beyond Forts Chambly and Saint Johns. Brown and Allen joined them as liaisons.

On September 17, Continental soldiers landed on the mainland again, bolstered by recent reinforcements. General Montgomery and several hundred men established a new camp south of Fort Saint Johns, while Major Brown led about fifty of them around the enemy post to join a similar number of armed Canadians as a "Corps of Observation" in the north. Late that night, Brown's men ambushed a British supply convoy at the key road junction connecting Saint Johns, Montreal, and Fort Chambly, seizing all the carts, goods, and cattle.

To recover the lost convoy, British major Preston sent two hundred men out—redcoats with a cannon, Canadian volunteers, and Indians. They temporarily drove Brown's "corps" off but retreated back to the fort when their flank was threatened by New Hampshire rangers sent north into the fight by Montgomery. Preston's sortie party had suffered two dead and two wounded. The Continentals and Canadians had fourteen casualties but retained the captured supplies and key road junction. The following day, Montgomery sent additional Continental detachments around the fort to establish a proper blockade, and Montreal citizens were soon shocked to peer across the Saint Lawrence and see rebel soldiers marching from their new camp in Laprairie. Despite the army's recent progress, General Schuyler had to leave his army and return to New York to recover from a debilitating "bilious fever and violent rheumatic pains."[2] Montgomery took operational command, and within a week siege efforts advanced when newly arrived New York artillerymen opened bombardment of Fort Saint Johns.

Meanwhile, Ethan Allen ranged the Richelieu Valley with patriot Canadians and a couple dozen Continentals. He soon cast his eyes on Montreal, a weakly defended, politically divided city that he had long felt could be taken with just a show of force. He coordinated a scheme with Major Brown and Canadian rebel Thomas Walker to cross from three different points onto the Island of Montreal and unite for a final advance on the city. Allen assembled Continentals and Canadians at Longueuil, Brown led the Continentals at Laprairie, and Walker rallied rural Canadian militia north of the island. Through a planning error, or perhaps in a deliberate choice to reap all the glory himself, Allen crossed a day earlier than expected.

Mid-morning on September 25, a Canadian spotted Allen's hundred men approaching Montreal and raised the alarm. Thirty-four redcoats and about two hundred Loyalists quickly formed to meet Allen's "Banditti." Surprised by the opposition, Allen withdrew to defensible terrain in the village of Longue Pointe as many unarmed patriot Canadians took flight. Allen and some die-hards prepared for a last stand, but when the battle was clearly lost, he surrendered with seventeen Continentals and sixteen Canadians—ten wounded. Seven patriot Canadians died at Longue Pointe, opposite two dead and two wounded Loyalists. Allen's defeat immediately dampened Continental and patriot Canadian morale, while Carleton saw a concomitant surge in militia and Indian support.

Over the next two weeks, Montgomery's ill-disciplined troops bickered and second-guessed their leaders as the artillery bombardment made little apparent impact on Fort Saint Johns and powder and shot stores ran low. Finally, on October 13, Brown challenged Montgomery for action to advance the campaign, and Livingston proposed taking Fort Chambly. To facilitate the effort, Continentals and Canadians floated two cannon past Fort Saint Johns at night—those guns could crack Chambly's thin but musket-proof stone walls.

In the early hours of October 17, three hundred Canadians and fifty Continentals surrounded Fort Chambly and opened artillery fire. Even though the defenders did not suffer casualties, once shot breached the walls the British commander judged that his post was lost and surrendered in just one day. The victory raised Continental and patriot Canadian spirits and provided desperately needed ammunition from the fort's stores. Four days later, eighty-three Chambly prisoners and army families sailed past Fort Saint Johns under a negotiated cease-fire, destined for the rebel colonies.

By the end of October, General Carleton saw that Fort Saint Johns would soon surrender if not relieved. In desperation, he called additional militia and Indian allies into Montreal to cross the St. Lawrence by force and march to break the rebel siege. Carleton coordinated efforts with Colonel Allan Maclean, who was already advancing up the Richelieu from Sorel with one hundred Royal Highland Emigrants, a few dozen redcoat regulars, and some shaky Canadian militia. Patriot Canadians and Continentals harassed the Loyalists and removed bridges in their path. Maclean's column advanced eighteen miles in three days—not halfway to the apparent rendezvous point in Chambly.

General Carleton launched his assault on October 30. Six hundred Canadians, one hundred and thirty redcoats, and about eighty warriors were in high spirits as they embarked from Montreal on forty boats in the late morning. On the opposite shore at Longueuil,

Colonel Seth Warner skillfully deployed three hundred Continentals. Every time enemy boats approached the shore, Warner's men forced them off with musket fire and grapeshot from a single cannon—killing or wounding perhaps fifty British and Canadians. A bold Indian–Canadian party waded across from a river island, but even they failed to establish a beachhead. Carleton ordered the boats back to Montreal in defeat. Without incurring a single serious casualty, Warner's men achieved a resounding victory at Longueuil. Carleton abandoned hope of relieving Fort Saint Johns and ordered Maclean back to Quebec City.

The defenders in Fort Saint Johns had taken fairly minor losses over two months—twenty killed and twenty-three wounded—but they were low on provisions, and shelter had been shredded as winter approached. The final blow came on November 1, when Montgomery sent two Canadian prisoners taken at Longueuil to the fort, proving that Carleton's relief had failed. On November 3, Preston surrendered the battered fort with its 680 defenders and auxiliaries. With Montgomery's men crossing the St. Lawrence on November 11, General Carleton evacuated troops, supplies, government officials, and prominent Loyalists from Montreal aboard eleven ships bound for Quebec City. Montgomery led victorious Continentals into Montreal two days later.

Carleton's ships traveled fewer than fifty miles. Adverse winds and fog slowed them to a crawl, and at Sorel a six-gun Continental battery and two small gunboats threatened the fleet's passage. Seizing upon the enemy's plight, the Americans initiated surrender negotiations. On the night of November 16, Governor Carleton successfully slipped away in a whaleboat, escaping to Quebec City with a couple of aides. British general Richard Prescott remained behind, surrendering the trapped ships, men, and supplies to the rebels three days later, capping the Continentals' productive fall campaign.

In two months' fighting, Montgomery's ragtag, ill-disciplined army had driven the "tyrannical" British government into a last stronghold at Quebec City. With the assistance of Livingston's Canadians, the rest of the Province of Quebec was nominally in patriot control. Carleton had little to show at the end of his passive and hesitant campaign, but Preston's brave Fort Saint Johns defense tied the rebels to the Richelieu Valley through the fall fighting season.

The Battle of Quebec City

Long before Schuyler's invasion began, Benedict Arnold departed Crown Point in a command dispute and went to Cambridge, where General Washington soon placed him in charge of the second advance into Canada. Maps showed a usable route up the Kennebec River, over the Appalachians, and down the Chaudière River to the St. Lawrence, near Quebec City. By friendly Canadians' reports, that city was weakly guarded, with many patriot-friendly citizens. Like Schuyler, Arnold was to treat the Canadians and Indians as "Friends and Brethren," and free them from the "Tools of Despotism."[3]

On September 13, Arnold left Cambridge with about one thousand men—volunteers from various New England regiments and three Pennsylvania and Virginia rifle companies. Sailing from Newburyport, on September 20 they fell upon supplies collected at Fort Western (Augusta, Maine). Five days later, the first division headed upriver. Upstream travel was slow, and supplies were lost in leaky and overturned boats. Provisions were already running low when lead parties had traveled just one hundred miles, reaching Dead River on October 13. Lieutenant Colonel Roger Enos, commanding the trail division, assessed the supply situation and turned his men back on October 25, removing about one quarter of Arnold's strength without consultation.

With horrible weather flooding the Appalachian highlands, Arnold's starving, soaked, and freezing soldiers struggled to find the route into Quebec, and men began to fall out of the march. Arnold finally reached the summit on October 27, and ragged survivors followed him onto the Chaudière and into Canada, appearing "more like ghosts than men."[4] In contrast to Montgomery's Richelieu Valley experience, locals did not rush to arms, but were still glad to supply food, shelter, and transportation at a price. On November 7, the advanced guard reached Pointe Lévi on the St. Lawrence, across from Quebec City. Arnold sent messengers to inform Montgomery of his arrival and waited as more than six hundred men rejoined him in the next few days.

Quebec City officials had done little to improve their defensive posture for much of the fall. A dramatic change came on November 11, though, when Colonel Maclean arrived from his aborted Richelieu Valley effort. He rallied sullen Anglo citizens, reorganized defenses, and encouraged military commitment to defend the city at all costs.

On the night of November 13, Arnold's corps crossed the St. Lawrence in boats, past two nearby British warships. Then the men retraced General James Wolfe's 1759 route up the steep hillside to the Plains of Abraham outside Quebec City's western walls. By dawn, with some men still waiting to cross, Arnold found that his force had arrived too weak and too late for a surprise assault, so his men paraded outside the city in hopes of prompting the city to fight or surrender. The garrison, emboldened by Maclean's vigorous leadership, greeted them with cannon fire.

Arnold resorted to a crude blockade, but soon received reports that Maclean was preparing to attack from the city with superior numbers and artillery. Arnold had only 680 men with just five shots each. So, on November 19, they withdrew twenty miles upriver to Pointe aux Trembles (Neuville), where the men safely recuperated among friendly locals. On the same day that Arnold's corps left Quebec City, Carleton returned after escaping the ship surrender off Sorel. Three days later, he purged dangerous pro-rebel citizenry by ordering all able-bodied men to take up arms or leave.

Upriver at Montreal, most of General Montgomery's fall campaign soldiers rushed home before the imminent expiration of their enlistments. With noble appeals and generous enticements, the general re-enlisted just seven hundred for five months. He formed ad hoc regiments of New Yorkers, Connecticut men, and a Massachusetts–

New Hampshire conglomeration under Major Brown. James Livingston also recruited a newly authorized Canadian Continental regiment. Montgomery led five hundred soldiers from Montreal to join Arnold, many traveling aboard the ships captured off Sorel.

When Montgomery's shipborne contingent landed at Pointe aux Trembles on December 1, Arnold's men were overjoyed to have reinforcements and enjoyed new uniforms and supplies brought from captured British stocks. Montgomery procured local sleigh transportation for men and supplies, and the army moved to the Plains of Abraham. On December 6, the Continentals reestablished their Quebec City blockade.

Inside the fortress city's walls, Carleton tallied about 1,300 defenders—British regulars, Royal Highland Emigrants, ships' crews, and militia—facing about 1,000 rebels. Yet even with numerical superiority and a well-defended base, Carleton planned a deliberate defensive fight. He refused to repeat past generals' mistakes of fighting outside the walls, where the fates were fickle. Instead, he kept the garrison inside, ready to repel attacks but otherwise awaiting relief from England in early May, when the St. Lawrence River's ice broke. Officers calculated that city food supplies could feed both defenders and inhabitants until then.

After early failed attempts to prompt a surrender, Montgomery prepared to fight for Quebec City. Cannon opened fire from a makeshift Plains of Abraham ice battery on December 15, but made little impact. The Americans had a little more success from the northern Saint Roch suburb, where Captain Daniel Morgan's riflemen sniped at enemy sentries and mortars lobbed small rounds over city walls.

In contrast to Carleton's patient, calculated plan, Montgomery felt rushed to act. Patriot Canadians confided that until Quebec City fell, most fellow colonists would not rally behind the invaders or form their own government. Additionally, Arnold's irritable New England troops were preparing to leave upon their enlistments' expiration at year's end, so Montgomery intended to storm Quebec City before then.

He waited for a snowstorm to screen a night assault, and conditions appeared promising on December 23. Aware of his tenuous control over Arnold's men, the general specifically obtained their assent before proceeding. In the Christmas Eve predawn darkness, troops formed for action, but the general called them back to quarters after a deserter compromised the plan. The army impatiently waited another week until a snow squall blew in on December 30, giving Montgomery an opportunity to attack on the last practical day.

Quebec City was well-prepared for the coming onslaught. The main city, Upper Town, was protected by imposing western stone walls facing the Plains of Abraham. Fortifications protected remaining approaches up steep hillsides in other directions. On the riverfront below, to the northeast, Lower Town was far more exposed—a narrow strip of merchant stores and warehouses—but defenders had barricaded both ends. Sentries kept regular watch and men slept on arms, ready to scramble to rallying points upon alarm.

Montgomery weighed different attack options, but focused his New Year's Eve effort on Lower Town. It was a more practical objective, and if its valuable trade goods were at risk by capture, citizens might demand the entire city's surrender. The general was desperate, steeling himself with the proverb "Fortune favors the brave." Montgomery split his force into three independent columns. Livingston and Brown would make feints against Upper Town while Arnold and Montgomery led separate assaults on Lower Town, from north and south respectively.

Around 4:00 a.m. on New Year's Eve, Continentals shuffled through steep drifts toward assembly points in a near whiteout. Quebec City sentries sounded the alarm after spotting traces of light through the blizzard on the Plains of Abraham, and Livingston's Canadian Continentals approached to set a blaze at Saint John's Gate but withdrew under musket and cannon fire. Brown's men shot at the Cape Diamond bastion but never left their initial positions. The defenders soon saw that this was not the main effort.

Unobserved by defenders above, Montgomery led his New Yorkers along the icy riverside road below Cape Diamond. The general led from the front, clearing Lower Town's first barricades uncontested. Then, as he called for help removing the next barriers, cannon fire flashed from a house. Montgomery, his aide, and six soldiers were killed by grapeshot. Shocked by their brave leader's death and challenged by seemingly formidable defenses, the senior colonel withdrew rather than pressing ahead. The southern attack was over.

Arnold's column started a little late, missing the signal rocket in the blowing snow. As his men moved beyond Saint Roch, Upper Town defenders fired down, striking Arnold with a serious leg wound. He tried to carry on, but heavy bleeding forced him back to the hospital. Intrepid Kennebec Expedition veterans drove into Lower Town, and the battle quickly devolved into ferocious house-to-house fighting. Captain Morgan led a drive that took some barricades and threatened the heart of the town.

Carleton, however, discerned that this was the only fight and sent one hundred men out Palace Gate at dawn. Attacked in the rear, the Continentals briefly fought on until it became clear that they were unmistakably trapped and outnumbered. After the rebels reluctantly surrendered, British and Loyalist defenders rounded up 372 prisoners and 33 wounded. Thirty-five of Arnold's men lay dead in Lower Town's streets and buildings. Despite the resounding victory, Carleton held to his plan and remained behind Quebec City's walls to wait for either the rebels or winter to break.

The Cedars, Trois Rivières, and Withdrawal

After Montgomery's demise, Benedict Arnold took every practical measure to sustain the Quebec City blockade with the army's weak remnants. He requested immediate reinforcements from his new superior, Brigadier General David Wooster in Montreal—but there were few to send. Despite the circumstances, surprising numbers of

Canadians responded to Arnold's local appeals for supplies and men to join the blockade.

Even though Carleton's troops remained inside Quebec City, Arnold's army faced another deadly enemy—smallpox. The first cases appeared in early December, and Montgomery had already established a smallpox hospital to isolate victims. Yet many soldiers inoculated themselves against orders, taking the disease with less deadly symptoms but often inadvertently spreading it as a result. Up to half of Arnold's men were sick and unavailable for duty at any time.

Wooster remained back in Montreal to secure lines of communication while appealing near and far for immediate reinforcements. Lacking meaningful occupation guidance, he improvised policies, vainly trying to placate friendly Canadians and suppress Loyalist agitators. With great controversy, he banned annual fur trade shipments to the Great Lakes. While those wares could be used to encourage Indians to join the British in the west, they were also Montreal's economic lifeblood.

Far away in Philadelphia, Congress had been slow to address Northern Army needs from the beginning. Despite Schuyler and Montgomery's repeated appeals in the fall for troops, money, and supplies, Congress waited until January to authorize six additional regiments for Quebec. Combined with troops still in Canada, they only totaled about half of Schuyler's ten-thousand-man recommendation. The Quebec City camp suffered at the end of a fragile six-hundred-mile logistics chain that failed to meet basic needs. Since Canadians refused to take Continental paper money, Arnold resorted to unpopular requisitions to feed his men.

In mid-January, word of Montgomery's tragic defeat distressed the united colonies, but Congress still dithered. It waited months to appoint both a new commander, Major General John Thomas, and a much-needed congressional commission to deliver patriot political leadership assistance to Canada. As a result, the commander and the commissioners traveled north during the spring thaw and arrived far too late.

At the end of April, Wooster finally joined the Quebec City siege, and Arnold—now a brigadier general—left for Montreal. Wooster struggled to keep soldiers in camp until properly replaced, sometimes past their enlistments. Yet when Major General Thomas finally reached the camp on May 2, he found just two thousand men, half on the sick rolls. Brigadier General William Thompson was on the way with a two-thousand-man brigade from Cambridge but was still hundreds of miles away. So, on May 5, General Thomas made a difficult decision to abandon the untenable siege. That very night, signal fires warned that British ships were coming up the St. Lawrence.

Carleton had patiently awaited relief. Over winter, British leaders responded to Canadian setbacks with pragmatic determination. In just a few months, they assembled a ten-thousand-man expedition under General John Burgoyne, and its first wave crossed the Atlantic early enough to venture up the St. Lawrence as soon as river ice cleared.

The first five vessels reached Quebec City on the morning of May 6 and promptly unloaded soldiers. By noon, Carleton led almost nine hundred men out to drive off the already disordered enemy. Americans fled in panic, leaving weapons, supplies, and sick comrades. Carleton's troops gathered up abandoned, incapacitated rebels but made no immediate pursuit.

Initially, General Thomas hoped to halt the American flight north of the St. Maurice River, but the army was too disorganized and ill-supplied. After a 125-mile retreat, officers restored order at Sorel. The army established a fortified camp there, hoping to hold the Richelieu Valley and Montreal.

Back at Montreal, Continental leaders had long been warned that British troops and Indians were preparing an attack from the west. In late April, Arnold responded by ordering a regiment-sized force of New Hampshire and Connecticut reinforcements to build a fort in the westernmost parish of the Cedars (Les Cèdres) to control western approaches on the St. Lawrence. One hundred and sixty Iroquois and Mississauga warriors gathered at the British Fort Oswegatchie, 125 miles west of

Montreal. Encouraged by Loyalists and Indian Department officers, they aimed to attack the rebels around Montreal for many reasons, including a desire to restore the trade-goods flow on the St. Lawrence that was being blocked by the Americans. On May 14, the Indian force headed downriver along with Oswegatchie's redcoat garrison company.

One hundred Seven Nations of Canada warriors joined the expedition as it approached the Continentals at Fort Cedars. On May 18, more than two hundred Indians, forty British, and some Canadian Loyalists attacked that fort. Its commander—terrified of "savages" and suffering from smallpox—surrendered with four hundred men the next day. On May 20, an Indian and Loyalist detachment met and ambushed a fatally delayed Continental relief column. The one hundred Americans suffered a couple dozen battle casualties in an hour-long fight. They surrendered when their retreat path was blocked, having killed just one Indian and wounding two. The five hundred combined American prisoners were pillaged and tormented by their Native captors for a week.

Despite his prisoner burden, the British commander proceeded on toward Montreal until Arnold threatened to counterattack with superior numbers on May 24. The Indians and British withdrew as the Continentals lagged in pursuit. Two days later, the captain negotiated a controversial prisoner-exchange cartel with Arnold, saving captives' lives while giving Indians and redcoats safe retreat. The Cedars affair was a highly embarrassing American defeat.

Meanwhile, General Carleton's army moved slowly upriver. Following a strategic hearts-and-minds approach, Carleton sought to spare rebel soldiers so they could return home in defeat, spreading tales of the king's generosity and gross Continental incompetence. As a result, the British advanced just eighty miles by land and river in a month—half the distance to Montreal.

The Continental army recovering at Sorel was vexed by familiar problems: inadequate supplies, smallpox, poor discipline, and a lack of hard money. Command was further complicated as General Thomas succumbed to smallpox, leaving Wooster, Arnold, and Thompson to conditionally lead the army. On June 1, the winds of war seemed to shift when Brigadier General John Sullivan reached Fort Saint Johns with another brigade from Washington's main army. As the senior brigadier, Sullivan took command. Soldiers' spirits improved at Sorel and local Canadian support resurged. Then, on June 6, General Sullivan received promising intelligence of three hundred British soldiers exposed at the head of Carleton's advance in Trois Rivières, above the St. Maurice River.

Late the next night, General Thompson and 1,600 men crossed the St. Lawrence to attack Trois Rivières and stem the British advance. The general led his troops inland to avoid observation by British warships, but they became disoriented and were misrouted that night on swampy, wooded paths. The advanced guard did not reach Trois Rivières's outskirts until dawn on June 8. Redcoats sounded the alarm and manned defensive works outside the city to fend off the rebel advanced guard. Unbeknownst to Thompson, over the past couple days the British had brought two thousand troops to Trois Rivières. With supporting fire from Royal Navy ships, those regulars efficiently routed the disorganized Continentals, driving them into the woods. The British suffered about twenty casualties, and a few dozen Americans were killed or wounded. Over the next few days, Loyalist Canadians and Indians brought more than two hundred prisoners from the woods, including General Thompson.

With the humiliations at the Cedars and Trois Rivières, General Sullivan abandoned hope for Canada. On June 11, the army withdrew from Sorel, and four days later, Arnold left Montreal. On June 18, Sullivan began moving the entire army back to Crown Point to recover and defend the thirteen colonies at the other end of Lake Champlain. The retreat was complete on July 1.

The Northern Army's retreat essentially guaranteed that Carleton would attack in the summer of 1776, but Continental leaders took important steps to delay that prospect. The army left no intact watercraft for the British to use on Lake Champlain. Carleton had to assemble a new navy at Fort Saint Johns while the American built their own ships in a summer naval construction race. In early October, Carleton finally advanced with a superior fleet. Arnold skillfully contested British lake superiority with a Continental squadron, eventually incurring a tactical naval defeat at Valcour Bay on October 11 and 12. However, Arnold strategically delayed the British advance long enough that Carleton decided it was too late in the season to continue on to Crown Point and Ticonderoga. The British Army went back to Canada. The British invasion was postponed into 1777, buying the struggling Continental cause valuable time.

Significance

In the summer of 1776, the Continental Congress assigned a committee to review the Quebec campaign disaster. Its report identified three principal causes for the defeat. The first was short enlistments—Montgomery was compelled to attack Quebec City before his army disappeared; and he, Wooster, and Arnold repeatedly remade and improvised an army on campaign. Second was the want of hard money; the colonies simply lacked sufficient hard currency to pay for army requirements in a remote land that would not accept Continental paper. Last was smallpox, which kept one-quarter to half the army on the sick rolls in 1776.

Despite these findings, the campaign's core failures were truly rooted in Philadelphia. Overconfident in the power of revolutionary zeal and virtue, Congress had approved an invasion with insufficient thought to the requisite forces, supplies, and finances. Quebec proved the limits of the thirteen colonies' strategic reach—they lacked the wealth of imperial resources and military expertise that Great Britain had used to conquer the same province in 1759–1760. Even if Montgomery or Arnold had managed to take Quebec City, Britain's naval superiority and vast means, as well as Canada's near-total economic dependence on the St. Lawrence, meant that the king's forces could inevitably have retaken the entire province if desired.

Still, Congress never completely abandoned hope that Canadians would join the Continental confederation. Common historical analysis often asserts that French-Catholic inhabitants never would have supported the American patriot cause because of seemingly insurmountable historical, ethnic, and religious differences. Yet during the invasion, military, economic, and geographic realities seemed to be far more significant factors. The 1775–1776 campaign demonstrated that, like many other colonies, Canada had active Loyalist and patriot factions, even as the largest segment of the population generally sought to avoid active commitment.

In 1776, Carleton "saved" the province by holding Quebec City until relieved, but his most important contribution may have been made after the province was recovered. He deliberately restored order and reasserted control with generous, balanced policies that minimized future dissent. His hearts-and-minds approach with rebel invaders did not pay off as well, though. Given time, distance, and the shocks of the 1777 invasion, many Canadian campaign veterans returned to the patriot cause with vigor.

The Quebec campaign further challenged the short-war myth popular on both sides of the Atlantic. Instead of shrinking from their bloodying at Lexington, Concord, and Bunker Hill, the Americans launched an offensive that almost took Canada. Similarly, even when the northern province appeared to have fallen to the rebels, the king and Parliament did not opt for reconciliation. The British responded with even greater military commitment and ruthless, punitive policies that included loosening restraints on Native American–allied warfare. In the colonies, defeat in Canada persuaded many American leaders that they ultimately required foreign assistance—financial, material, and military. Since European powers were more likely to assist a new nation rather than rebellious colonies, the campaign encouraged those inclined to independence and helped prompt the birth of the United States, just three days after the Canadian invasion concluded.

Statistics
1775 Campaign Participants

Patriot
Northern Army Continentals (Connecticut, New York, New Hampshire, Massachusetts, Green Mountain Boys): 4,750
Kennebec Expedition Continentals (New England, Virginia, Pennsylvania): 680
Canadians: 200–600

British, Loyalist, and Allied Indians
British Regulars (3 regiments and artillery): 975
Provincials (Royal Highland Emigrants): 200–360
Canadian Volunteers: 80
Canadian Militia: <1,200
Allied Indians: 80–500

1776 Campaign Participants

Patriot
Continentals in Quebec (New York, Connecticut, Massachusetts, New Hampshire, Canadian): 1,060
First Wave Continental Reinforcements, January–April (New Hampshire, Connecticut, Massachusetts, Green Mountain Boys, Pennsylvania, New Jersey, Canada): 3,835
Thompson's Continental Brigade, May–June (Massachusetts and New Hampshire): 2,500
Sullivan's Continental Brigade, June (New Hampshire, Pennsylvania, New Jersey): ~2,000
Canadian Militia: 200–400
Allied Indians: 30

British and Loyalist
British Regulars: 8,000
Hessians: 3,000
Provincials: 350
Militia: 600–900
Allied Indians: 200–350

Total Quebec Campaign Casualties

Patriot Losses
Killed in Action: 138
Killed by Disease: ~1,000
Wounded: 79
Captured/Paroled/Exchanged: 1,258

British, Loyalist, and Allied Indian Losses
Killed: 60
Wounded: 100
Captured: 923

Further Reading

Anderson, Mark R. *The Battle for the Fourteenth Colony: America's War of Liberation in Canada, 1774–1776*. Lebanon, New Hampshire: University Press of New England, 2013.

Desjardin, Thomas. *Through a Howling Wilderness: Benedict Arnold's March to Quebec, 1775*. New York: St. Martin's Press, 2006.

Fenn, Elizabeth. *Pox Americana: The Great Smallpox Epidemic of 1775–82*. New York: Hill and Wang, 2001.

Watt, Gavin K. *Poisoned by Lies and Hypocrisy: America's First Attempt to Bring Liberty to Canada, 1775–1776*. Toronto: Dundurn, 2014.

About the Author

Mark R. Anderson is an independent historian and retired U.S. Air Force officer. He earned his B.A. in history from Purdue University and his M.A. in military studies from American Military University. He is the author of *The Battle for the Fourteenth Colony: America's War of Liberation in Canada, 1774–1776* (2013); *The Invasion of Canada by the Americans, 1775–1776: As Told through Jean-Baptiste Badeaux's Three Rivers Journal and New York Captain William Goforth's Letters* (2016); and a forthcoming book on the Affair of the Cedars and the first Indian battles of the Revolutionary War. Visit his website at https://markandersonhistory.net.

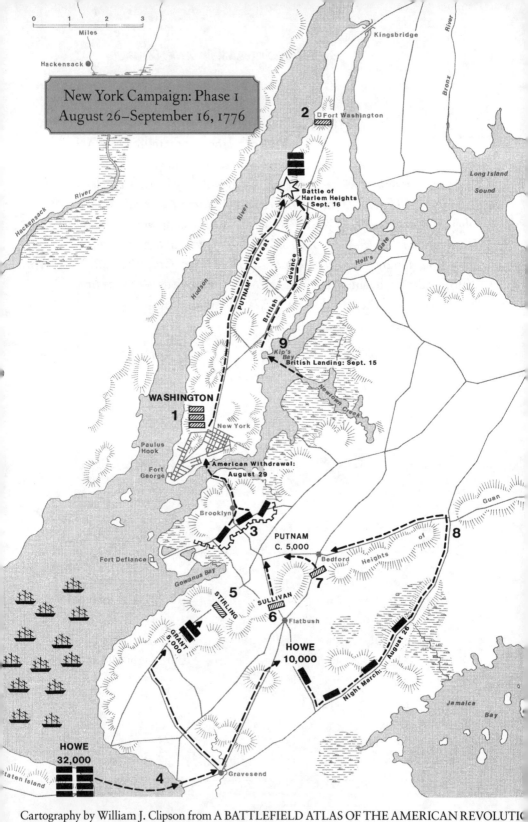

New York Campaign: Phase 1
August 26–September 16, 1776

Kingsbridge

Hackensack

2
Fort Washington

Long Island
Sound

Battle of
Harlem Heights
Sept. 16

Hudson River

Harlem River

Hell's
Gate

Bronx
River

PUTNAM's retreat

British Advance

9
Kip's
Bay
British Landing: Sept. 15

Newtown Creek

WASHINGTON

1

New York

Paulus
Hook

Fort
George

American Withdrawal:
August 29

Brooklyn

3

PUTNAM
C. 5,000

Bedford

Heights

of

Guan

8

Fort Defiance

Gowanus Bay

7

5
STIRLING

SULLIVAN

6
Flatbush

HOWE
10,000

Night March, August 26

HOWE
32,000

GRANT
6,000

Gravesend

4

Jamaica
Bay

Staten Island

Hackensack

Miles

Cartography by William J. Clipson from A BATTLEFIELD ATLAS OF THE AMERICAN REVOLUTION
published by Savas Beatie, www.savasbeatie.com

All London Was Afloat

BY TODD W. BRAISTED

For those who awoke early in the morning of July 1, 1776, there was a light breeze in lower Manhattan. Residents who wandered out toward the tip of the island likely could not see far into the harbor on that foggy Monday. Hugh Gaine's *New-York Gazette* and the *Weekly Mercury* for that day offered only the slightest clue that something momentous stood just offshore. Buried toward the bottom of the "New-York" byline for that day was a simple matter of fact sentence: "The Number of Transports now at Sandy-Hook, we hear amounts to 113 Sail, and we have not the least Reason to doubt, that General Howe is in this Fleet." Daniel McCurtin, a recently discharged Maryland soldier in the city, summed it up much better when he saw the massive British fleet off the New Jersey shore: "[I]n about ten minutes, the whole bay was full of shipping as ever it could be. I declare that I thought all London was afloat."[1] The war that started outside of Boston in April 1775 had finally come to New York City.

That a British fleet started arriving off Sandy Hook at the end of June should not have been a surprise to most people. When the British Army in America under General William Howe evacuated Boston on March 17, it did not signal an end to the conflict, but merely that the scene of war would be moving elsewhere. Howe and the army regrouped in Halifax, Nova Scotia, awaiting large numbers of reinforcements before opening the campaign. The British would be stretched thin. Troops were required in Canada, which was then under siege from an invading American army, and also to launch an expedition to strike at the southern colonies, principally Charleston, South Carolina.

New York made perfect sense as the next target. The harbor would be an excellent base for the Royal Navy; Loyalists were said to be far more common there than in New England; and the rivers and waterways would make defense by Washington's troops problematic, given their lack of a naval force. The extensive coastline provided the British with every advantage in terms of mobility.

Howe's troops, about 9,000 in number including some Highlanders newly arrived from Scotland, left Halifax on June 10, convoyed by Royal Navy warships. Over the next month, the army would grow in size and diversity. Many of the Highlanders arrived off Sandy Hook below New York in seven transports on July 21. On August 1, Howe's second-in-command, General Henry Clinton, arrived with General Charles Earl Cornwallis at the head of 2,900 British troops, including a company of Loyalist Black Pioneers recruited in North Carolina. The fleet accompanying them consisted of fifty ships under Sir Peter Parker. Parker and Clinton had lately conducted a failed campaign to capture Charleston, South Carolina. On August 12, 1,000 men drawn from the elite Brigade of Guards arrived, along with the first division of Hessian troops, about 7,800 men, under Lieutenant General Leopold von Heister. The fleet bringing these regiments consisted of some 107 transports, storeships, and warships. A ragtag assortment of British and Loyalist troops from Virginia—the debris of forces once serving under royal governor Lord Dunmore—and some very weak British regiments from the West Indies rounded out the army. Now totaling around 24,000 men under Howe, it would be ready to commence operations by the third week in August.

With the arrival of the British off Sandy Hook, Staten Island became indefensible and was ordered evacuated by Washington. The British Army then took possession of its first foothold in New York, much to the delight of its royal governor, William Tryon, who wrote to London on July 8: "I have the Satisfaction to acquaint Your Lordship...[that] General Howe disembarked the Troops under his Command on Staten Island the 2d Instant without Opposition, on which Occasion the Inhabitants of the Island came down to welcome the Arrival of their Deliverers, & have since afforded the Army every Supply & Accommodation in their Power. On Saturday last I reviewed the Militia of the Island, at Richmond Town, where near four Hundred appeared, who cheerfully, on my Recommendation, took the Oath of Allegiance & Fidelity to His Majesty."[2]

British expectations of encountering sympathetic Americans met with some initial success as Loyalists from both New Jersey and Long Island clandestinely made their way to Staten Island to join them. On July 23, Ambrose Serle, secretary to Admiral Lord Richard Howe, "met several People who had just escaped out of Long Island from the Tyranny of those insolent Demagogues, who, under pretences of superior Liberty, are imposing upon all about them the worst of Bondage. It excited one's Sympathy to see their poor meagre Faces, and to hear their Complaints of being hunted for their Lives like Game into the Woods and Swamps, only because they would not renounce their allegiance to their King and affection for their Country."[3]

The British Army arrayed against Washington included some American troops, raised the previous winter by Loyalists, primarily from Dutchess and Westchester Counties along the Hudson. Massachusetts Loyalist Edward Winslow, muster-master general of the American provincial forces, described their early plight: "The first provincial recruits that join'd the army was a party call'd the York Volunteers. They were collected about the North River before the Troops appear'd in that quarter, and...escaped to the King's Ships at Sandy-Hook, after some months they were forwarded to Hallifax, where they arriv'd a few days before the embarkation of the Troops. There they were review'd & form'd into two companies.... At that time it was say'd that no provision was made, or fund establish'd from which these unfortunate men cou'd be cloathed or accoutred, and they embark'd with the troops, with only the wretched remnant of apparel in which they had escaped from the rebels six or eight months before. In this distress they landed at Staten-Island—a few small articles were bestow'd on them while there— but nothing to relieve 'em essentially."[4]

With every indication that New York City would be the intended target of the 1776 British campaign, Washington had months to make defensive preparations. By August 3, his Continentals and state troops mustered some 20,537 officers and men, with thousands more on the march to join him. His army was then composed primarily of the numbered Continental regiments Congress had established at the beginning of the year, although they often went simply by their commander's name. Brigades typically consisted of five or more regiments, usually commanded by a brigadier general or colonel.

While Washington could take comfort in numbers, there were any number of worries to vex him. Despite an assembly of troops that would never be equaled again in the course of the war in point of numbers, his army could not concentrate in one place. The New York City area encompasses long stretches of coastline, including Manhattan and Staten and Long Islands, not to mention New Jersey, Connecticut, and the Hudson River Valley. All would need protection from the Royal Navy and Howe's troops. A brigade of soldiers would be required to defend the Hudson Highlands, particularly Forts Montgomery and Constitution. A brigade each would have to build and occupy Fort Lee in New Jersey and its sister, Fort Washington, on the opposite side of the Hudson. Further troops would be needed south of Fort Lee, at Paulus Hook (modern Jersey City) and Bergen Point (Bayonne).

Brigadier General Hugh Mercer, meanwhile, took charge of thousands of men serving in Pennsylvania's "Flying Camp," garrisoning such places as New Brunswick, Perth Amboy, and Elizabethtown, New Jersey.

Flying Camp troops were raised in New Jersey, Pennsylvania, Delaware, and Maryland for the purpose of providing a mobile force that could move from place to place on the defensive, covering such areas where the British might land. They served primarily, but not exclusively, in New Jersey, particularly as the campaign progressed.

Scattered among Washington's troops were companies and regiments of rifle-bearing troops. While the majority of long-arms used in the war, by both sides, were smoothbore muskets, each made use of rifles. A rifle differed from a musket in that its barrel was grooved, making the projectile spin when fired, increasing both its range and accuracy. Rifles were not universally adopted heretofore because of the increased time they took to load and their general unsuitability for holding a bayonet fixed onto the barrel.

The reputation that riflemen enjoyed as marksmen became almost mythical, prompting the British to adapt "loose files" (eighteen-inch intervals) between the soldiers and often to discard lace and other signs of distinction that could attract undue attention. One Irish officer serving in the British Army noted the unique "Rifle dress, which is a frock & Trowsers of linnin, fringed with Knotting which in warm weather is worn singley; in cold, covers their Body Clothes & is very convenient for the woods."[5] Some of these riflemen were initially posted to New Jersey, where they were among the first to make contact with the British. Some took the opportunity to desert, as noted by New Jersey Loyalist Stephen Kemble, a British Army officer, on July 15: "Two Rifle Men Came in with two Inhabitants from Rahway; the Rifle Men Desert every day."[6] Other riflemen may have let their reputation get the better of their judgment, as indicated in this anecdote written by a soldier in Elizabethtown on July 25: "Yesterday a rifle-man crossed the river, and when within fifteen yards of the enemy's out posts, desired them to surrender; at that instant he received a ball thro' his head, which killed him on the spot."[7]

While preparations for war commenced in New York's vicinity, there was also talk of peace. On July 12, HMS *Eagle* arrived, carrying Admiral Lord Richard Howe, brother to General William Howe. The Howe brothers were empowered by the Crown to act as commissioners for restoring peace in America. They had not expected the nature of the conflict to change fundamentally before they had any chance to carry out this assignment. Unbeknownst to them, Congress had, in one historic declaration, changed its objective from seeking redress of grievances with the British Crown to establishing a new, independent country. Informed of the historic event on July 9, Washington wrote to John Hancock:

> I perceive that Congress have been employed in deliberating on measures of the most Interesting nature.... It is certain that It is not with us to determine in many Instances what consequences will flow from our Counsels, but yet It behoves us to adopt such, as under the smiles of a Gracious & All kind Providence will be most likely to promote our happiness; I trust the late decisive part they have taken is calculated for that end, and will secure us that freedom and those privileges which have been and are refused us, contrary to the voice of nature and the British Constitution. Agreable to the request of Congress I caused the Declaration to be proclaimed before all the Army under my Immediate command and have the pleasure to inform them that the measure seemed to have their most hearty assent, The expressions and behavior both of Officers and men testifying their warmest approbation of It.[8]

A jubilant crowd of soldiers, Sons of Liberty, and residents showed their approbation in a more tangible way by marching to Bowling Green and pulling down the statue of King George III, which had stood six years. The physical embodiment of the monarch was trundled off to Connecticut to serve the needs of the forces of the new United States of America by being melted into musket balls.

While the British still could conceivably land anywhere, Long Island seemed the most logical place. This was confirmed by British deserters

and escaped American prisoners, no doubt transmitting camp gossip rather than factual knowledge of future maneuvers. Some reported the intended movement of the troops to be sometime between August 23 and 25, covered by gunboats with the fleet. This estimate was not far off the mark. Early on the morning of August 22, scores of flatboats, bateaux, and galleys, filled with British, Hessian, and Loyalist troops clad in red, blue, and green, landed in seven debarkations near Gravesend (now wholly within Brooklyn, at the time of the Revolution Kings County encompassed the villages of Brooklyn, New Utrecht, Flatlands, Gravesend, Bushwick, and Flatbush). The gunboats proved unnecessary, as the fifteen thousand or so troops were unopposed. One witness noted, "The Soldiers & Sailors seemed as merry as in a Holiday, and regaled themselves with the fine apples, which hung every where upon the Trees in great abundance."[9]

Washington had not been inactive. With New Jersey seemingly less of a target, in mid-August the Continental commander started drawing off troops from Amboy and other places opposite Staten Island, some of which would have a prominent role in the upcoming fighting: namely, the two Pennsylvania rifle battalions and Colonel Atlee's musketry regiment. Hugh Mercer, commanding in New Jersey, would see his command siphoned off throughout the campaign as the situation in New York evolved.

The British landing at Gravesend led to rumors and some action between the warring parties. One New England soldier, picking up gossip he had heard in Manhattan, wrote to his brother in Massachusetts that the British were "in a hollow and our men on the hills around them" which was true enough. He continued, however: "Last week four men were poisoned to Death Down in the City with Chocolate by the Tories...it is said that their [sic] was six more killed in the same manner."[10] There had been actual plots in the city against George Washington. The uncovering of a traitorous correspondence involving a senior officer, Lieutenant Colonel Herman Zedwitz of the First New

York Regiment, led to a court-martial which lent credence to the rumor-mongering. There were, however, no known factual reports of death by chocolate.

There was death by musket and rifle ball, however. Each side used its light troops to skirmish with the other. Such actions buoyed up spirits, with the *New-York Gazette* reporting on August 26, "An advanced Party of the Regulars are encamped a little to the North-West of Flatbush Church, and have a Battery somewhat to the Westward of Mr. Jeremiah Vanderbelt's, from whence they continue to fire briskly on our People, who often approach and discharge their Rifles within 200 Yards of their Works. We have had only 4 Men wounded since the Enemy landed; but we are certain many of them fell; one, a Hessian, was killed last Friday: Several Dollars were found in his Pocket, and he had an excellent Rifle."[11] On the opposing side, Howe noted in his general orders for August 25 that he "highly approved of the Spirited behaviour of Capts. Campbell & Grant & [the] Detachmt. of New York Compys. Upon the Scouting partys of yesterday."[12] The time for skirmishing soon came to an end. The main event was at hand.

The British plan for the early morning hours of August 27 involved feints, deception, and perhaps some luck. On their far left (the American right, anchored on Gowanus Bay to the north), advancing from the Narrows past Yellow Hook, were the Fourth and Sixth British brigades, along with the Forty-Second Highlanders, New York Companies, and ten pieces of cannon all under the command of Major General James Grant. This was a feint. In the center, Lieutenant General Leopold von Heister commanded the Hessian brigades that would attack at Flatbush, amidst the "Heights of Guan," with Cornwallis and additional British troops in reserve. The main British force, in two divisions led by Clinton and Hugh Earl Percy, would take ten thousand men on a wide sweep beyond the right of the British line toward Bedford, slip through the unguarded Jamaica Pass, and bring the bulk of the army behind the American left flank.

The first indication of the British came on the American right, where 120 men of Atlee's Pennsylvanians formed a guard at the Red Lion Inn, a tavern along the coast of Gowanus Bay. There, at 1:00 a.m., General James Grant's troops smashed into the guard, who retreated back after a few shots, leaving a lieutenant and fifteen men behind as prisoners. While many of Washington's troops remained in the extensive fortifications opposite Manhattan, thousands more now moved forward to block any British advance. The American line formed with Sullivan facing von Heister in the center and Lord Stirling in front of General Grant's force. The rifle troops under Colonel Miles and Lieutenant Colonel Brodhead that had been on the left moved to reinforce Stirling's division, which now included Smallwood's Maryland Regiment under Major Mordecai Gist, the Delaware Regiment under Colonel John Haslet, and the Pennsylvanians under Atlee. The removal of the riflemen to the right of the line would prove to be unfortunate.

Soon after daybreak, von Heister and his corps commenced a cannonade upon Sullivan's troops, followed up by the advance of his blue-coated Hessian brigades. With both Stirling and Sullivan fully engaged, the British under Clinton then appeared behind them. Confronted only by a patrol of officers, which the British captured, Clinton and Percy's troops poured through the pass between Sullivan and Stirling's forces and their fortifications. The rout soon commenced.

The fighting had so far raged between Stirling's troops and those of General Grant on the left of the British line. The British suffered some of their heaviest losses of the day where their light troops fought against many of the Pennsylvania rifle troops. One British captain wrote home to his mother: "I was lucky in my Escape for I had my right hand Man wounded and left hand Man kill'd, I had three kill'd and Six wounded in my Company in about three minutes having fallen in with about 400 Rifle men unawares, they are not so dreadfull as I expected or they must have destroyed me and my whole Company before we were supported by anybody else."[13] The casualties among the Americans were just as heavy. "Our Lieutenant Colonel [Caleb] Parry was shot through the head," wrote an officer of Atlee's regiment.[14]

With Clinton's force closing the noose around the two American divisions, the race was on to retreat back to the safety of the fortifications. For some, the choice was to surrender or attempt escape via Gowanus Creek. Isaac Pier, a soldier in Van Cortlandt's battalion of Heard's Brigade, "had to retreat to make his Escape & forded a creek watter up to his neck."[15] The retreat was covered by the Maryland troops. "We had not retreated near a quarter of a mile," wrote one Marylander, "before we were fired upon by an advanced part of the enemy, and those upon our rear were playing upon us with their artillery. Our men fought with more than Roman virtue, and I am convinced would have stood until they were shot down to a man. We forced the advanced party, which first attacked us, to give way; through which opening we got a passage down to the side of a marsh, seldom before waded over, which we passed, and then swam a narrow river, all the time exposed to the fire of the enemy." The right wing of the battalion, unable to cross the water, was shot down or surrendered. The Maryland Regiment, with about 400 effective rank and file, lost 259 officers and men killed, wounded, or taken. With the retreat into the fortifications by the defeated American troops, the battle was done. At a cost of just 41 British dead and some 257 wounded, along with less than thirty Hessian casualties, Howe had achieved an overwhelming victory over some of Washington's best troops.

For the nascent army of the fledgling United States, the battle was a rough coming-of-age experience, pushing men without much training or experience to the limits of their endurance. Rifleman James Karr of Pennsylvania "underwent the most severe and arduous duty, having in the course of the day, between the post where they were stationed in the morning, and the Flatbush road, encountered and fought five or six different detachments of the enemy."[16] There was no shortage of blame going around among both officers and men. "Less Generalship never was shown in the Army since the Art of War was understood," complained Lieutenant Colonel Daniel Brodhead of the riflemen.[17] The

Pennsylvania battalions had been thrown into chaos, marching and countermarching as new information appeared. When they tried to stand, the troops to their front from New England and New Jersey threw them into disorder by retreating through their lines.

The New Jersey troops, some 1,600 or so, were a five-battalion state corps under Brigadier General Nathaniel Heard, raised less than two months before the battle. These troops had been part of Sullivan's force. Matthias Riker, a twenty-year-old Bergen County soldier in Colonel Philip Van Cortlandt's Battalion, survived his ordeal, but not unscathed: "They had to retreat with great loss...the order was every man should make the best of his way.... He retreated through the woods and saw the Pennsylvania Troops taken...on his retreat, he was wounded in the Knee by a ball."[18] The other battalions of the brigade were bloodied as well, including the one commanded by Colonel Philip Johnston, who "received a ball in his breast, which put an end to the life of as brave an officer as ever commanded a battalion."[19] Another battalion commander in the brigade, Colonel Ephraim Martin, received a similar wound but survived to fight another day.

Howe's Loyalist troops fought well; however, their lack of uniforms would prove fatal—a reminder that "friendly fire" is never actually friendly. Their exploits were witnessed by army surgeon Thompson Forster, who noted:

> The New Yorkers...merited the confidence the General [Howe] reposed in them by their very gallant Behaviour on this occasion. The only mark of distinction the New Yorkers had to be known from the Enemy in the Field was a Red Cross they wore on their hats or rather caps, this distinction was scarcely sufficient as an accident in this engagement disagreably proved...the Light Infantry and New Yorkers were ordered to dash into the thickest of the wood, by which means they surprised the enemy in the Rear, drew them out absolutely with the Bayonet with great slaughter; the New

Yorkers were so hot in the pursuit that they followed them
out of the wood on to the Plain, where they were unfortunately mistaken by our Battalion [of Light Infantry] for the
enemy, and received one fire before they were known.[20]

A testament to their service was provided by (then) Sergeant Richard
Vanderburgh of Dutchess County, who "received seven severe and dangerous wounds, [and] was rendered for a considerable time incapable of
serving."[21]

The Hessian troops under General von Heister also acquitted themselves satisfactorily in the battle, losing just two killed and twenty-six
officers and men wounded. "The Hessians distinguished themselves
[against] the best of their troops and rifleman," one regimental commander boasted. "If [the Americans] are all as bad as they were on that
day, this will be more of a hunt than a war. It will still be too bad for
many an honest fellow who can be killed by these knaves. Several days
after the battle which frightened them so, they still shiver at the word
Hessians."[22] That fear would not last the rest of the war.

While the battle was a terrible drubbing for Washington's troops,
the loss was not complete—indeed, it could have been catastrophic for
the Americans if the British had immediately pushed their success. General Henry Clinton believed the numerous works and trenches built by
Washington's men opposite Manhattan were only occupied by eight
hundred men, over an extent he considered as needing over seven times
that amount to adequately defend. "I had at the moment," Clinton wrote
afterwards, "but little inclination to check the ardor of our troops when
I saw the enemy flying in such a panic before them. I was also not without
hopes that His Excellency [William Howe], who was on a neighboring
hill and, of course, saw their confusion, might be tempted to order us to
march directly forward down the road to the ferry, by which, if we succeeded, everything on the island must have been ours."[23]

To be fair, neither Howe nor Clinton could have known with any
certainty how many troops manned the fortifications, and Clinton's

estimate was well below the thousands Washington actually had there. The most recent major battle Howe had fought, on a fortified hill outside Boston in June 1775, had cost the British some nine hundred killed and wounded, losses that could not easily be replaced. One Hessian officer witnessing the rout noted:

> The enemy retreated in small groups and in great confusion toward the Brooklyn lines, where they have built fortifications strong enough to withstand an assault of fifty thousand men. On both wings they have zigzag trenches, casemated and supplied with provisions for 350 men. In front of these fortifications is a picketed double trench. In this manner they have raised one work behind another as far as the sea. On their right wing, moreover, is a woods with many trenches and strong abates. On the highest spot of a small peninsula called Red Hook, they have raised a battery to keep the New York channel clear and prevent us from occupying the woods.[24]

Howe freely admitted in his official report that the American works could have been carried by his troops "whom he had to prevail upon to desist from the Attempt…but as it was apparent the Lines must have been ours at a very cheap Rate by regular Approaches, I would not risk the Loss that might have been sustained in the Assault."[25]

The days following the battle featured heavy rain and minor skirmishing between the light troops of each side. Washington was perhaps not thrilled with the former but welcomed the latter, hoping it would give his shaken troops some renewed confidence. This allowed for some time to count up the losses and inform Congress of the defeat. No one could accurately tabulate the casualties, however, and Washington held out hope that many of the missing would return into the lines. Four days after the battle, John Hancock and Congress were informed that the loss to the army, in killed, missing, and prisoners, was perhaps between 700 and 1,000 officers and men. The actual losses were nearly twice that. A

British return made out after the battle tallied 1,097 American officers and men taken prisoner, 67 of whom were wounded. Among the prisoners were Continental generals John Sullivan and Lord Stirling, along with wounded New York militia brigadier general Nathaniel Woodhull, who would die in New Utrecht within a few weeks. The capture and death of the last mentioned officer remains a mystery to this date, steeped in legend and lore of a defiant patriot. According to the common report at the time, he was wounded in the hand and arm for not turning over his sword.

The Americans grasped for glimmers of success. In one instance, a captured officer's hat marked "Grant" led to reports of the death of British general James Grant in the battle. The hat actually belonged to Lieutenant Colonel James Grant of the Fortieth Regiment of Foot, who was indeed killed in action. The general, who was still alive and well, related the fact to a friend in England: "Those cursed Saints put me in the News Papers as being killed, & rejoiced exceedingly at getting rid of a man who had abused them in Parliament."[26] The Americans would have to settle for a lieutenant and twenty-one British marine grenadiers who mistook a well-uniformed party of blue-coated Continentals for Hessians and ended up as prisoners. The number of American dead and wounded was never ascertained, with estimates running from 500 to 1,800.

With the imminent danger of the Royal Navy cutting off reinforcement or evacuation, Washington convened a council of war to discuss the situation and formulate the next step. The wind had so far prevented the British warships from advancing up the East River, but that would not last much longer. The heavy rain had ruined ammunition and provisions. Above all, the defeat on the Twenty-Seventh had caused "great confusion and discouragement among the Troops."[27] The eight generals present unanimously voted in favor of immediately evacuating the troops to New York City.

The evacuation proceeded as quietly as possible. Soldiers helped those in need of assistance, such as Pennsylvania rifle ensign George Owrey: "We crossed over in the night from Long Island to New York. I had received in the Battle a flesh wound in my right thigh, made with the Sabre of a Light Horseman when they broke our ranks, and lay in one of the wagons, on account of weakness from the loss of blood, until the proper time for embarking, when the men carried me to the Boat."[28] The crossing from the fortifications on Brooklyn Heights to Manhattan was aided by both nature and man. With a heavy fog rolling in off the water, small craft with muffled oars went unheard and unseen by the British, ferrying Washington's troops to safety.

The men doing the rowing were primarily from one corps raised in the vicinity of Marblehead, Massachusetts, the Fourteenth Continental Regiment, commanded by Colonel John Glover. The colonel and his men miraculously evacuated the entire remaining force in Brooklyn, perhaps over eight thousand men, for which they "received the thanks of all the Generals, for the attention, dispatch and regularity which they manifested through the whole night."[29] One Connecticut soldier summed it up well when years later he recalled that "while the enemy was yawning, we were quietly paraded and drawn off."[30]

The scale of the American defeat could not remain secret forever. The *New-York Gazette* and the *Weekly Mercury* for September 9, 1776, published a list of captured officers who had requested their baggage and money be sent to them. It included dozens of names, principally Colonels Samuel Miles and Daniel Brodhead's Pennsylvania riflemen, Samuel Atlee's Pennsylvanians, William Smallwood's Marylanders, and Jedediah Huntington's Seventeenth Continental Regiment. The paper likewise informed its readers that "a Flag [of Truce] came from the [British] Fleet with a Return of those Officers that were made Prisoners in the late Attack on Long-Island; who we hear are treated with Civility by the British Officers."

On August 29, General Lord Stirling wrote to Washington from aboard HMS *Eagle* to inform him that he had been taken prisoner by the Hessians under General von Heister. His fellow Continental general in captivity probably carried Stirling's letter personally to Washington. "On Thursday [August 29] General Sullivan came up on his Parole, and confirms the Account of General Lord Stirling, and the greatest Part of our Men that were missing being Prisoners, and very humanely treated. He returned on board that Evening, but came up again next Morning and set out immediately afterwards to the Congress at Philadelphia."[31]

Within a few days, there would actually be far fewer prisoners in British hands. Among those serving with the British were recruiters for the Royal Highland Emigrants, a Loyalist regiment then stationed in Nova Scotia, commanded by Major John Small. On September 3, "Major Small ordered the [Maryland Loyalist] Robert William Walker to go amongst the Rebel Prisoners to try what number he could inlist for the Regiment when he inlisted 173 Men and took them all safe to Halifax."[32]

Sullivan had specifically been paroled to bring a message to Congress on behalf of Admiral Lord Howe, wishing the two sides to meet to discuss peace. Congress agreed, sending three delegates, Benjamin Franklin, John Adams, and Edward Rutledge. The meeting took place on September 11 at the home of Loyalist colonel Christopher Billopp on Staten Island. The outcome was preordained, as the issue of independence could not be negotiated. In the words of Lord Howe's secretary, Ambrose Serle, "They met, they talked, they parted."[33] The war would continue.

The remainder of the New York campaign, despite American bravado and the numerous fortifications dotting the New York area, was a foregone conclusion. Manhattan was still an island, and without a proper American navy to defend the surrounding waterways, the British could place troops when and where they wished. General John Morin Scott knew all too well what would happen when he wrote Washington on August 31: "I have very little apprehension that the Enemy will attempt to land in [the city] while we are here; as I think they can drive us out of it without that Risk; and we never I am convinced can prevail on the Troops to stand a Bombardment & Canonade."[34]

New York City was completely untenable. Manhattan Island is just over two miles wide, meaning any retreat from the city could be easily blocked, unless fortifications and disciplined troops existed in such numbers as to prevent the British landing. They did not. On September 15, thousands of British and Hessian troops pushed off from Newtown, Long Island, into the East River toward Manhattan, protected by five Royal Navy frigates in Kip's Bay. Ahead of them, from the quiet of the water, the British saw breastworks "filled with men" and columns of troops advancing to reinforce them. Germans in the boats sang hymns. British troops cursed.

On command, the ships opened fire. "They began the most tremendous peal I ever heard," one British officer wrote. "The breastworks were blown to pieces in a few minutes, and those who were to have defended it were happy to escape as quick as possible through the neighbouring ravines. The columns broke instantly, and betook themselves to the nearest woods for shelter. We pressed to shore, landed, and formed without losing a single man."[35]

Although the men of Douglas's Brigade of Connecticut Militia, the troops tasked with manning the breastworks, fled despite the exhortations of Washington and his staff to hold, the defeat could have been much worse. Despite wishing to hold the city, Congress allowed Washington leave to evacuate, staying there not "a moment longer than he shall think it proper."[36] This gave Washington time to remove vital stores, march off the bulk of his troops, and start building new works on the northern tip of the island. Despite the British not extending their line across the island before the bulk of the army escaped, another 371 officers and men fell into British hands, along with ordnance and stores that had not yet been removed.

While New York City had fallen into British hands and would remain the headquarters for their army in America through November 1783, they would not enjoy all of it, at least not as it stood when Washington left it. As far back as July 27, Cortlandt Skinner, a New Jersey Loyalist then raising a regiment for the British, opined, "tis probable the N. Englanders will burn the Town to prevent its being a Station for us."[37] It is still debated today what happened, and by whose hand, but soon after midnight on September 21, flames erupted in New York City, devouring such landmarks as Trinity Church. Enraged residents, soldiers, and sailors sought not only to douse the flames but to catch the perpetrators as well. Rumors swirled of arsonists being caught with combustibles and others cutting the handles of leather fire buckets. Such as were apprehended were said to have received summary justice on the spot. When the flames were finally extinguished, over 10 percent of the city had burned to the ground, principally between Broadway and the Hudson River.

For the next two months, Washington and Howe continued the campaign, with the British again leapfrogging forward from their shipping, first at Throg's Point (or Neck) and then, on October 18, at Pell's Point, a few miles to the northeast on the Long Island Sound. The men under John Glover, the Third, Thirteenth, Fourteenth, and Twenty-Sixth Continental Regiments, once again did great service to the cause of independence, holding off a superior British force five times their number, giving Washington time to remove his remaining forces from below that point and redeploy into Westchester. The two sides maneuvered around until fighting an inconclusive battle at White Plains on October 28.

The end of October saw the Americans in possession of Fort Washington, commanding Kingsbridge and northern Manhattan, along with its sister post, Fort Lee, to the southwest across the Hudson River in New Jersey. Over the past four months, the British had occupied all of Staten Island, Long Island, New York City, and Paulus Hook. In November, Washington divided his forces, leaving New York and New England troops in the Hudson Valley and upper Westchester while personally leading the troops from New Jersey and southward to take post at Fort Lee and Bergen County, New Jersey. Fort Washington, heavily defended by troops from Pennsylvania and New England under Colonel Robert Magaw, appeared to be safe from further British interest. Most American officers thought the campaign season was over and the fighting done until spring. Writing to his wife on November 10, artillery commander Henry Knox said, "This Campaign I think may be term'd a loosing Campaign not that I think the enemy have gained infinite advantages over us—It has been a Tragic Comedy of errors on both Sides."[38]

To the surprise of Washington and his staff, however, the British were not done. On November 15, they summoned Colonel Magaw and Fort Washington to surrender, and were refused. The wiser response would have been to evacuate the garrison to New Jersey as it could no longer be safely supported. General Nathanael Greene, however, commanding at Fort Lee, instead chose to double the troops in Magaw's post, a decision that would come back to haunt him. The day following Magaw's refusal to surrender, a large force of British and Hessians, the latter led on by Lieutenant General Wilhelm von Knyphausen, attacked and quickly captured the fort, which was renamed in honor of the Hessian commander. Over 2,800 officers and men were captured, virtually the entire garrison. Washington could only watch helplessly watch from Fort Lee.[39]

Washington perhaps thought this action had closed the campaign, but he made the prudent decision to start evacuating the large stock of provisions and stores from Fort Lee prior to abandoning it. The fort, intended to be used in conjunction with Fort Washington in blocking the Hudson River to the Royal Navy, was now useless. It had never actually stopped British ships from sailing past, despite withering fire from the heavy guns at each post. On November 20, just four days after the fall of Fort Washington (and before the latest evacuation could be completed), 5,000 British and Hessian troops under Lord Cornwallis landed unopposed about six miles above Fort Lee. Thanks to the alertness of a lieutenant in Heard's Brigade on guard duty, the garrison was warned and able to cross the Hackensack River at New Bridge to the west, thereby escaping entrapment. The British captured the post with virtually all its artillery, tents standing and breakfast on the fire, without firing a shot.

The British had taken 4,430 officers and men prisoner since that August day in Brooklyn. Washington and his divided army now faced defeat in detail by the recently knighted Sir William Howe. As pamphleteer Tom Paine, who marched with Washington's troops, would write, these were the times that tried men's souls. The Americans would need a major reversal of fortune to achieve their cause of independence—and soon.

Further Reading

Braisted, Todd. *Grand Forage 1778: The Battleground around New York City*. Yardley, Pennsylvania: Westholme, 2016. (This book is about future actions.)

Fischer, David Hackett. *Washington's Crossing*. New York: Oxford University Press, 2004.

Gallagher, John J. *The Battle of Brooklyn 1776*. New York: Book Sales, 2003.

Martin, Joseph Plumb. *A Narrative of a Revolutionary Soldier: Some Adventures, Dangers, and Sufferings of Joseph Plum Martin*. Originally published in 1830.

O'Donnell, Patrick K. *Washington's Immortals: The Untold Story of an Elite Regiment Who Changed the Course of the Revolution*. New York: Atlantic Monthly, 2016.

About the Author

Todd Braisted is the author of *Grand Forage 1778: The Battleground around New York City* (2016), *Bergen County Voices from the American Revolution: Soldiers and Residents in Their Own Words* (2012), and *The Loyalist Corps: Americans in the Service of the King* (2011). He is a researcher of Loyalist military studies. His primary focus is on Loyalist military personnel, infrastructure, and campaigns throughout North America. Since 1979, Braisted has amassed and transcribed over 40,000 pages of Loyalist and related material from archives and private collections around the world. He has authored numerous journal articles and books, as well as appearing as a guest historian on episodes of Who Do You Think You Are? (CBC) and History Detectives (PBS). He is the creator of royalprovincial.com, the largest website dedicated to Loyalist military studies. Braisted is a fellow in the Company of Military Historians and a past president of the Bergen County (NJ) Historical Society.

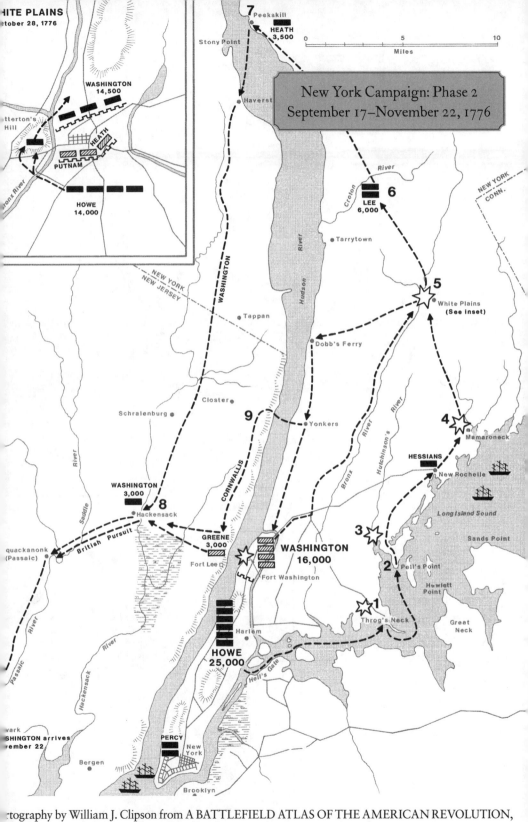

WHITE PLAINS
~~October~~ tober 28, 1776

WASHINGTON
14,500

~~Chatterton's~~ tterton's
Hill

HEATH

PUTNAM

HOWE
14,000

7 • Peekskill
HEATH
3,500

Stony Point

• Haverst~~raw~~

NEW YORK
CONN.

Croton River

6
LEE
6,000

• Tarrytown

5
White Plains
(See inset)

NEW YORK
NEW JERSEY

• Tappan

• Dobb's Ferry

Hudson River

• Closter

Schralenburg •

• Yonkers

9

4
• Mamaroneck

HESSIANS

• New Rochelle

Long Island Sound

Sands Point

WASHINGTON
3,000

8
• Hackensack

~~quackanonk~~
(Passaic)

British Pursuit

CORNWALLIS

GREENE
3,000

Fort Lee

Bronx River

Hutchinson's River

3

2 • Pell's Point

Hewlett
Point

WASHINGTON
16,000

Fort Washington

Saddle River

1
Throg's Neck

Great
Neck

• Harlem

HOWE
25,000

Hell's Gate

Hackensack River

Passaic River

~~Newark~~ ark
~~WA~~SHINGTON arrives
~~Nov~~ember 22

PERCY

New
York

• Bergen

• Brooklyn

New York Campaign: Phase 2
September 17–November 22, 1776

0   5   10
Miles

~~Car~~tography by William J. Clipson from A BATTLEFIELD ATLAS OF THE AMERICAN REVOLUTION,
~~pub~~lished by Savas Beatie, www.savasbeatie.com

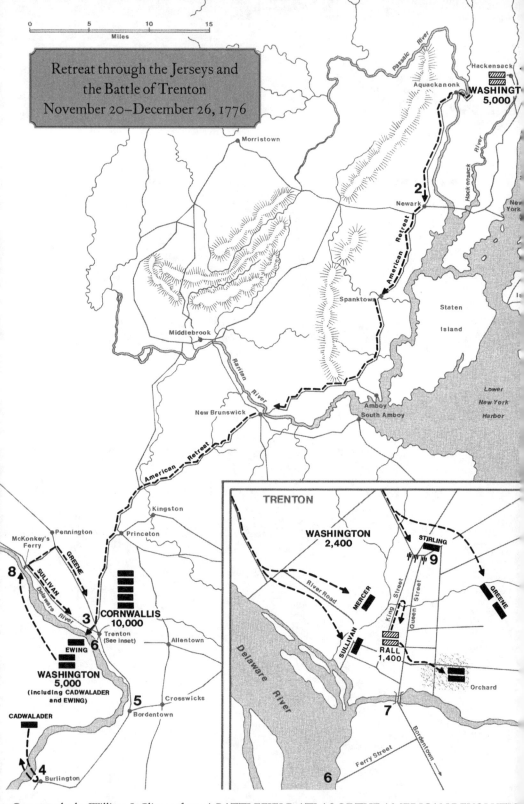

Retreat through the Jerseys and
the Battle of Trenton
November 20–December 26, 1776

Cartography by William J. Clipson from A BATTLEFIELD ATLAS OF THE AMERICAN REVOLUTIC
published by Savas Beatie, www.savasbeatie.com

The Times That Try Men's Souls: The Crossing and the Ten Crucial Days

BY WILLIAM L. KIDDER

Following their daily routine, Thomas Clarke and his sister Sarah, along with their enslaved woman Susannah, awoke early on Friday morning, January 3, 1777, on their farm located about a mile south of the village of Princeton, New Jersey. Beginning their chores, they unexpectedly heard and then saw a long column of Continental soldiers and militiamen marching up the little-used dirt road that passed a short distance from their front door. As they watched, about three hundred soldiers turned left from the column and marched across the crop stubble of the Clarkes' frozen farm fields and toward the bare orchard on their brother William's farm.

These peaceful Quakers watched an intense battle flare up when the American troops encountered about four hundred to five hundred British troops coming toward them. After an hour of heavy combat on their farm, as the battle sounds became more distant, Thomas and Sarah's relief changed to shocked grief when some American soldiers came to their door carrying several wounded, heavily bleeding men, including one identified as a high-ranking officer. The Quaker siblings accepted these wounded men into their home for treatment, knowing there were more wounded and dead lying in their fields who also needed help.

This battle took place during the times that Thomas Paine described as trying men's souls, but also at a moment of transition. On December 25, 1776, the war for independence had seemed all but lost. Just ten days later, however, the American patriots had gained a feeling of renewed confidence that their cause was just and they could succeed. Simultaneously, the British and their Loyalist supporters began questioning their ability to win.

■   ■   ■

After abandoning Fort Lee on the northeast edge of New Jersey in mid-November 1776, Washington's army retreated across New Jersey, pursued by a British force commanded by Lord Charles Cornwallis. The ordinarily aggressive Cornwallis followed Washington's troops with restraint as ordered by his commander, General William Howe, who wore a second hat as a peace commissioner and felt the war was essentially over.

Howe's restraint allowed Washington to reach Trenton and use its ferries and other boats to cross the Delaware River to Pennsylvania during the first week of December. Washington took aggressive action to remove any boats the British could use to cross the river after him and move against Philadelphia. He dispersed his troops among posts established in Bucks County for over twenty miles along the Delaware River, from Coryell's Ferry (today's New Hope) in the north to Bristol in the south. If British troops somehow found boats and tried to cross the river at any point, they would encounter American troops ready to resist and quickly spread the alarm.

Stymied, General Howe decided to end the campaign and establish winter quarters, assigning troops to a string of cantonments across New Jersey. About fifteen hundred Hessians under Colonel Johann Rall manned the westernmost post at Trenton, and another fifteen hundred Hessians and British under Colonel Carl von Donop were stationed in the Bordentown/Burlington area. This arrangement put much of central New Jersey, along with the New York City area, under apparently firm control of the largest expeditionary force ever assembled by Britain. The young New Jersey State government ceased functioning, and patriots felt abandoned while Loyalists felt empowered and protected by the British Army. The British recognized the low rebel morale and hoped that the Loyalists could help them against the rebels.

For the next two and half weeks, small bands of patriot troops crossed the Delaware River on a near-daily basis to harass the British troops at both western posts. This prevented the British and Hessian troops at those posts from settling into winter quarters, recovering from the fatigue and illnesses of the fall campaign, repairing equipment, and receiving fresh clothing and shoes. The soldiers felt they were still on campaign, not standing down in winter quarters. Sickness increased, in addition to wounds and violent deaths.

In the Trenton area, groups of fifty or fewer militiamen and Continentals carried out harassing attacks. Hessian outposts, foraging parties, messengers, and patrols experienced hit-and-run skirmishes that took a mental as well as physical toll. In the area south of Trenton, around Bordentown, Burlington, Moorestown, and Mount Holly, a series of skirmishes occurred during the week before Christmas. At Moorestown, Virginian Colonel Samuel Griffin gathered a small group of Virginia artillery and about five hundred New Jersey militiamen from Cumberland, Salem, and Gloucester counties. Griffin arrived at Mount Holly on December 20 and found the enemy had abandoned it, leaving supplies behind and fires burning. Griffin set out after the British, but local Loyalists kept the British informed of his progress. The British had about seven hundred men and three cannon at Black Horse.

On December 22, Colonel Griffin led his men in a skirmish at Petticoat Bridge near Mount Holly, killing several Hessians and forcing them to retreat rapidly and abandon their knapsacks and other gear. British reinforcements advanced the next morning with seven or eight cannon, and the Americans retreated in good order. In a firefight that evening at Mount Holly on Iron Works Hill, the Americans lost two killed and seven or eight wounded. Most of the American forces were then at Moorestown, while Colonel Donop made his quarters at Mount Holly on December 23.

These actions fatigued Donop's troops but gave them confidence that the small American force could be easily defeated. They also led Donop to center his attention on Mount Holly rather than Bordentown, increasing his distance from Trenton and widening the dispersal of his troops. Although not connected to Washington's larger plan, Griffin's actions therefore materially supported it by hampering Donop's ability to support Rall. The constant small attacks north and south of Trenton convinced the British and Hessians that they could expect a long and exhausting winter of harassment, but also that the Americans were in no condition to mount a significant attack.

Washington, meanwhile, developed a plan to reverse the downward course of the war, based on his belief that he needed to cease retreating, achieve a symbolic battlefield victory, and at least partially drive the British forces out of New Jersey. The continuing daily loss of men to illness, enlistment expiration, and desertion complicated that objective. Down to a tiny fraction of the 20,000 men with which he had begun the year's campaign, and needing to assemble as large a force as possible, he had repeatedly ordered General Charles Lee to bring on his troops that had remained near New York during the autumn retreat. Only after the British captured Lee on December 13, however, did his successor, General John Sullivan, move to reunite the army several days before Christmas. Washington's force then numbered about 2,400 cold, hungry, tired, and sick men, but even that was temporary since most Continental troops had enlisted only until the end of the year. The Continental Congress had initiated the creation of a new Continental Army several months earlier, but recruits were hard to come by in a time of despair.

The plan Washington secretly developed with his generals aimed to defeat the outnumbered Hessians at Trenton and simultaneously attack the Hessians and British dispersed in the Bordentown/Mount Holly area. He hoped to follow up with an attack on Princeton and other cantonments before the British could react by consolidating their troops. As long as British forces remained dispersed, Washington's small army outnumbered the enemy at each of their cantonments.

In addition to his main force encamped between Coryell's and Yardley's ferries, Washington had approximately 1,500 Pennsylvania and New Jersey militiamen with General James Ewing, opposite Trenton. The New Jersey militia system was in complete disarray. These men had joined Washington's force individually and in small groups before being organized into makeshift companies. Many knew Trenton and the area he would be traversing to attack it, and their knowledge would prove valuable. A third group of approximately 1,500 men at Bristol, under Colonel John Cadwalader, was composed of a mixture of Pennsylvania militia and New England Continentals originally assembled to help defend Philadelphia and the surrounding area from British control. General Israel Putnam was working in Philadelphia to collect additional Pennsylvania militiamen who would join with Cadwalader's force to attack Colonel Donop's force south of Trenton.

Washington planned to cross the Delaware River with his army about nine miles north of Trenton, beginning on the afternoon of December 25, and march overnight to attack the town around dawn on December 26. Simultaneously, Ewing's men would cross at ferries just south of Trenton to support Washington and prevent any Hessians from escaping to alert and join their forces near Bordentown. Cadwalader's force would cross at a ferry near Bristol to at least distract Donop's Hessian and British forces, preventing them from supporting Colonel Rall. Hopefully, Donop's dispersed units would pull back and allow Cadwalader to join forces with Washington and continue attacking additional vulnerable cantonments.

Colonel Johann Rall commanded approximately 1,500 Hessians at Trenton. They comprised one grenadier and two fusilier infantry regiments, a company of about fifty light infantry Jäger, three artillery companies with a total of six cannon, and about twenty British light dragoons. These men had served with skill and courage in the fall campaign. Their posting at Trenton put them in a position of honor following military tradition, although contemporaries and historians could question Howe's wisdom in placing soldiers who did not speak English at such an advanced post. Although acknowledged as a skilled battlefield commander, at Trenton Rall refused to build redoubts and did not provide his officers with a coordinated plan for defending an attack on the town. He simply did not believe that Washington had sufficient numbers or quality of troops to mount a significant attack.

Washington put his plan of attack into operation on the afternoon of December 25, hoping to get all troops and equipment across the river by midnight and attack Trenton before dawn. The Continentals, with eighteen artillery pieces and their horse-drawn ammunition and supply wagons, formed up to cross the Delaware from McConkey's Ferry to Johnson's Ferry. The crossing required several types of rivercraft. Approximately eighteen to twenty Durham boats that normally carried heavy bulk cargoes up and down the river, varying from forty-five to sixty-five feet long, could carry troops and cross anywhere on the river. But the Americans also needed flat ferry barges to carry horses, artillery, and wagons.

Washington chose this crossing point because of its appropriate distance from Trenton and also because the ferry owners were solid New Light Presbyterians and staunch patriots. To manage the boats while crossing, he would rely on the multiethnic seafaring men of Colonel John Glover's Fourteenth Massachusetts Regiment, the Marbleheaders, and local militiamen who knew how to operate the tricky ferry boats, which were attached to overhead lines that kept them on course. The day before the crossing, Washington selected from Ewing's camp a group of about two dozen New Jersey militiamen who lived in the area and knew well the roads between Johnson's Ferry and Trenton. Two of these men were assigned to each brigade as guides.

Even before the crossing commenced, the plan began to unravel. In Philadelphia, Putnam decided he needed to stay put with the very few militia troops he had gathered. The frigid weather deteriorated, and a storm set in that turned into an ugly nor'easter. The weather and the nature of the Delaware River created different ice conditions at each crossing point. Where Washington crossed about nine miles above Trenton, the river flowed continuously south, and various-sized floating fragments of sheet ice that had formed upriver and broken off came downstream. These ice chunks were annoying and potentially dangerous, but not prohibitive to the crossing. At Trenton, where Ewing was to cross, the rapids in the falls at the river's head of navigation combined with the tidal nature of the river below the falls to produce packed ice, with only treacherous narrow lanes of rushing water. No one from Ewing's force was able to cross. At Bristol, the wider and tidal river caused ice to form from the banks toward the river's center. In places near the shore, ice was thick enough to support a man walking to a boat secured at the outer edge of the ice. The boat could cross to the opposite ice shelf where the men could then walk across the ice to the shore. However, the ice was nowhere consistently thick enough to support horses, artillery, and wagons. Cadwalader did get some men across but then recalled them when others, and especially artillery, could not follow. So, Washington's force was the only one to cross successfully. Even he was considerably delayed by the river ice and the intense storm that developed.

Despite the delay, Washington persisted in crossing everything, even the artillery. He had agreed with Colonel Henry Knox, his artillery commander, to take eighteen artillery pieces, knowing that the Hessians only had six. Despite the significant difficulties and delays encountered while crossing the artillery, Washington wanted to inspire his troops with the confidence provided by artillery support and demoralize the Hessians. As the weather deteriorated with wind-driven snow, sleet, and rain, the artillery took on even greater importance as the "foul weather weapon." It was easier to keep the bagged powder dry and fire an artillery piece in wet conditions than it was for the infantrymen to keep their musket powder dry.

The crossing took until about 3:00 a.m. to complete, putting Washington three hours behind schedule. Two advance companies of forty men each were sent on toward Trenton to set up roadblocks and prevent locals or any British patrols from learning of the crossing. Close to 4:00 a.m., the army began its march from Johnson's Ferry to Trenton. Despite the darkness, weather conditions, and dirt roads, the militia guides kept the men and horses on course. After marching uphill for about a mile, the column turned right toward Trenton and onto more level ground, with the wind no longer directly in their faces.

A ravine encountered at Jacobs Creek, which the guides had no doubt warned Washington about, slowed the march considerably while the men helped the horses, wagons, and artillery down the steep slope, across the swift, deep creek, and then up the opposite slope. Once past the ravine, the army continued its march to the small crossroads village of Birmingham, about four miles from Trenton. There, Washington had his officers synchronize their watches with his, and he split the force into two divisions. General Nathanael Greene's division turned left and took the Upper Ferry Road to the Scotch Road and then the Pennington Road to arrive at the northern end of Trenton. General John Sullivan's division continued straight out of Birmingham on a route paralleling the Delaware River to enter the town at its southern end. Both divisions reached and drove in the advanced Hessian guard posts almost a mile outside town at about 8:00 a.m. The battle began with the heavily outnumbered Hessian guards retreating into town.

The Hessian troops quartered throughout the town, so they could not quickly turn out and form up for battle. Their dependents may have quartered in the stone barracks in the southern end of town. Two regiments, the Rall and von Lossberg, managed to assemble under Rall near the center of Trenton on King Street while being attacked by Greene's division from the north and west, including pouring artillery fire down the two main streets, King and Queen. Other elements of Greene's division continued to the northeast side of town to block Hessian escape to, or British reinforcement from, Princeton. Colonel Rall led his two outnumbered regiments east across Queen Street and into the area of an apple orchard, where they attempted to defend themselves and break out to the north. Finding himself nearly surrounded, Rall tried unsuccessfully to return into town. His men continued to fight in the orchard area until he received a fatal wound and his two regiments surrendered.

The third Hessian regiment, the Knyphausen, formed up nearer to the southern end of the village and met Sullivan's division after it chased the fifty Jäger from their outpost into town and over the bridge at Assunpink Creek. After some maneuvering, this regiment also surrendered, thus ending the short Battle of Trenton. No Americans were killed and only a few were wounded. These included Lieutenant James Monroe, who was severely injured with a severed carotid artery while attacking and capturing a Hessian cannon on King Street early in the fighting. Twenty-two Hessians were killed and eighty-three were wounded, in addition to about nine hundred men captured. Several hundred Hessians had been able to escape by crossing the Assunpink Creek, which was undefended due to Ewing's failure to get across the river, and fleeing to either Bordentown or Princeton. The town suffered much structural damage, and the street fighting had terrified the civilian residents.

Word of the victory at Trenton led Donop to order his troops to abandon the area and head toward the vicinity of Princeton. This allowed Cadwalader to cross his troops the next day and prepare to join with Washington. Washington had won a significant victory, mainly because his enemy had dismissed him and his army as incompetents. The battle did not diminish the British Army's ability to pursue the conflict, but it did inflict a psychological wound and enhanced the reputation of Washington and his force.

Immediately after the battle, Washington attempted to ferry his prisoners and their wives and children across the river to Pennsylvania, where they could be taken to Philadelphia and kept under guard. However, river ice prevented their removal. Not knowing his exact situation or that of the enemy forces at Bordentown and Princeton, Washington marched his exhausted troops and their prisoners back to Johnson's Ferry and crossed back to Bucks County through that night and into the morning. He left about twenty-eight severely wounded Hessians, several of whom would die within a few days, at Trenton under the care of paroled Hessian medical officers.

Washington spent the next several days removing his Hessian prisoners to Philadelphia and preparing his troops for further action in New Jersey. Because he could not risk appearing to retreat to safety in Pennsylvania, he returned his army to Trenton on December 30–31, and began preparations to defend the town. His army was growing in strength with the arrival of New Jersey and Pennsylvania militia units encouraged by the victory at Trenton. At the same time, though, he was only hours away from losing his Continentals at the end of their enlistments. He and his officers pleaded with them to extend their enlistments for six weeks, telling them that in doing so, they could "render that service to the cause of liberty, and to your country, which you probably never can do under any other circumstances." He also offered them a ten dollar bonus, equivalent to an extra month's pay, in addition to their regular pay. About half the veterans agreed to stay while the rest left.

With his forces stationed at Trenton and Cadwalader's nearby at Crosswicks, Washington sent out scouting parties toward Princeton who informed him that British forces were concentrating there and planned to attack him on January 2. He also learned about a little-used back road, called the Sawmill Road, leading to the outskirts of Princeton. Between December 30 and January 1, his troops established fighting positions on Mill Hill on the south side of Assunpink Creek, which ran through Trenton. On January 1, he sent out about a thousand men to set up several defensive positions where creeks crossed the main road to Princeton. Positioning troops on the rise behind each creek gave them the advantage of high ground and the stream as a barrier. These small delaying parties would not fight for long against the vastly more numerous British. However, they could temporarily halt the enemy, force them to deploy for battle, exchange volleys, and then fall back to another position while the British reformed their marching column.

On the night of January 1, Washington called for all of Cadwalader's troops at Crosswicks to join him by morning for the expected showdown. He would then have almost seven thousand men, including remnants of veteran Continental regiments who had extended their enlistments, together with a large number of militiamen who had not fought at the Battle of Trenton. Most of the militiamen had not been in a significant battle. This mixed force would oppose approximately eight thousand veteran British and Hessian troops under Cornwallis.

Early on the morning of January 2, Cornwallis began marching his troops from Princeton in one long column down the main road to Trenton, leaving behind about 1,500 men as a rearguard and 1,500 more as reserves at Maidenhead between Princeton and Trenton. The combination of American delaying tactics and deep muddy roads, which resulted from temperatures rising into the forties and melting the ice and snow, caused his troops to use almost the entire day to march the twelve miles to Trenton. Pennsylvanian Colonel Edward Hand organized the very effective delaying actions. By the time the British chased Hand's forces back through Trenton and across the Assunpink Creek bridge to Mill Hill, it was beginning to get dark.

The two sides exchanged pounding artillery fire, and the British made three unsuccessful and bloody attempts to cross the bridge. Finally, darkness led General Cornwallis to suspend the assault and prepare to fight in the morning. He dispatched an order back to Princeton to leave just one regiment behind very early the next morning and send two regiments down to Trenton, along with some artillery, light dragoons, and a group of transient men looking to rejoin their regular units.

When the fighting ceased, British and American soldiers set up camp for the night, building fires for warmth and cooking. Both forces had suffered significantly higher casualties than in the first battle on December 26. The Americans had about 100 killed and wounded, the

Hessians about 140, and the British about 225. The town had suffered damage from artillery exchanges, further terrorizing civilians. But, unlike Rall, Washington had prepared well and survived to fight another day.

However, neither side looked forward to the morning. The outnumbered Americans had their backs to the Delaware River, and the British could take advantage of several fords further up the Assunpink Creek to outflank them. For their part, the British faced substantial American forces holding the high ground and supported by a large amount of artillery. Fighting an enemy entrenched on high ground presented a distasteful recipe for high casualties, like at Bunker Hill in 1775. Each side posted sentries and kept an eye on the other.

Late in the evening, Washington called a council of war at the house of Alexander Douglass. The dangerous situation they were in was evident to each of his officers. No one wanted to retreat, but neither did they want to risk a tragic defeat at Trenton that could cripple the war effort. Considering that the British only had about 1,500 men at Princeton, the number he had defeated at Trenton, and knowing about British defenses and the little-used road, Washington and his officers put together a plan to make an all-night march to Princeton by a route that kept them well away from the British troops at Trenton. They called in several local militiamen and interviewed each separately to compare their recommendations for a roundabout route avoiding the British. The chosen route, for which the men were designated guides, followed a road used by Quakers to travel between the Princeton and Crosswicks meetinghouses, and joined the little-used back road that would allow them to surprise the British at Princeton.

Following this route, Washington would avoid renewed battle with Cornwallis and instead take on an enemy force that he significantly outnumbered. After defeating that Princeton force, he could capture supplies the British left at New Brunswick and then march his troops to Morristown in northern New Jersey. There they could take up defensible positions in the Watchung Mountains, monitor the British in New York, and be on the flank of any British forces attempting to cross New Jersey during that winter or spring.

The council of war broke up, and the officers returned to camp and quietly gave the orders to break camp and form up to march. Some militiamen were assigned to stay behind and keep the fires burning all night. The American troops were not completely successful in concealing their departure from the British sentries. But when informed of perceived American movements, Cornwallis discounted any danger. He simply thought the troops were moving to defend the fords up the Assunpink Creek or were preparing to cross those fords and surprise the British on their flank in the morning. Cornwallis's only response was to reinforce his troops at those crossings.

The Americans departed so secretly that even some Americans did not get the word. Among these was Dr. Benjamin Rush and several of his assistants, who were tending to wounded men in a house he had converted into a makeshift hospital. In the middle of the night, they discovered that the army had departed for parts unknown and hurriedly got their patients into wagons and took them to Bordentown, thinking Washington had gone there.

Overnight the temperature dropped into the twenties and refroze the muddy roads, turning them into a rough, slippery, concrete-like surface. After traversing the icy roads all night, the leading American units arrived around daybreak at the junction of the Quaker Road and the Sawmill Road. Here Washington split the army into three divisions. General Mifflin would continue along the Quaker Road toward the main highway. An advance group of about five hundred men under Colonel Nicholas Hausegger would move out first to cross the main road and proceed on farm lanes to the northwest side of Princeton, ready to help take the town and prevent the escape of British soldiers. Approximately one thousand men under Mifflin would wait and then follow as far as the main road, where a bridge at a large gristmill crossed Stony Brook. They would destroy that bridge to delay Cornwallis from getting back to Princeton until after the battle there had ended.

Another large division with several thousand men under General Sullivan would follow the Sawmill Road to just behind Nassau Hall, on the campus of today's Princeton University, and attack the center of town. The third division, with about 1,800 men, led by General Hugh Mercer, would begin marching on the Sawmill Road but then break off and approach the town from the center so that the troops there would be hit on three sides, much as the Hessians at Trenton had been.

While Washington formed up his troops, British lieutenant colonel Charles Mawhood led some five hundred to eight hundred troops out of Princeton, heading down the main road toward Stony Brook Bridge and Worth's Mill to support Cornwallis at Trenton. After crossing the bridge, the vanguard of light dragoons ascended a hill known locally as Cochran's Hill. About the time they reached the hilltop, the rising sun on that bright, crisp morning glinted off some shiny metal associated with the troops of Sullivan's division on the Sawmill Road, about a mile away. A dragoon officer distracted by the glint saw the troops and reported to Colonel Mawhood. At about the same time, American troops likewise were distracted by a glint and saw the dragoons on Cochran's Hill, thinking they were just a routine morning patrol sent out from Princeton.

To investigate the unknown troops heading toward Princeton, Mawhood sent a dragoon officer down the hill to determine their identity and numbers. Washington ordered General Mercer to detach his brigade of about three hundred men to cut off the perceived British patrol and prevent it from notifying the troops in Princeton. Upon learning that he faced a considerable force of Americans, Mawhood turned his column around and led his regiment, along with his mounted and dismounted dragoons, and some of his transient troops toward the Clarke farms to intercept the enemy troops that he now knew outnumbered him.

Mercer's and Mawhood's troops met on William Clarke's farm, and the battle ignited. After an exchange of volleys, a British bayonet charge forced Mercer's men, who generally lacked bayonets, to retreat. In the melee, Mercer's horse went down. He fought on foot, refusing to surrender until surrounded and repeatedly stabbed in the abdomen. Cadwalader's brigade of about 1,500 men, who were mostly volunteer militia known as the Philadelphia Associators and included a multiracial force of Pennsylvania marines, entered the fray to support Mercer. Mercer's retreating brigade and the advancing British disrupted Cadwalader's men. However, the Americans stabilized things with the high-quality assistance of Captain Joseph Moulder's two-gun Associator artillery company.

As the melee developed, Washington noted that the action was more significant than anticipated. He pulled out two brigades of Pennsylvania and Rhode Island Continentals and personally led them in a counterattack on the left British flank. Washington rode between the two armies exchanging fire and miraculously escaped being injured or killed, earning the deep respect of his men for his courage. About the same time, General Mifflin sent some men from Quaker Road to engage the right British flank. Attacked on three sides by larger forces, the British had to retreat. It became a rout, and the Americans took many prisoners.

Both the William and Thomas Clarke farmhouses, along with others near the battlefield, became makeshift hospitals for the wounded of both sides. Thomas Clarke's house received the mortally wounded General Mercer, and he was cared for there until his death on January 12. The fighting continued as Washington's forces advanced on the town, and the one British regiment left there made a brief effort to stop them before being completely overwhelmed. Mop-up actions took place in and about town, and more British became prisoners. The final action seems to have been at Nassau Hall, where a few British troops had taken refuge. After American artillery opened fire on the building and several cannonballs came through the windows, they surrendered. The British had lost some 450 killed and wounded, along with 200 to 300 taken prisoner. Thirty to forty Americans were killed, and about the same number wounded.

Just as British troops began arriving from Maidenhead and Trenton, Mifflin's men destroyed the Stony Brook Bridge. Washington withdrew from Princeton but found that his men were so exhausted from the night marches and two days of battles that he could not ask them to march to New Brunswick. He decided instead to go directly to Morristown. When Cornwallis came back through Princeton, he headed straight to New Brunswick, fearing that Washington would take the supplies there. This decision allowed Washington to get to Morristown unmolested, although it took several days.

After these ten days of fighting, the British did not try to reoccupy Princeton or Trenton. Instead, they withdrew some units to New York while maintaining cantonments at New Brunswick and Perth Amboy. This pullback removed significant numbers of British soldiers from New Jersey. The state government reconvened while Washington rebuilt his army at Morristown, allowing the patriots to feel protected while the Loyalists felt more exposed. In addition to the main camp at Morristown, Washington established military posts at Trenton and Princeton. For the rest of the winter and into the spring, American troops harassed British foraging parties sent out from New Brunswick and Perth Amboy. The resulting skirmishes, referred to as the Forage War, kept the British soldiers on a campaign footing, and the men suffered greatly.

News of these ten days of victory spread first by word of mouth, followed by letters and newspapers. After arriving home in Connecticut later in January, Captain John Chester wrote, "You cannot conceive the joy and raptures the people were universally in as we passed the road[.] 'Tis good to be the messenger of Glad Tidings…they make an amazing alteration in the faces of men & things.'"[1] A year later, Chaplain David Avery commented that news of Trenton and Princeton "flew upon the wings of the wind—and at once revived the hopes of the fearful, which had almost fled! How sudden the transition from darkness to light; from grief to joy!"[2] Supporters of independence gained confidence in ultimate victory, interpreting the successes as proof of God's will that America should be independent and that Washington's seemingly miraculous victories were preordained.

Looking back on the ten crucial days, British officers acknowledged both Washington's leadership qualities and their commanders' mistakes. Captain Johann Ewald wrote that they had intended to resume battle at Trenton on the morning of January 3, but "Washington spared us the trouble." He credited Washington with realizing that Cornwallis would seek to atone for his mistake in not using the Assunpink fords to attack the American flank on January 2. Therefore, Washington had broken camp, and "since he could not risk returning across the Delaware, he made such a forced march under cover of darkness that he arrived at daybreak at Princetown." Cornwallis had thus contributed to Washington's reputation as an "excellent general" by "simply and solely" refusing to march his army in two columns from Princeton and outflank Washington at Trenton. Twice at Trenton and then at Princeton, "the enemy was despised, and as usual we had to pay for it."[3] Lord George Germain commented to Parliament in 1779 that things had looked very positive in December 1776, "[b]ut all our hopes were blasted by that unhappy affair at Trenton."

Not long after hearing of the climactic victory at Yorktown in 1781, the citizens of Annapolis published a letter to Washington. It proclaimed that "the successes at Trenton and Princeton, laid the corner stone of our freedom and independence, and that the capture of earl Cornwallis and his army has completed the edifice, and secured the temple of liberty to us and our posterity."[4] These ten crucial days comprised one of the ten crucial campaigns of the American Revolution, turning the tide of the Revolution and allowing it to continue for another six and a half years to a successful conclusion.

Further Reading

Fischer, David Hackett. *Washington's Crossing*. New York: Oxford University Press, 2004.

Kidder, William L. *Ten Crucial Days: Washington's Vision for Victory Unfolds*. Lawrenceville, New Jersey: Knox Press, 2019.

Price, David. *The Road to Assunpink Creek*. Lawrence Township, New Jersey: Knox Press, 2019.

Maloy, Mark. *Victory or Death: The Battles of Trenton and Princeton, December 25, 1776–January 3, 1777*. El Dorado Hills, California: 2018.

For more on the effect of the battle on Trenton and its context in the entire Revolution, see Kidder, William L. *Crossroads of the Revolution: Trenton, 1774–1783*. Lawrence Township, New Jersey: Knox Press, 2017.

For more on the effect of the battle on Princeton and its context in the entire Revolution, see Kidder, William L. *Revolutionary Princeton: The Biography of an American Town in the Heart of a Civil War*. Lawrence Township, New Jersey: Knox Press, 2020.

For more on the Trenton area militia in the ten crucial days and the entire Revolution, see Kidder, Larry. *A People Harassed and Exhausted: The Story of New Jersey Militia Regiment in the American Revolution*. CreateSpace, 2013.

About the Author

William L. Kidder is a retired high school history teacher and U.S. Navy veteran. He is a board member of the Princeton Battlefield Society and is active in several historical associations, including the Association for Living History, Farm, and Agricultural Museums. In addition to his four books on the American Revolution, Kidder has contributed chapters for several books on the Revolution in New Jersey. He frequently speaks to a variety of historical and civic groups.

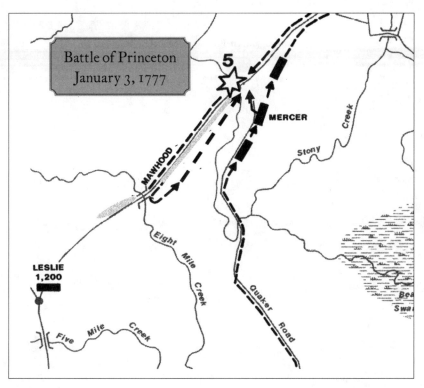

Cartography by William J. Clipson from A BATTLEFIELD ATLAS OF THE AMERICAN REVOLUTION, published by Savas Beatie, www.savasbeatie.com

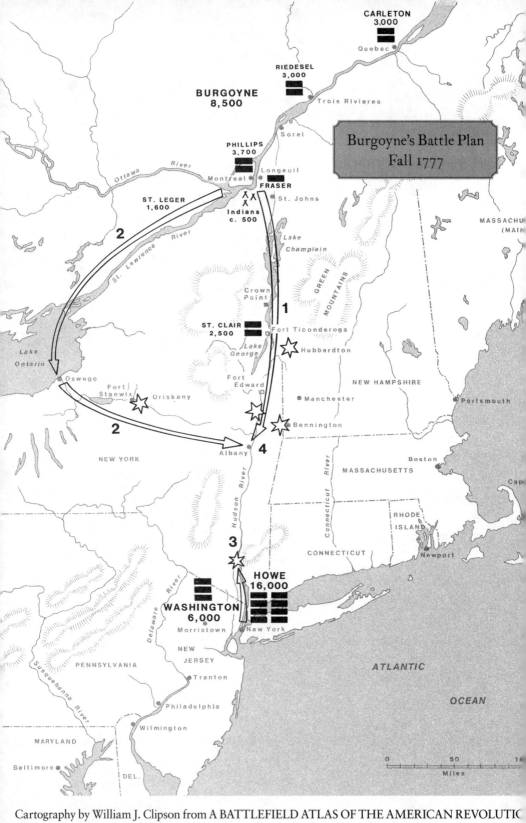

CARLETON
3,000

Quebec

RIEDESEL
3,000

Trois Rivieres

BURGOYNE
8,500

Sorel

PHILLIPS
3,700

Longeuil

Montreal

FRASER

Burgoyne's Battle Plan
Fall 1777

St. Johns

ST. LEGER
1,600

Ottawa River

St. Lawrence River

Indians
c. 500

Lake
Champlain

MASSACHU
(MAIN

2

GREEN
MOUNTAINS

Crown
Point

1

ST. CLAIR
2,500

Fort Ticonderoga

Lake
Ontario

Hubbardton

Lake
George

NEW HAMPSHIRE

Oswego

Fort
Stanwix

Oriskany

Fort
Edward

Manchester

Portsmouth

2

Albany

4

Bennington

NEW YORK

Boston

MASSACHUSETTS

Hudson River

Connecticut River

Cap

RHODE
ISLAND

3

CONNECTICUT

Newport

HOWE
16,000

WASHINGTON
6,000

Morristown

New York

Delaware River

NEW
JERSEY

ATLANTIC

OCEAN

Susquehanna River

PENNSYLVANIA

Trenton

Philadelphia

Wilmington

MARYLAND

DEL.

Baltimore

0   50   1
|___|___|___|___|___|
Miles

Cartography by William J. Clipson from A BATTLEFIELD ATLAS OF THE AMERICAN REVOLUTIC
published by Savas Beatie, www.savasbeatie.com

Gentleman John Burgoyne's Great Gamble: Ticonderoga to Saratoga

BY JAMES KIRBY MARTIN

John Burgoyne, born in 1722, was one of the most flamboyant characters of the American Revolutionary era. He possessed boundless energy and enthusiasm, was cocksure of himself, and never met a colonist for whom he felt much respect. For him, the Americans were outlanders and bumpkin-like inferiors in comparison to the "better sort" of favored folks, especially the lords and ladies of their parent nation Britain.

Somehow, the upstart colonists were suffering from the same problem that Burgoyne failed to recognize in himself, a mounting sense of self-importance. They had lost sight of their proper place in the empire, having gone too far in resisting what Burgoyne believed to be, holding as he did a seat in Parliament in 1761, the reasonable taxation plans embodied in the Stamp Act (1765), the Townshend Duties Act (1767), and finally the Tea Act (1773). The obstreperous Americans needed a good dosage of military discipline, and Burgoyne was sure that he knew how to help administer the imperial spanking.

Gentleman John was, in fact, an upstart himself. Born into a respectable though not wealthy family, he may well have been the illegitimate son of Robert Benson, 1st Baron Bingley, who served as young Burgoyne's godfather. When Bingley died in 1731, he provided handsomely for his godson's future. By the 1750s, Burgoyne had established his basic life patterns. He bought an officer's commission but had to sell it to pay off his gambling debts. He carefully maintained his ties with influential members of England's aristocracy. In 1751, he eloped with Lady Charlotte Stanley, the youngest daughter of Sir Edward Stanley, 11th Earl of Derby, who had extensive political connections and sat in the House of Lords. Derby was not happy about the elopement, having wanted his daughter to marry someone of more respectable social status. Eventually, he and Burgoyne reconciled, which opened many more doors among the ranks of powerful persons in class-conscious England.

Keeping up his military career, Burgoyne won accolades for leading a successful cavalry charge in Portugal during the Seven Years' War. Supposedly, his fair-minded treatment of soldiers in an era when brutal discipline was meted out to the rank and file won him the affectionate title of "Gentleman." Perhaps it was his dapper personality or ability to lose with grace, as he so often did with his gambling addiction. Whatever the reason, his peers liked him, as did King George, whose interests he actively supported in Parliament.

In 1772, Burgoyne, who had kept his military career going, received a promotion to major general. Then, in early 1775, the king persuaded him to join two other major generals in sailing to America to put an end to the incipient rebellion brewing in Massachusetts. Along with Generals William Howe and Henry Clinton, he departed England without much fanfare. As one doggerel in a London paper sneered:

> Behold the Cerberus the Atlantic plough
> Her precious cargo, Burgoyne, Clinton, Howe,
> Bow, wow, wow![1]

Arriving in Boston late in May 1775, Burgoyne contributed little and complained a lot. Supposedly he quipped, in his usual disdainful manner, that he would make plenty of "elbow room" for British soldiers then entrapped in the city after the Lexington and Concord engagements. The local populace, in turn, dubbed Burgoyne "General Elbow Room," an image that would have ironic meaning for him in another two years.

Frustrated as the infrequently consulted junior major general of the "bow, wow, wow" team, Burgoyne received permission to sail back to London. He returned to gambling while also caring for his wife, Lady Charlotte, who was in bad health. He also used his personal charm—and political connections—to talk his way into a better wartime assignment. In early April 1776, Burgoyne joined a flotilla of vessels carrying troops from England to the Quebec Province in Canada. There he was to serve as second-in-command under Governor Guy Carleton, also a major general, whose military experience included beating French forces on the Plains of Abraham in September 1759, securing Quebec City for the British Empire. Suffering a head wound in that engagement, Carleton went on to play a pivotal role in managing the transition of Canada from French to British sovereignty, as agreed to in the 1763 Treaty of Paris that ended the Seven Years' War in Europe and America.

At first, Burgoyne relished his new assignment, which was to assist Carleton in driving an American rebel invading force out of Canada. Seeking to have Quebec Province become the fourteenth colony in rebellion, two patriot forces had invaded the province during the fall of 1775. One detachment, under the command of the wealthy New Yorker Major General Philip Schuyler, with a recently retired British officer, Richard Montgomery, serving as second-in-command, moved north up Lake Champlain from Fort Ticonderoga and in mid-November captured Montreal. The second column, led by Colonel Benedict Arnold, marched through the Maine wilderness and along the Chaudière River toward Quebec City. Schuyler, suffering from debilitating health issues, returned to New York. Montgomery and Arnold linked their forces together in early December only to suffer an overwhelming defeat in a desperate attempt to capture the walled city of Quebec early in the morning of December 31, 1775.

Montgomery was killed, and Arnold was seriously wounded. The Canadian campaign never recovered from this defeat. Even though the

Continental Congress gamely ordered hundreds more patriot troops into Quebec Province during the spring of 1776, they could not match the twelve thousand British and Hessian soldiers who poured into Canada that spring, with Burgoyne himself reaching Quebec City in early May. A devastating outbreak of smallpox helped finish off the rebel campaign, with all the surviving American troops retreating all the way back to Fort Ticonderoga by mid- to late June.

Carleton and Burgoyne worked harmoniously together during that spring and summer. They were now participants in an overall British strategic plan to cut off New England, the original center of the rebellion, from those colonies west and south of the Hudson River–Lake Champlain water corridor. Home government leaders were working to concentrate a large force of thirty-five thousand troops in the New York City area under William Howe, now commander in chief of all British forces in North America. Adding more than twelve thousand troops in Canada represented a massive overall commitment to crushing the rebellion, hopefully by the end of 1776.

To implement this strategy, Howe was to move a sizable force up the Hudson River toward Albany, and Carleton was to float a naval-land force southward across Lake Champlain to capture Fort Ticonderoga and then move on to Albany. As for Burgoyne, he was to command the ground troops, reporting only to Carleton. Once united, the two armies would march eastward toward Boston, wiping out any lingering rebel holdouts along the way. Royal naval forces would bottle up any resisters in the various port towns along the Atlantic seaboard, in effect squeezing the American rebels into begging for the Crown's forgiveness.

This Hudson River–Lake Champlain strategy, given the sizable land mass of the thirteen colonies, was straightforward, easy to understand, and possibly doable, despite significant geographic obstacles in the region. The problem, however, was not so much reckoning with the logistical challenges of moving large forces across waterways and over swampy, hilly terrain, but with the generals themselves.

More or less on his own, Howe decided he could end the war more quickly—and with greater personal glory—by chasing after George Washington's Continentals and grinding them into the ground as they fled for their lives across New Jersey and over the Delaware River to Pennsylvania. Clinton objected, so Howe sent him off to establish a winter naval base in Rhode Island.

Carleton, for his part, was the most cautious of them all, not wanting to proceed south until he had a powerful enough naval fleet to clear Lake Champlain of any potential resistance. By the time he finally moved his flotilla onto the lake in early October, the number of days for sustained campaigning were almost gone, with colder autumn weather coming into play and frigid winter conditions lurking in the background. In sum, the British generals, pulling this way and that, had nothing to show for their campaign activities in 1776 despite so much effort on the part of the Crown to get them thousands of troops and enough military supplies to crush the ever growing rebellion before it was too late.

As for Burgoyne, he was now having doubts about Carleton's cautionary leadership and also thinking about greater martial glory for himself. Placed in charge of land forces that followed along after Carleton's fleet, he could not believe that the governor stopped his southward movement at Crown Point, some twelve miles north of Fort Ticonderoga. Carleton, after considering such basics as maintaining a secure supply line back to Canada over the winter, as well as having been impressed by the fighting prowess of the patriot fleet defending the lake, decided to pull back all his land and naval forces to regroup for a timelier invasion in 1777.

All along the way, Burgoyne studied the terrain and gained an impression of how easy movement by water through the Champlain region would be with a large, well-equipped army and proper naval support, especially with what he surmised would be insignificant rebel resistance. He just couldn't bring himself to believe that the Americans had any sustained fighting capacity, despite the incredibly brave stand by Benedict Arnold's much weaker fleet at Valcour Island on October 11 and Arnold's death-defying stand at Split Rock two days later.[2]

Carleton did understand the American's abilities, and he had backed off for the winter season. Unlike Burgoyne, he recognized the rebels' capacity to put up a good fight—even with inferior numbers and equipment. Just as importantly, the governor wanted to defeat his adversaries but leave them with enough self-respect to be able to rejoin the British Empire with some dignity left.

Burgoyne, on the other hand, was an inveterate gambler who too often wagered his bets without taking his opponents very seriously. His mistake in 1776 was his reckless pride in assuming that the likes of Benedict Arnold and other rebel defenders on Lake Champlain would cut, run, and hide in the face of superior—in numbers and weaponry—British forces. After all, as Burgoyne reported in July to General Clinton, the American retreat from Canada "was most unsoldierlike and disgraceful," and in November he crowed about "the compleat victory obtained over the enemy's fleet" on the lake."[3] In hindsight, he was wrong on both counts.

In this second letter to Clinton, Burgoyne wrote about the passing of his wife, whose various ailments had cut her life short back in June 1776. Her death became a reason to return to England that winter to attend "to a few duties yet remaining to the memory of Lady Charlotte." Further, he claimed to have a "constitution unfitted to [the] severity of cold" Canadian winter weather. He needed to "seclude" himself from "this country…for the next six months." Since his motives for returning home were purely magnanimous, all "[i]nterest, ambition" and the "animation of life" did not motivate his return home. He was flattering himself, of course, as his dominant reason was to secure a more important military assignment. He added that serving in "a secondary station in a secondary army is at no time agreeable" for a man like himself, one so full of military talent.[4]

Making a quick passage home to London, Burgoyne was soon meeting with none other than King George III, who in turn commended him to

Lord George Germain, secretary for American affairs and chief strategic planner for ending the rebellion. Burgoyne tried to be coy, pretending that he was not complaining about Carleton's supposed dilatoriness when he was invariably damning the governor with faint praise. Naturally, the king and Germain, who despised Carleton for other reasons, wondered whether Burgoyne could put together an operational plan that would assure success during the upcoming campaign season. With outward humility, he assured them he was just the person to do so.

Burgoyne's "Thoughts for Conducting the War, from the Side of Canada," bore the date February 28, 1777. As in 1776, the objective of this plan was to move a substantial army at a rapid pace from Montreal to Albany, which was a little over two hundred miles. There this force would "effect a Junction with General Howe" before charging through New England. Burgoyne recommended that Carleton, whom he implied was a little decrepit for the task and obviously slow-moving, should receive orders to stay in Canada with three thousand troops to protect Quebec Province from a possible enemy incursion. What Burgoyne was really saying was that, this year, he intended to be the star of the military show, never again just a "secondary" general off campaigning in some obscure theater of war.[5]

Burgoyne went on to insist that he needed at least 11,000 troops and up to 1,000 Canadian Indians, along with 2,000 Canadian auxiliaries, some with enough nautical skills to move this huge army by water southward to the lower end of Lake Champlain. To facilitate his own rapid movement, Burgoyne recommended a divisionary force of 1,500 or more regulars, loyalists, Hessians, and hundreds of Indians drawn from the Six Nations, including Mohawks and Senecas, to sweep southeastward from Lake Ontario. They were to take control of the western end of the Mohawk Valley, then sweep eastward toward Albany, some 100 miles away. The presence of this detachment would force the American resisters to defend on two fronts, thus dividing what strength, if any, they might have left to slow down the British advance. Lieutenant Colonel

Barry St. Leger, an experienced veteran of warfare in the Canadian region going back to the Seven Years' War, would take charge of this diversionary column with the brevet rank of brigadier general.

Burgoyne would obtain what he most craved: overall command of the whole operation. Lord Germain, however, did not guarantee him the 11,000 troops he had requested, especially with 3,000 assigned to stay behind in Canada. As finally constituted, this grand northern army consisted of 3,576 British, 2,919 German, and 511 artillerists (all designated as fit for duty), for a total of 7,006 combat soldiers. Burgoyne had hoped to enlist about 1,000 Indians, but only about half that number—Wyandots, Ottawas, Abenakis, and Canadian Mohawks—agreed with some reluctance to sign up for scouting duty. About 800 Canadians came along as militia, day laborers, and boat crewmen, not the 2,000 Burgoyne expected. The total force, including consorts, wives, and children, was an estimated 10,000 persons, about two-thirds the number that Burgoyne had indicated—but not insisted—that he needed to assure complete success in reaching Albany in a timely fashion.[6]

Among the strengths of this expeditionary army were the talented general officers assisting but not upstaging Burgoyne. At the age of forty-six, Major General William Phillips was among the most gifted artillery officers in the British Army. In direct charge of the Hessian soldiers, many of them Brunswickers, was Major General Baron Friedrich Adolf von Riedesel, age thirty-nine, a skillful leader who politely put up with Burgoyne's pomposity. Also highly competent was Brigadier General Simon Fraser, age forty-eight, who repeatedly showed no fear in leading the way in combat situations against the American resisters—for which he ultimately paid the price with his life.

As for Burgoyne, he bubbled over with confidence. Even before he had gained official approval to lead the expedition, he had the temerity to place a wager with a friend—the price of a pony—that he would be back in England crowned with great laurels of victory before the end of 1777. One London observer dubbed him "General Swagger." Gentleman John was acting as if he were about to embark on a summer camping adventure. Obviously, he felt compelled to bring along all the comforts of home, which amounted to several wagonloads of essentials, apparently including several uniform changes and the family silver tea service. For his additional well-being and personal pleasure, he arranged to secure a mistress by awarding her obliging husband some advance in rank as a commissary officer.[7]

On June 14, 1777, Burgoyne , having gathered all participants and equipment, including 138 artillery pieces, ordered the expedition to move out at Saint Johns on the Richelieu River. According to his "Thoughts for Conducting the War," the army's first objective was to capture Fort Ticonderoga. Within a week and a half, Fraser's advance corps had crossed Lake Champlain and reached Crown Point, a distance of some 200 miles (actually about halfway to Albany). The rest of the army arrived there by June 30. Amid the ruins of a once mighty British fortress, everyone rested for a couple of days before moving out to attack Fort Ticonderoga some twelve miles by water to the south.

Burgoyne, using his gift for condescendingly florid prose, issued a public proclamation on June 24, warning all rebel bumpkins in his army's path to give up their "phrenzy of hostility" or suffer the direst of consequences. As he explicated, "the present unnatural Rebellion" rested on "the most compleatest system of Tyranny that ever God in his displeasure suffered for a time to be exercised over a forward & stubborn Generation." To continue to resist his mighty army, best appreciated as true "Messengers of justice & of wrath," was to guarantee "devastation, famine & every concomitant horror" for every colonist who did not submit to the unstoppable military machine under his command.[8]

The taking of Ticonderoga seemed to verify Burgoyne's locked-in perception that breaking the patriot will to fight would be easy. The extensive grounds at the fort, including outlying redoubts, lacked the troop strength at this point in the war to be properly defended. The commander in charge, Major General Arthur St. Clair, a Pennsylvanian not known for his military prowess, had only 2,200 defenders, about one-fourth of Burgoyne's numbers. They were short of weapons and ammunition as well as basic supplies, including food. Ripe to be over-run—and overrun they were.

By July 4, Burgoyne had his force ready to strike from various angles. The Hessians were sweeping down on the east side of the lake to cut off any rebel retreat through Vermont territory. Moving south on the extreme right was General Phillips with an artillery column. He had decided that cannons could be placed near the top of Sugar Loaf Hill (today's Mount Defiance), which rose 750 feet and literally overlooked the fortress from the southeast. Phillips supposedly quipped: "Where a goat can go a man can go, and where a man can go he can drag a gun."[9] On the afternoon of July 5, the fort's defenders observed the artillery battery that could easily fire cannon shots down on them. Obviously overwhelmed on all sides and now outflanked, St. Clair wisely issued orders to retreat, which took place under cover of early morning darkness on July 6.

Hardly firing a shot, Burgoyne had the rebels on the run—easy pickings indeed. And run the rebels did. Some escaped into Vermont territory, where the next morning they engaged in a bloody battle at Hubbardton against Fraser's advance corps.[10] Those who got away eventually made it to Fort Edward, located about forty miles away along the east side of the Hudson River. St. Clair, meanwhile, led a fleeing contingent of about five hundred men in boats, first to the lower end of the lake at Skenesborough (today's Whitehall), where they burned everything in sight. Then they proceeded overland for twenty-four miles to Fort Edward, where they regathered with the Vermont group and local militia that the overall Northern Department commander, Philip Schuyler, was beginning to pull together as a fighting force to resist, at all costs, what so far had been the rapid advance of Burgoyne's army.

As for Gentleman John, he was ecstatic. In a feigned attempt at personal humility, he wrote to Lord Germain from Skenesborough: "The instruments I have to employ are so good that my merit will be small."[11] As he had convinced himself over and over again, the rebels lacked the physical, mental, and military capacity to fight effectively against the likes of "General Elbow Room." As he considered matters, it had taken his army little more than three weeks to move more than 60 percent of the way toward his target. From Skenesborough, the distance left to reach Albany was about seventy miles.

What Burgoyne could not imagine was that his rapid southward movement was all but over. If someone had told him that he would never reach Albany, he would have scoffed at them. Nor would he have believed that over two months later his army would still have more than thirty miles of backwoods terrain to cover before reaching Albany.

Once they had subjugated Fort Ticonderoga, about everything that could go wrong for Burgoyne and his minions did. It was almost as if the wilderness started to devour the British-Hessian army alive as it reckoned with traversing the landscape below Lake Champlain, which was much more of a debilitating enemy than a cooperating friend.

Back in 1776, Burgoyne had traveled no farther south than Crown Point, with perhaps a quick scout of the Ticonderoga area. He had no knowledge of the terrain beyond this point or of the possible difficulties of moving overland through jagged hills, across streams, and through swamps to reach the Hudson River. In his "Thoughts for Conducting the War," he took it for granted that no significant geographic obstacles could possibly cause serious problems for his mission. Making this assumption was a major blunder on Burgoyne's part.

The logistical challenge was how to move his soldiers and weaponry southward to Fort Edward. Burgoyne had two choices. He used both. In a retrograde movement back to Ticonderoga, he issued orders to have a portion of his artillery pieces and heavy baggage shipped up Lake George, basically paralleling Lake Champlain to the west. After reaching Fort George at the lower end of the lake, everything had to be unloaded, placed on gun carriages, carts, and wagons, then hauled by pack animals overland sixteen miles to reach Fort Edward. This operation proved to be a logistical nightmare, and the weaponry did not reach Burgoyne until around September 10.

As for Burgoyne, he and the bulk of his troops sailed back to Skenesborough to begin an overland trek to Fort Edward that would take them three weeks, a distance of about twenty-four miles. This little-used route was not easy traveling under any circumstances, and it was now to be made even more treacherous by the harassing tactics of bands of rebels, including militia companies from New York and Massachusetts. Acting as well-organized partisans, they cut down trees and rolled large boulders into the crude pathway. Since the weather was rainy that month, they opened spillways from swamps to produce flooding conditions, and they took potshots at the enemy troops when possible. They engaged in a delaying firefight at Fort Anne, about halfway to Fort Edward, all of which slowed Burgoyne's army to moving forward little more than a mile a day.

Burgoyne remained resilient through it all, as if losing so much time was not a problem—but he should have been worried. As already indicated, patriots in the region were rallying to the standard of Northern Department commander Philip Schuyler, who was operating out of Fort Edward in early July. Thanks to George Washington, he received significant leadership support from Benedict Arnold, whom the commander in chief considered his best fighting general. Arnold, who played such a key role in Carleton's decision to retreat from Lake Champlain in 1776, rendezvoused with Schuyler on July 21. Together, they devised a fallback strategy that had Schuyler organizing additional troops to the south of Fort Edward while Arnold would direct a small detachment in picket duty designed to gauge the enemy's movements while continuing with delaying tactics.

During Arnold's assignment, the murder of Jane McCrea was observed, an incident fraught with implications. On July 27, Arnold sent out a picket company to determine the whereabouts of Burgoyne's force. While watching at Fort Edward, they were suddenly overrun by a large party of Indians, along with an advance column of British regulars. They retreated, but not fast enough to avoid having six of their number "killed & scalped." As they gained some distance, they observed some Wyandots drag two women out of a house, one of whom was beautiful, young Jane McCrea. Supposedly she was waiting there to meet her betrothed, a Loyalist officer named David Jones. The Wyandots argued over which one of them she belonged to and then settled the matter, as Arnold reported, when they "Shot, scalped, stripped & Butchered" her "in the most shocking Manner."[12]

Burgoyne insisted on punishing the responsible Wyandot, but the Indian chiefs demurred. In council, they told him to back off or they would start returning to Canada. He mollified them with alcohol, but only temporarily. Over the next several days, his Indian allies started drifting away, bored the with slow pace of the march and the lack of promised opportunities to plunder the countryside.

Before August was over, Burgoyne had less than one hundred Indian scouts still available to stalk rebel pickets and provide intelligence about growing rebel resistance. His Canadian auxiliaries were also heading back north by the hundreds. To keep supply lines back to Canada open he had assigned close to a thousand soldiers to garrison duty at Fort Ticonderoga and Fort George.

Still, Burgoyne insisted that the Americans "cannot finally impede me," and he expected that "successful progress" would allow his shrinking army to reach Albany by August 23 at the latest.[13] Exuding complete confidence, according to Baroness von Riedesel, who was traveling with her husband and their children, Burgoyne was "having a jolly time" carousing at night while "amusing himself in the company of the wife of a commissary, who was his mistress and, like him, loved champagne."[14]

Indulgence in champagne no doubt helped Burgoyne to discount the reality of the campaign that was collapsing around him. During August he suffered three major blows, one of which was definite news that General Howe would, as in 1776, not be playing his intended part in the Hudson-Champlain strategy. Before the end of July, Howe had ordered fifteen thousand troops onto troop transports in New York Harbor. They would sail out to sea, then move up through Chesapeake Bay, where they would land. Then they would march toward Philadelphia with the idea of catching Washington's Continentals in a major set piece battle that would destroy the main rebel army—and, in theory, end the war.

Ever confident, Burgoyne acted as if he really didn't mind since he was sure that he could make it to Albany all on his army's own. Then they would rest over the winter while preparing for a major assault on New England in 1778. Clearly, Burgoyne believed, or pretended to believe, that under his brilliant leadership his army could do it all.

The second blow resulted from a decision to send out a detachment of 750 soldiers, half of them Hessians, under the command of Lieutenant Colonel Friedrich Baum to plunder Vermont territory for horses, wagons, and cattle and try to alleviate the food shortages. What Burgoyne did not expect was that Baum's force would run into a column of 1,500 New Hampshire militiamen operating under the highly competent John Stark, with some Green Mountain Boys under Seth Warner thrown in. The Battle of Bennington on August 16 turned into a rout that cost Baum and more than 200 of his soldiers their lives—along with 700 taken prisoner, a devastating loss of about 15 percent of Burgoyne's fighting force.

"General Elbow Room" was beginning to feel a squeeze. Vermont, he declared, contained the "most active and most rebellious race of the continent and hangs like a gathering storm upon my left."[15] At this juncture, he had not yet learned about an even bigger storm on his right, the collapse and retreat of his diversionary force.

By early August, Barry St. Leger's detachment had reached the western Mohawk Valley and had placed Fort Stanwix (called Fort Schuyler during the Revolutionary War) under siege. St. Leger had nearly 1,000 Indians with him, led by the powerful Mohawk warrior Joseph Brant (Thayendanegea). In addition, the King's Royal Regiment of New York, the "Royal Greens" operating under the prominent Mohawk Valley landlord Sir John Johnson, was part of this raiding force. Once the fort, defended by 750 Continentals, capitulated, nothing in terms of significant rebel resistance would be able to block St. Leger's eastward thrust toward Albany.

Local Tryon County militiamen rallied under Nicholas Herkimer and marched northwest along the course of the Mohawk River to relieve the fort. Early on the morning of August 6, Brant's Indians and Johnson's Royal Greens, along with a few British regulars and Hessians, surprised and attacked the patriot column about six miles short of the fort. The Battle of Oriskany was a gory bloodbath, with an estimated 385 of the 750 militiamen killed. Local Oneida Indians fought alongside the valley's defenders, also losing a few of their warriors in an engagement that divided the once-united Six Nations confederacy of Indians into angry opponents over resisting or supporting the Revolution.[16]

Once Philip Schuyler learned about this crushing defeat, he ordered a relief column from his immediate ranks to go west and drive off St. Leger's column. Benedict Arnold stepped forth and led nine hundred Continentals up the valley. As they got to within thirty miles of the fort, Arnold learned that his soldiers, having heard lurid stories about the slaughter at Oriskany, would go no farther. Searching for a solution, he convinced a captured local Loyalist named Hon Yost Schuyler to rush into St. Leger's camp with news that a huge Continental force, numbering three thousand, was nearby and ready to launch a full-scale attack. Panic ensued, and before evening on August 22 the diversionary force was in rapid retreat.

Arnold's deceptive action not only relieved Fort Schuyler and its defenders but seriously weakened Burgoyne's invasion plan. With both his left and right wings now shorn off and rebel forces building in significant numbers between his army and Albany, Gentleman John knew he had to get his army in motion before it was too late. On September 12, with his artillery and baggage having finally arrived at Fort Edward, he gave orders for his depleted columns to move south. By September 15, they had crossed over the Hudson and marched into a village named Saratoga (today's Schuylerville). There they rested while burning local property, including Philip Schuyler's summer residence, before proceeding south along a crude river road toward Sword's Farm, where they arrived on September 17. This property was Burgoyne's final bivouac location until the morning of September 19, when Gentleman John moved his forces forward to combat with what had recently become Major General Horatio Gates's Northern Department army.

Civilian leaders in the Continental Congress, especially those from New England, had long harbored doubts about Schuyler's capacity to head the army's Northern Department. The loss of Ticonderoga, which some of them viewed—without good reason—as the irreplaceable Gibraltar of America, naturally caused them to blame Schuyler and St. Clair. The delegates ordered them removed from command in favor of their much-admired Gates.

On August 19, Gates met with Schuyler on Van Schaick Island, ten miles north of Albany, where he indecorously took over the northern command. Having contributed nothing so far to the resistance campaign, Gates was now in position to claim full glory for Burgoyne's final defeat, which the Herculean labors of Schuyler, Arnold, Stark, Warner, and others had made possible in setting up Gentleman John for defeat. In early September Gates began moving his army north to a stronger defensive position on Bemis Heights, about four miles south of Sword's Farm and thirty miles north of Albany. There his Continentals and militia dug in as they prepared to defy any onslaught from Burgoyne.

Bemis Heights, located on rising terrain extending westward from the Hudson River, represented a strong defensive position that Burgoyne's troops would have to punch through if they were going to succeed. Gates, a defensive-minded general with real doubts about the fighting prowess of his American rebels, wanted his troops to hold their position on the heights as Burgoyne's columns attacked them. Arnold, who was in command of Gates's left wing, believed strongly that the Continentals could be effective fighters in open-field combat. He feared that if Burgoyne's troops gained enough momentum in striking the American position, they could literally shove them back to the Hudson River, where they might have to face surrender.

Gates, for his part, had come to dislike Arnold, considering him a rival for Washington's favor, which was true. Still, he listened to Arnold's pleas on September 19 and allowed him to send out troops to challenge the advancing enemy. Colonel Daniel Morgan's rifle regiment led the way. The fighting that day took place about a mile north of Bemis

Heights on partially cleared land known as Freeman's Farm. Burgoyne's troops managed to hold the ground, but barely. What saved the day for him was a decision to call up troops under Baron von Riedesel from the river road, which stabilized his line. Gates, in turn, kept fretting whether "foolhardy" Arnold would be too aggressive. Late in the day, he removed Arnold from the field, which left American troops leaderless. Only the approaching darkness saved them from taking more serious casualties.

Burgoyne rightfully claimed a technical victory by holding the battlefield at Freeman's Farm. He later wrote to Germain that "no fruits, honour excepted, were attained" that day.[17] His force was still thirty miles from Albany, with food supplies now running gravely low. With forward momentum all but gone, he sat and debated options for possibly proceeding or, worse yet, trying to retreat to Canada.

What little hope there was for relief depended on a sizable force under Henry Clinton moving up the Hudson River from New York City to divert Gates's attention. This effort happened with too few troops and too late to offer any assistance. Finally, Burgoyne decided to launch a reconnaissance in force to gather grain in a nearby wheat field and to view the rebel position on Bemis Heights, hoping to find some opening to outflank the left end of the American lines.

The fighting that occurred on October 7 represented the beginning of the end for Burgoyne's army. The troops, about two thousand in number, marched out from the British defenses at Freeman's Farm and easily reached the wheat field. Not long thereafter, Morgan's riflemen and various Continental units engaged them. Arnold, although embroiled in personal disagreements with Gates, joined the fray and mounted a charge, facilitated when one of Morgan's men, allegedly Timothy Murphy, fired a shot that mortally wounded Simon Fraser.

With even Burgoyne retreating, Arnold pushed forward and found a weakness on the extreme right of the British defenses, a redoubt held by troops under Hessian colonel Heinrich Breymann. Charging in on his horse, he was an easy target for the defenders, who shot down his horse and wounded his lower left leg, the same limb that had taken a musket ball back at Quebec City. Other Continentals were soon pouring into the redoubt. Just as darkness fell, the British line buckled, which resulted in a full-scale retreat.

Ten days later, Burgoyne, trying to escape northward, finally ran out of elbow room. Surrounded by some 15,000 patriot troops, he capitulated his battered, near-starving force, which was now reduced to less than 5,800 British and Hessian soldiers. The surrender site was a hillside overlooking the Hudson River, about a mile south of Saratoga. Gates, a former British officer who had moved to Virginia partially because he lacked the connections to advance beyond the rank of major, could fairly gloat in victory over so favored a British subject as Gentleman John. Graciously offering respectful surrender terms, Gates refused to accept Burgoyne's sword and invited him to a light repast after the ceremony that saw his soldiers lay down their arms with the honors of war—their flags still flying.

Daniel Morgan was there at the surrender, as was defrocked Philip Schuyler, whose scorched-earth tactics had played such a pivotal role in frustrating Burgoyne's advance from Ticonderoga. Benedict Arnold, who provided critical on-the-field leadership, was then writhing in an Albany area military hospital while the doctors debated whether to cut off his severely damaged leg—they didn't when he threatened their lives. On the British side, William Phillips was present, but Simon Fraser had died and was buried just north of the battlefield. Burgoyne, suffering from acute embarrassment, maintained his composure and only asked to be returned to London, where he knew he would be greeted with loud boos rather than his dreamed laurels of great victory.

Foolishly, Gates worked out a surrender "convention" that would allow the captured soldiers to return to England and sit out the war. Of course, once they were back in the British Isles, Lord Germain could then release an equal number of local defenders to sail for America and restrengthen British ranks. Both General Washington and Congress repudiated this agreement, and most of Burgoyne's soldiers sat out the rest of the war in a camp near Charlottesville, Virginia—except for a small number of them who enlisted in the Continental army in exchange for promised pay and their freedom.

Gates's adoring delegates in the Continental Congress declared him the hero of Saratoga, but Burgoyne stated that Arnold was the general who had done the most to defeat his army. In recent years, Schuyler has regained recognition as a critical player, having overcome the bad rap laid on him regarding the loss of Fort Ticonderoga.

Most important was the impact of this stunning American victory. Burgoyne's failed campaign opened the door to direct French intervention in the American cause. The victory proved that, with persistence, the patriot rebels could succeed in winning their independence. Key officials in France agreed. In February 1778, they signed two treaties declaring themselves good and faithful allies, more than ready to provide additional critical assistance in the form of war matériel and land and naval forces to defeat their hated foe, the ever growling British lion.

After Burgoyne's "turning-point" Saratoga campaign disaster and direct French involvement, the British would be hard-pressed to find some way to regain political control of their rebellious North American colonies. However, leaders in England refused to give up. In 1778 they began to develop a new strategy for victory; they turned to military campaigning in the southern colonies, the subject of other essays in this volume.

As for Gentleman John, he refused to fault himself for getting trapped in the American wilderness. He was full of face-saving excuses, including blaming Lord Germain's decision to let Howe go after Washington's army rather than following the approved British strategic plan for 1777. Over time, Burgoyne regained some social favor and dabbled in politics. He fathered four children with his mistress (not the commissary's wife) and continued his literary career. As he aged, he appeared less often in public, and he died unexpectedly in 1792. His remains lie in Westminster Abbey next to Lady Charlotte's. He is remembered not as the military hero he dreamed of being but as an overly confident general officer who helped to lose America.

Further Reading

Ketchum, Richard M. *Saratoga: The Turning Point of America's Revolutionary War.* New York: Henry Holt and Company, 1997.

Martin, James Kirby. *Benedict Arnold, Revolutionary Hero: An American Warrior Reconsidered.* New York: New York University Press, 1997.

Martin, James Kirby, and David L. Preston. *Theaters of the American Revolution: Northern, Middle, Southern, Western, Naval.* Yardley, Pennsylvania: Westholme Publishers, 2017.

Schnitzer, Eric, and Don Troiani. *Don Troiani's Campaign to Saratoga—1777: The Turning Point of the Revolutionary War in Paintings, Artifacts, and Historical Narrative.* Guilford, Connecticut: Stackpole Books, 2019.

Battle Information:
First Saratoga, September 19, 1777

Estimated Combatants:

British/Hessian Estimated: 2,500

American Estimated: 2,000–3,000

Casualties:

British/Hessian: 556 killed, wounded, captured, missing

American: 311 killed, wounded, captured, missing

Second Saratoga, October 7, 1777

Estimated Combatants:

British/Hessian Estimated: 2,500–3,000

American Estimated: 2,000–3,000

Casualties:

British/Hessian: 618 killed, wounded, captured, missing

American Estimated: 130

British Commanders in the Field:
John Burgoyne
Baron von Riedesel
William Phillips
Simon Fraser

American Commanders in the Field:
Horatio Gates
Benedict Arnold
Benjamin Lincoln
Daniel Morgan

About the Author

James Kirby Martin is the author or editor of fourteen books, including *Men in Rebellion* (1973); *In the Course of Human Events* (1979), now in an updated edition; *Insurrection: The American Revolution and Its Meaning* (1919); *Benedict Arnold, Revolutionary Hero An American Warrior Reconsidered* (1997); *Forgotten Allies: The Oneida Indians and the American Revolution* (2006, with J. Glatthaar); and *A Respectable Army: The Military Origins of the Republic, 1763–1789* (3rd ed., 2015, with M. Lender). Martin has taught at Rutgers University, the University of Houston, The Citadel, and the United States Military Academy, West Point. He served as the Hugh Roy and Lillie Cranz Cullen University Professor of History, now emeritus, at the University of Houston. Among other activities, Martin has served on the Board of Trustees of the Fort Ticonderoga Association and as a historian consultant to the Oneida Indian Nation of New York. He has appeared as a talking head on television programs aired by the History Channel, American Heroes Channel, and Fox News Network. He remains active in writing projects and public speaking engagements.

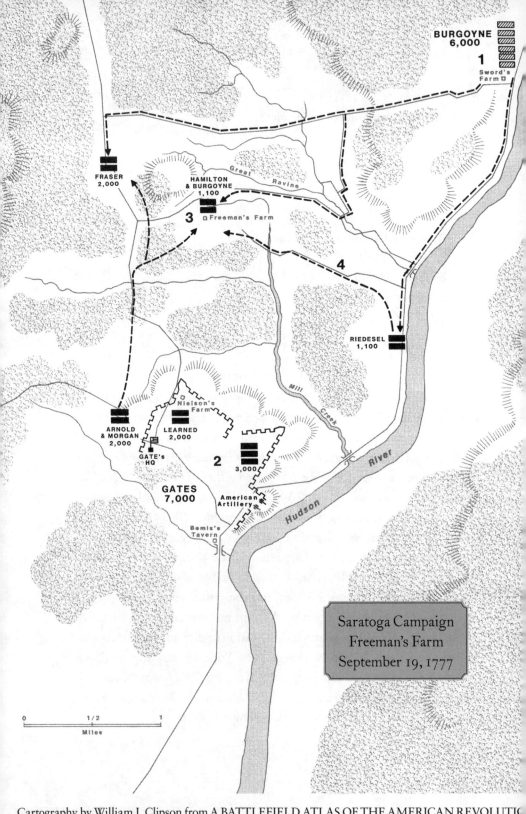

BURGOYNE
6,000

1

Sword's
Farm

FRASER
2,000

HAMILTON
& BURGOYNE
1,100

Great Ravine

3

Freeman's Farm

4

RIEDESEL
1,100

Nielson's
Farm

ARNOLD
& MORGAN
2,000

LEARNED
2,000

GATE'S
HQ

2

3,000

GATES
7,000

American
Artillery

Mill Creek

Hudson River

Bemis's
Tavern

Saratoga Campaign
Freeman's Farm
September 19, 1777

0   1/2   1
Miles

Cartography by William J. Clipson from A BATTLEFIELD ATLAS OF THE AMERICAN REVOLUTIO
published by Savas Beatie, www.savasbeatie.com

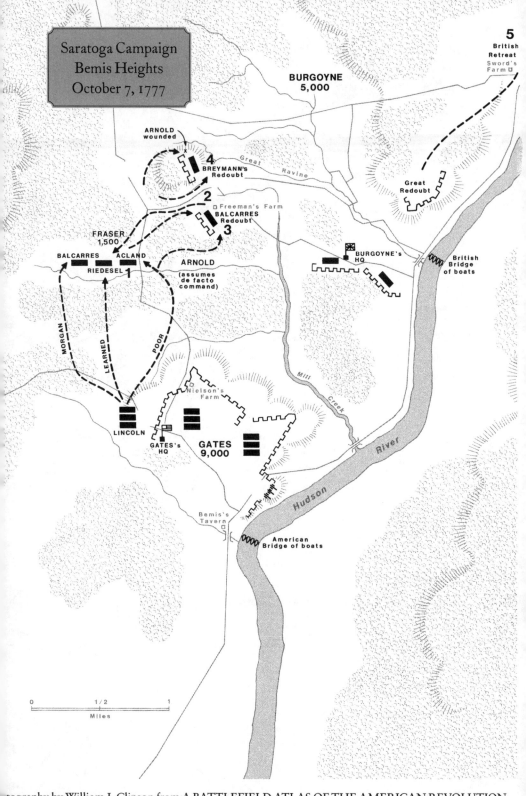

Saratoga Campaign
Bemis Heights
October 7, 1777

BURGOYNE
5,000

ARNOLD
wounded

4
BREYMANN'S
Redoubt

Great
Ravine

5
British
Retreat
Sword's
Farm

Great
Redoubt

2
☐ Freeman's Farm
BALCARRES
Redoubt

3

FRASER
1,500

BURGOYNE's
HQ

British
Bridge
of boats

BALCARRES   ACLAND
RIEDESEL   **1**

ARNOLD
(assumes
de facto
command)

MORGAN
LEARNED
POOR

Nielson's
Farm

Mill
Creek

River

LINCOLN

GATES's
HQ

GATES
9,000

Hudson

Bemis's
Tavern

American
Bridge
of boats

0   1/2   1
Miles

tography by William J. Clipson from A BATTLEFIELD ATLAS OF THE AMERICAN REVOLUTION,
lished by Savas Beatie, www.savasbeatie.com

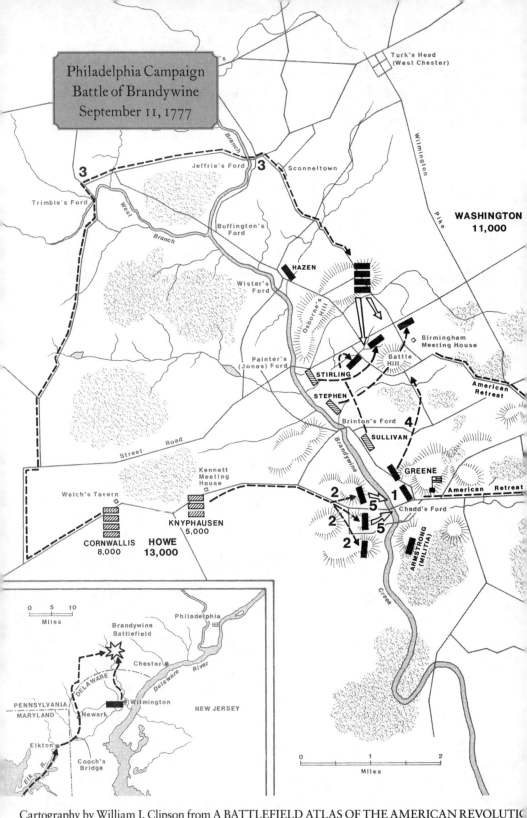

Philadelphia Campaign
Battle of Brandywine
September 11, 1777

Turk's Head
(West Chester)

Jeffrie's Ford

Sconneltown

Trimble's Ford

West Branch

Branch

Buffington's Ford

WASHINGTON
11,000

HAZEN

Wistar's Ford

Osborne's Hill

Birmingham
Meeting House

Painter's
(Jones) Ford

Battle
Hill

STIRLING

American
Retreat

STEPHEN

Brinton's Ford

SULLIVAN

Street Road

Kennett
Meeting
House

GREENE

American Retreat

Welch's Tavern

Chadd's Ford

KNYPHAUSEN
5,000

ARMSTRONG
(MILITIA)

CORNWALLIS
8,000

HOWE
13,000

Brandywine

Creek

0   5   10
Miles

Brandywine
Battlefield

Philadelphia

Chester

PENNSYLVANIA
MARYLAND

DELAWARE

Delaware River

NEW JERSEY

Newark

Wilmington

Elkton

Elk R.

Cooch's
Bridge

0   1   2
Miles

Cartography by William J. Clipson from A BATTLEFIELD ATLAS OF THE AMERICAN REVOLUTIC
published by Savas Beatie, www.savasbeatie.com

The Empire Strikes Back: Philadelphia Campaign 1777

BY MICHAEL C. HARRIS

Following his successes at Trenton and Princeton, General George Washington spent the next six months around Morristown, New Jersey, building a new army nearly from scratch. During the long and arduous process, Washington harassed British outposts scattered across northern New Jersey in a series of raids and skirmishes. Fortunately for him, British general William Howe was more concerned with strategic planning than with what he considered the minor doings of the Continental Army. Between January and June 1777, small-scale raids and skirmishes were the only military operations witnessed in northern New Jersey, giving Washington the precious time and space he needed to rebuild his weakened army.

General Howe intended to capture Philadelphia as rapidly as possible and return to New York to join forces with General John Burgoyne and the northern army. Defeating Washington in New Jersey and then marching to Philadelphia offered Howe the best chance to take the colonial capital and leave in time to aid Burgoyne in New York. Howe intended to draw Washington down from the high ground and offer him battle on the relatively flat country east of the mountain range. To Howe's dismay, Washington refused to take the bait.

Howe gave up the game and returned to New Brunswick on June 19. His half-hearted attempt in New Jersey was as baffling then as it is today. Even though he was on a tight schedule, he moved thousands of troops ten miles, went into camp and constructed earthworks, waited four days, and returned to his starting point a week later. He would reach Philadelphia by using the British fleet to transport his army.

Washington came down off the high ground and pursued Howe's retreating army, however, providing the British general with the opportunity he had been seeking. The Continental Army was on terrain suitable for engagement and Howe had his chance to attack. He did just that on June 25 by turning and assaulting Major General Lord Stirling's isolated and heavily outnumbered American division. The British pushed hard and forced Stirling's command back. The Battle of Short Hills bought precious time for Washington to move the balance of his army into the hill country to deny Howe the opportunity of the larger pitched battle he so craved. By June 28, Howe was back in Amboy, his attempt to defeat Washington in northern New Jersey at an end.

On the final day of June, Howe removed the last of his troops from New Jersey and returned to Staten Island, New York. He and his command were right back where they had started nearly a year earlier before their attack on New York City. Howe's withdrawal allowed Washington and his Continental Army to assume complete control of New Jersey.

The next move was up to Howe. Determined to use his fleet to reach Philadelphia, on July 8 the British general began the arduous process of loading his army onto transport ships. Howe believed he could ascend the Delaware River, gain Philadelphia, and still aid Burgoyne in a timely fashion. He also believed that moving by sea would freeze the Americans in place until Washington realized where Howe was going.

The deliberate British general sailed out of New York Harbor on an armada commanded by his brother, Admiral Richard Howe. American observers along the New Jersey coast speculated that the fleet was turning south, but at this point General Howe's target was still an open question. The lack of a Continental navy hampered Washington, who was forced to rely upon spotters scattered along the coastline to locate the ships and relay information. Until reliable intelligence arrived, Washington had no choice but to mark time in northern New Jersey.

General Howe's voyage promised to be long and slow. The journey was a miserable experience for man and beast alike. The heat and humidity were stifling, and brisk winds buffeted the ships. Meanwhile, the Continental Army headed for three separate crossings of the Delaware River to expedite the crossing into Pennsylvania, if warranted. When news of the fleet found its way to Washington, there was little doubt Howe was heading for Philadelphia.

The final days of July arrived with the British fleet tacking into the Delaware Bay to assess the current conditions and intelligence about Washington's army. When the news reached Washington about twenty-four hours later, he ordered his army to cross into Pennsylvania to block a move against Philadelphia. Almost simultaneously, the Howe brothers made what was perhaps the most critical decision of 1777, aboard bobbing ships in Delaware Bay.

The British general and admiral acted upon incorrect information that Washington's entire army was across the Delaware River and approaching Wilmington, Delaware, and that the Delaware River was heavily fortified below Philadelphia. Although William Howe was informed that Washington's army was west of the Delaware River, little if any of the Continental Army had yet to arrive in Pennsylvania, and there were few American defenses on the river. There was a clear and open path for the British to the American capital.

Despite easy access to Philadelphia, approximately ninety miles by ship, Howe decided to sail south to Chesapeake Bay, where he could put his troops ashore without molestation. On July 31, the fleet headed back to sea. Howe later claimed the move farther south benefited John Burgoyne by drawing Washington away from the Hudson River Valley. In reality, the moment William Howe gave the order to steer toward the Chesapeake, he eliminated any possibility of aiding Burgoyne.

When news of Howe's location in the upper Chesapeake Bay arrived on August 21, Washington scrambled to move the scattered elements of his army into a position to confront the British south of Philadelphia. On August 24, Washington paraded his troops through Philadelphia en route to Delaware. It was time to block Howe's approaches to the capital. The next morning, Washington crossed into Delaware. About the same time, Howe began off-loading troops into northeastern Maryland.

Now that Howe had landed, making a connection with the Delaware River was imperative. Throughout the war the British were in short supply of land transportation. Howe's logistical concerns were compounded because many of his horses had died during the voyage. This operational conundrum affected Howe's decision-making throughout the campaign. Had he landed in northern Delaware at the end of July, he would have had his connection with the Delaware River. Now, Howe was barely back on land, and he had no choice but to find and operate along the waterway.

Howe had been avoiding a pitched confrontation, but the campaign season was rapidly winding down and there was precious little to show for it. Washington had an outpost in northern Delaware at Cooch's Bridge on the Christina River, which Howe would have to deal with in order to reach Washington's main army. He did just that on September 3. The fitful fighting lasted some seven hours before the American detachment ran out of ammunition and fled across the bridge and eventually back toward Wilmington, leaving the British in command of the banks of the Christina River. The battle, which carried Howe one step closer to Philadelphia, was the largest land engagement in the history of Delaware.

On September 8, Howe gained the Pennsylvania border ahead of Washington. By late morning, the bulk of Howe's army was camped on the hills around Hockessin, Delaware, well above Washington's right flank. Out-generaled yet again, Washington scrambled to get his army in motion and into a blocking position to protect Philadelphia. In the middle of the night, he pulled the Continental Army from northern Delaware, marched north, and the next day began moving into positions on the east side of the Brandywine River near Chadds Ford in Pennsylvania.

Howe's army moved north parallel to Washington's position and camped about six miles west of the American army at Kennett Square. Washington had spent the long summer months attempting to hinder British movements with militia and other troops while seeking a favorable opportunity to make a stand should one become necessary. The terrain along the Brandywine River provided him with exactly that.

The Battle of Brandywine was the longest and largest single-day engagement of the war. The fighting on September 11, 1777, is also a study of contradictions. Washington hoped a stout defense along the rolling terrain hugging the Brandywine Creek would bar British access to Philadelphia. His goal was to defend its various crossings and prevent Howe from gaining access to the east bank. Although Washington had his troops in position east of the Brandywine a full day before the fighting began, he remained almost completely ignorant of the surrounding terrain and road network, failing to identify and guard all the fords available to the British. There was a lack of reconnaissance patrols. Even more alarming was that no one in a position of authority thought to speak to the many local residents serving in the Continental Army.

While Washington prepared for battle with little terrain knowledge and even less help from the locals, William Howe made his plans with the advantage of both. Pennsylvania Loyalist Joseph Galloway and others provided the British general with everything he needed to know about local terrain conditions and the road network. Howe recognized that a frontal assault against the American positions would be too costly. Instead, he sent Wilhelm von Knyphausen's division ahead to pin Washington in place and executed a wide left hook under the command of General Cornwallis that surprised the Americans beyond their vulnerable right flank. Washington discovered the move too late to prevent it, but he managed to shift the bulk of his army to oppose it and conducted a dogged defensive action that cost Howe dearly. Howe's success that day can be evenly credited to his good generalship and Washington's failures.

Washington's poor use of scouts and the intelligence they produced haunted him throughout that long day. Howe's flanking maneuver worked almost to perfection.

Late on the evening of September 11, Washington and his army were retreating in haste from the battlefield at Brandywine toward Chester, Pennsylvania. General Howe did little to interfere with Washington's efforts to regroup in the immediate aftermath of the battle. For four days, Howe kept most of his army on the battlefield instead of launching a vigorous pursuit. In truth, the British Army was exhausted. The soldiers had endured a long, tedious voyage, followed by hard marching and prolonged combat with sustained casualties. They were in no condition to drive ahead.

Washington needed to find fresh defensive ground to protect Philadelphia from Howe's victorious army. The Continentals left Chester, crossed the Schuylkill River at the Middle Ferry, and marched out toward Germantown, thus completing a nineteen-mile march. Moving the army north of the Schuylkill River put Washington behind the last natural barrier between the British and Philadelphia. As a defensive barrier, the river was less than ideal. If defending the numerous fords across the Brandywine had been difficult for Washington, then defending the fords across the Schuylkill, which were more spread out, would prove a Herculean task.

Moving into the Germantown area left Washington with a vexing conundrum. He felt duty-bound to defend the capital, but he could not leave the critical supply depots at Reading and other places in the backcountry unprotected. Moving northwest to protect the depots would expose the capital. Moving into position to protect Philadelphia exposed the supply centers upon which his army depended. It was now readily obvious that the loss at Brandywine made protecting the American capital nearly impossible. Protecting his storehouses had to take precedence over the most important city in North America.

Most of Howe's army, meanwhile, remained idle. Howe could have crossed the upper fords on the Schuylkill River with ease, cutting

Washington off from his crucial supply depots. But Howe had a history of unenthusiastic follow-through after successful battles. Brandywine's aftermath was no different.

On September 14, Washington's army left the Germantown area and recrossed the Schuylkill River. The Americans were now strategically positioned to block a British advance to the Schuylkill River. Although they had taken a roundabout route to get there, they were just ten miles from where they had fought at Brandywine.

On the night of September 15, Howe issued orders for the army to move into the Great Valley the following day. Rain had already moved into the area, turning the rutted dirt roads into a dense paste through which thousands of soldiers tramped. What Howe seems not to have known is that on the morning of September 16, Washington's army was moving from the Lancaster Road and ascending the South Valley Hill to block Howe from the Schuylkill River. The armies were once more on a collision course, and only five days after the conclusion of the largest single-day battle of the American Revolution.

The rain showers, which had been heavy but intermittent, were now blending into a nearly continuous downpour. As the British columns came together at Goshen Meeting, Washington sought to move his army south from the Lancaster Road and deploy along the crest of South Valley Hill to block Howe's advance. Howe and Cornwallis hoped to catch Washington moving west on Lancaster Road, along which the Continentals camped the night before—not south of that road. However, the two armies were marching toward each other.

The British soon pushed Washington out of the way. Since the majority of the Continental Army never started marching up the South Valley Hill, Washington quickly formed a line on the southern slope of the North Valley Hill approximately three miles north of where the two separate actions known as the "Battle of the Clouds" occurred. Other than some skirmishing and muddy maneuvering, however, there was no major clash of arms. To the dismay of Howe and his subordinates, the driving rain of a nor'easter prevented the British from exploiting their initial success. When the storm clouds cleared the next day, the path was clear to the Schuylkill River fords and an easy occupation of Philadelphia.

Faulty cartridge boxes led to the destruction of most of the Continental Army's ammunition supply. Washington decided to move to Warwick Furnace in northwestern Chester County to obtain a fresh supply. From the new position, the army was within reach of its depots at Reading. The position also left Washington well-placed to observe British movements and to move into blocking positions on the Schuylkill River, with the nearest ford nine miles from the army. When the army moved west, Washington left Anthony Wayne's Pennsylvania division behind to screen the rear of the army and keep watch on Howe.

After waiting out the rain, on September 18 the British shifted into Tredyffrin Township, not far from an iron production facility known as Valley Forge. Howe needed to wait for his opportunity to cross the Schuylkill River. Like every creek nearby, the river was above flood stage.

Meanwhile, he set his sights on Continental supply depots south of the river, including Valley Forge. "Lighthorse" Harry Lee and Washington's aide, Alexander Hamilton, were sent there with small detachments of dragoons on September 18 to move the supplies to the north side of the Schuylkill. That evening, Howe sent a column to seize the storehouse at Valley Forge. Lee and Hamilton escaped without injury, but the British seized the magazine.

Washington wanted to get into a blocking position north of the Schuylkill River near the fords around Valley Forge. With Wayne behind the British, Washington hoped to catch the British in a pincer movement. Most of the army camped along the east side of Perkiomen Creek after their grueling twenty-nine-mile march. Washington's movement left Wayne in a terrible position. He was now unsupported by the Continental Army with the main British Army between him and Washington.

The next day, Washington's army moved from Perkiomen Creek and marched ten to fifteen miles to take up positions along the Schuylkill on a nine-mile front. Just as he had done at Brandywine, Washington spread his army thin along a wide front, hoping to prevent the British crossing of a natural barrier. Despite defeat at Brandywine and near disaster at the Battle of the Clouds, Washington had seized the initiative again.

General Howe decided on the evening of September 20 that the problem behind him—Anthony Wayne's Pennsylvania division—had to be eliminated so he could focus on Washington's troops north of the Schuylkill River and achieve his objective of capturing Philadelphia.

Howe tapped Major General Charles Grey to command the operation. Hoping to achieve complete surprise, Grey ordered his men to remove the flints from their muskets and perform their dirty work with bayonets. While Wayne was forewarned, the situation quickly got away from him. The British Second Light Infantry Battalion swarmed through Wayne's camp and surrounded the American rear. Confusion spread through the ranks of Wayne's command. Men scattered to save themselves, climbing over fences and into the woods. Many were caught by the pursuing British while still on the fences and bayoneted. The affair would go down in history as the "Paoli Massacre."

Once Grey's column returned from the successful Paoli operation, Howe put his army in motion and moved ahead with his plans to cross the Schuylkill River. The British Army departed its camps and marched into the Valley Forge area. Howe now had six river crossings in front of him, with the Continental Army stretched for nine miles along the Schuylkill River fords.

It was painfully obvious to Washington that Anthony Wayne's loss at Paoli had altered the strategic situation. Washington had intended to prevent Howe's crossing of the Schuylkill by raiding his rear and seizing his baggage. He now faced a Hobson's choice, for the storehouses at Reading needed to be protected, but protecting them would uncover Philadelphia, which, politically speaking, could not be surrendered without a fight. To the poorly supplied army, protecting those backcountry regions was more important than the psychological loss of Philadelphia. It was obvious, however, that Howe could move rapidly west, capture the Continental supply centers, return for Philadelphia, and win both major prizes. No matter what Howe decided to do, Philadelphia was all but lost.

On the evening of September 21, Washington pulled away from the river fords and shifted his army west to better protect the supply center. The risky movement exposed the lower fords of the Schuylkill River to the British. The British drove across that night. Having duped Washington into moving west away from the fords, the British army crossed to the north side unopposed. The British were now firmly positioned between Washington and Philadelphia. No more combat was needed to seize the capital.

Howe held all the strategic cards except one: he desperately needed to be resupplied by the British fleet. If Washington could bar access to Philadelphia by the Royal Navy via the Delaware River, he might be able to starve Howe's army into submission.

On September 25, Howe marched his army in two columns eleven miles into Germantown, just five miles from Philadelphia. Although he had been beaten at Brandywine and maneuvered away from Philadelphia, Washington was eager to strike the British. The army's current position, however, precluded any attempt to do so. The Continentals were not within striking distance of the British position at Germantown.

Charles Cornwallis received the honor of leading a column of troops into Philadelphia on September 26. After their triumphant show-of-force parade, Cornwallis deployed his men to cover the city's approaches in Maryland.

Howe now needed to keep the Continental Army at bay while his command, with the assistance of the British fleet, endeavored to open the Delaware River to provisions and supplies for his army. The situation was rather simple. If the British could gain control of the Delaware River, Philadelphia would remain in the hands of the Crown. If they could not navigate the Delaware at will, they would not have sufficient supplies to remain in place and would almost certainly have to evacuate the capital.

On September 26, Washington and his army crossed Perkiomen Creek and arrived at Pennypacker's Mills, ten miles closer to Philadelphia but still more than twenty miles outside the city. The host of problems and decisions Washington had to make included the management of the vitally important American defenses along the Delaware River. This line consisted primarily of three forts: Mercer (on the east bank of the river at Red Bank in New Jersey); Mifflin (directly across from Mercer on a mud island on the Pennsylvania shore); and Billingsport, two miles downstream on the same side of the river as Mercer.

With American quartermasters stripping resources from the region surrounding Philadelphia and army patrols blanketing the area, it would only get progressively harder to obtain provisions from the countryside sufficient to supply the British Army. Winter was coming. The men would need cold-weather clothing, and the Delaware River would begin to freeze in early December.

General Howe decided to move first against the southernmost enemy position on the river at Billingsport, New Jersey.

October opened with the British seizure of Billingsport, which meant the loss of the first line of chevaux-de-frise river obstructions. The British Navy began removing the obstructions immediately, but the tedious process would require three weeks to complete.

Washington had the Continental Army moving again on October 2. The march took the men four miles beyond the crossroads in Worcester Township onto Methacton Hill. Washington was now fewer than twenty miles from the city limits and about half that from Germantown. If Washington could break through the British camp at Germantown, Howe would be hard-pressed to stop the Continentals short of Philadelphia. Washington and his staff calculated the remaining British forces in Germantown to number perhaps eight thousand men.

Washington planned his assault on Germantown and gained the full consent of his generals for the undertaking. Surprise was a key element of the plan, which would require a great deal of discipline, coordination, and good luck. Once approved, Washington intended to divide his army into four columns intended to meet on the northern and western edges of Germantown simultaneously at 5:00 a.m. on October 4. The columns would move silently through the darkness for fourteen to as many as twenty miles over a series of poorly marked roads. These movements would show whether the army was capable of a nighttime march and a coordinated surprise attack.

The Americans had tried to execute a similar plan at Trenton nearly nine months earlier, but two of the four columns had failed to reach their objectives. Washington had learned though hard experience that stand-up fights against the British were a losing proposition; thus, his preferred tactic was to strike isolated enemy detachments, which is precisely what he was attempting to do against the depleted British garrison holding Germantown. In truth—as Washington well knew—the plan was bold, complicated, and risky for an army like his to attempt. Washington hoped to drive into a major village along four different roads, using precise timing that his men would have to pull off in the dark.

Coordinating the movements of each column so that they would arrive in Germantown simultaneously was more than ambitious. On paper Washington counted nearly fourteen thousand men, but the army that marched and fought on October 4 six miles outside Philadelphia was much smaller; it had been bleeding stragglers and deserters throughout the campaign, and some men had to be left behind to protect the encampment and wagons. It was the first time during the war that Washington launched his own army in a major attack against the main British force.

To achieve maximum effect and complete surprise, it was imperative that each of the four columns reach its assigned location at the same time—a rather tall order given that each column had to march a different distance in the dark. Coordinating the timing of departure was crucial; any errors could throw the entire attack plan off and result in piecemeal assault, allowing the British to concentrate troops as each attack developed. A final key to the battle plan was destroying Howe's Germantown garrison before any reinforcements could arrive from Philadelphia, six miles away.

Once the engagement began, the British light infantry experienced a temporary breakdown of discipline and were overwhelmed by superior numbers and, at least early in the fighting, better tactical management. Their conduct disgusted Howe, but the superior overall discipline within the British ranks proved decisive in the end.

Thomas Musgrave's decision to save his regiment by moving into Cliveden (a stone house in Germantown) rather than surrendering proved fatal to Washington's attack.

Perhaps the most surprising achievement that day was that all four columns arrived where they were expected. Once the American columns arrived and the British line was collapsing, the pivot point of the battle rested on the decision made at Cliveden to surround and assault Musgrave's men holed up inside the house. Rather than make his own intuitive decision, Washington held an impromptu council of war on the field. Henry Knox insisted that the troops inside the house had to be neutralized before continuing to drive south into Germantown. It was a tactically flawed decision that tied up many hundreds of men and commands that would otherwise have continued the attack and kept the British off-balance.

Washington's decision turned the initiative over to the enemy. The men under Anthony Wayne and John Sullivan well to the front heard firing in their rear, believed they had been flanked, and reversed course. During the chaotic withdrawal, Americans fired into one another. The time wasted around Cliveden and the withdrawal of the two divisions in the middle of the American assault gave the British the time they needed to regroup.

The well-trained veteran British troops pushed back the confused and inexperienced Continentals, regained the lost ground, freed Musgrave's men from Cliveden, and drove the Americans off the field. The rank-and-file Americans did their duty and performed heroically. Once again, the choices made at the highest levels failed them. Just as poor intelligence had doomed the Americans at Brandywine, poor tactical decisions did the same at Germantown. Ultimately, Washington failed the army; the army did not fail him.

Philadelphia was now firmly in the grasp of the British. Washington was no longer in a position to recapture it or drive the British away from the colonial capital. His strategy turned instead to starving Howe out of the colonial capital. Nearly everything Howe's army needed—including military and medical supplies and food—was stored in the holds of British ships stuck downriver from Philadelphia near Chester, Pennsylvania. The Royal Navy was still unable to navigate the Delaware. Several rows of cheveaux-de-frise blocked the ships from ascending the river, as did the American forts Mercer (on the New Jersey side) and Mifflin (on the Pennsylvania shore on Mud Island).

Forts Mifflin and Mercer were crucial components of Washington's strategy to tighten the logistical noose around Philadelphia.

On October 7, the same day Burgoyne lost the second battle of Saratoga (Bemis Heights), British engineers began erecting batteries along the Pennsylvania shore of Province Island north of Fort Mifflin. The Continental Army, meanwhile, had no choice but to remain north of Philadelphia to prevent Howe from launching excursions against American supply depots in the Pennsylvania backcountry, which meant the naval elements and river forts had to keep the British fleet below the chevaux-de-frise.

Despite the importance of the Delaware River operations, Washington's subordinates had thus far done little to slow the efforts of British engineers intent on taking Fort Mifflin. Creating the necessary gun platforms was more difficult than the British anticipated because the Americans had cut the dikes on Province and Carpenter's Islands and created knee-deep, swamp-like conditions precisely where the platforms were most needed. The only viable place to build them was on the dikes themselves, which were more exposed to enemy fire. Conditions in Fort Mifflin on Mud Island were nearly as bad for the Americans as laboring on flooded Province Island was for the British. The island was cold and damp, and the men were poorly equipped. The British, who erected four batteries along the dikes of Province and Carpenter's Islands, officially opened the siege of Fort Mifflin on October 15.

General Howe was losing his patience with the slow progress along the Delaware. He realized that more than ships were needed to assault Fort Mercer in New Jersey. The change in strategy signaled the end of the occupation of Germantown. In order to free up troops for the Mercer operation, on October 19 Howe withdrew his units from the battle-scarred village and concentrated his army in Philadelphia. He intended to winter there and wanted his men safely in the city before winter set in. He also intended to personally supervise operations along the river.

Once the Germantown garrison moved into Philadelphia, Howe had eighteen thousand military personnel in need of food and other supplies. If the river remained closed much longer, the population faced the very real prospect of starvation. Despite their strength and their victory at Germantown, the Crown forces were in a noose, and Washington's forces kept tightening the rope through harassment. Both army commanders were aware that Forts Mifflin and Mercer depended upon one another to control passage along the Delaware River. The loss of one would necessarily lead to the fall of the remaining fort.

It had become imperative for the British to break the river blockade. With Fort Mifflin already under partial bombardment, Howe decided to launch an attack against Fort Mercer. The all-German assault force was led by Colonel Carl von Donop. Up to this point in the campaign, the German troops had done very little.

By midday of October 22, Donop arrived in the vicinity of Fort Mercer. After attempting to force the surrender of the fort, Donop launched an assault on the earthworks. The Hessians were bloodily repulsed. Colonel von Donop was severely wounded in the thigh (a wound from which he would die on October 29). The victory for the Americans was shockingly lopsided.

Apparently overcome with depression, William Howe wrote a letter of resignation on October 22 (the king accepted Howe's resignation on

February 4, 1778). Having led two successful campaigns that had not led to total victory and lacking full support from England, the general was disgusted and ready to head home. Washington continued to maintain a death grip on Philadelphia, hoping to starve out the British just as he had done in Boston.

On October 26, another nor'easter slammed into the region, flooding the camps of both armies and turning the Delaware and the Schuylkill into raging torrents. Mud Island and Fort Mifflin were flooded, with much of the island being under two feet of water. In the midst of all the despair in the British camps, Howe received confirmation of Burgoyne's surrender.

On November 2, Washington's army moved forward to Whitemarsh and encamped. The army was positioned on a series of hills. For the next month, the armies settled into a lull that included a constant string of guerilla engagements in no-man's-land.

All reports from Philadelphia indicated that the population was on the verge of starvation and that the army never had more than two days' provisions on hand at any time. After the river froze, even this trickle of provisions would cease. Fort Mifflin started to take a beating. The palisades were shattered and the barracks were rendered useless. The men began huddling under the western wall. Despite this, the garrison appeared tenacious to Howe.

The British were having their own problems. Suffering was widespread among the British troops. Provisions, clothing, and firewood were in short supply. Many horses had succumbed to the hard work in the heavy mud and cold weather without pasture or grain.

As dawn broke on November 16, the American flag was still flying above Fort Mifflin, but no troops remained within its ruins. The British sent a detachment to the work, removed the American flag, and raised a British standard. The river was finally quiet. Fort Mercer would also be abandoned in short order.

Washington's army was in desperate condition and unable to sustain the two river forts. The campaign had worn down the men and their materials beyond their limits. The army had marched over four hundred miles, and supplies were trickling in from New England and Virginia with New York and Philadelphia cut off. With the river finally opened, British supplies began to flow into the city.

Howe determined to launch one last offensive. On December 5, he led ten thousand troops in two columns out from Philadelphia. Howe determined that attacking the American position on its series of hills would not prove advantageous. Rather, he opted for a flanking movement toward Cheltenham Township and Jenkintown. The march was conducted during the night of December 6, and the British moved to a position near Edge Hill.

On the morning of December 7, Howe's men marched to the top of Edge Hill. After pushing the American militia and riflemen back, Howe halted and looked across the valley to the main American line on the Whitemarsh Hills. The line appeared well-entrenched and fortified, with fifty artillery pieces looking down at him. Washington showed no signs of coming down off the hills. Having failed to draw Washington out from his encampment, Howe returned to Philadelphia the next day. Washington did learn a lesson from the fighting around Whitemarsh. His army was too close to Philadelphia and both flanks were vulnerable.

By mid-December, campaigning was quickly coming to a close. A discussion occurred between Washington and several of his officers over where a winter encampment should be located. Wilmington, Lancaster, and Reading were suggested. However, moving farther away from the British Army would open more of the region to depredations and increase local support for the British. Staying close to Philadelphia to deter Howe, but far enough away to avoid surprises, was a more probable political and military solution.

On the morning of December 19, Washington's army marched into their Valley Forge encampment, eighteen miles from Philadelphia. Howe's army officially went into winter quarters on December 30. Things did not look good for the American army and the American cause. Nevertheless, the future would see the transformation of the Continental Army at the hands of Baron von Steuben. The army that marched out of Valley Forge the following spring would go on to fight competently at Monmouth and ultimately force the surrender of the British Army at Yorktown in 1781.

Further Reading

Harris, Michael C. *Brandywine: A Military History of the Battle That Lost Philadelphia but Saved America, September 11, 1777.* El Dorado Hills, California: Savas Beatie, 2014.

Harris, Michael C. *Germantown: A Military History of the Battle for Philadelphia, October 4, 1777.* El Dorado Hills, California: Savas Beatie, 2020.

McGuire, Thomas J. *Philadelphia Campaign: Brandywine and the Fall of Philadelphia.* Mechanicsburg, Pennsylvania: Stackpole Books, 2006. Vol. 1.

McGuire, Thomas J. *Philadelphia Campaign: Germantown and the Roads to Valley Forge.* Mechanicsburg, Pennsylvania: Stackpole Books, 2007. Vol. 2.

Reed, John F. *Campaign to Valley Forge: July 1, 1777–December 19, 1777.* Philadelphia: University of Pennsylvania Press, 1965.

Smith, Samuel Steele. *Fight for the Delaware 1777.* Monmouth Beach, New Jersey: Philip Freneau Press, 1970.

About the Author

Michael C. Harris is a graduate of the University of Mary Washington and the American Military University. He has worked for the National Park Service in Fredericksburg, Virginia; Fort Mott State Park in New Jersey; and the Pennsylvania Historical and Museum Commission at Brandywine Battlefield. He has conducted tours and staff rides of many East Coast battlefields. Michael is certified in secondary education and currently teaches in the Philadelphia region. He lives in Pennsylvania with his wife, Michelle, and son, Nathanael. His first book, *Brandywine*, was awarded the American Revolution Round Table of Richmond book award in 2014.

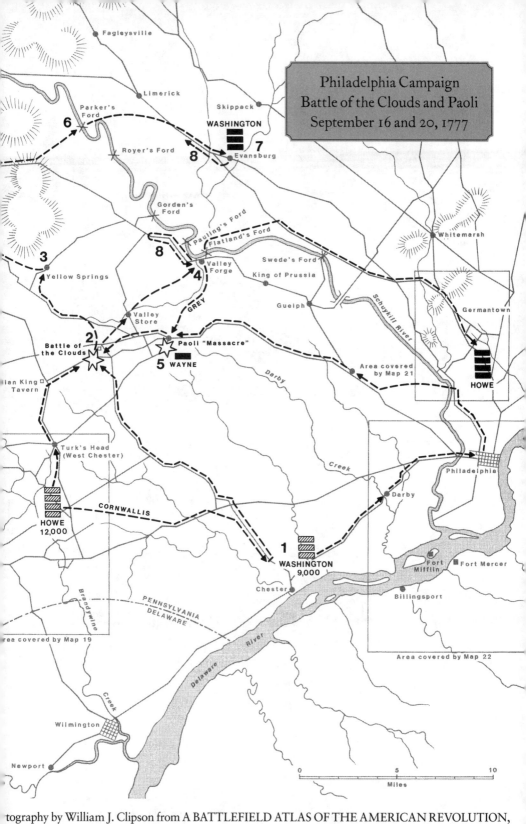

Philadelphia Campaign
Battle of the Clouds and Paoli
September 16 and 20, 1777

Fagleysville

Limerick

Parker's
Ford

6

Royer's Ford

Skippack

WASHINGTON

7

Evansburg

8

Gorden's
Ford

Pauling's Ford

Flatland's Ford

Whitemarsh

3

Yellow Springs

8

Valley
Forge

4

Swede's Ford

King of Prussia

Germantown

Valley
Store

GREY

Gueiph

Schuylkill River

Area covered
by Map 21

HOWE

2

Battle of
the Clouds

Paoli "Massacre"

5 **WAYNE**

Darby

ian King
Tavern

Turk's Head
(West Chester)

Creek

Philadelphia

HOWE
12,000

CORNWALLIS

Darby

1 **WASHINGTON**
9,000

Fort
Mifflin

Fort Mercer

Chester

Billingsport

Brandywine

PENNSYLVANIA
DELAWARE

rea covered by Map 19

Delaware River

Area covered by Map 22

Creek

Wilmington

0   5   10
Miles

Newport

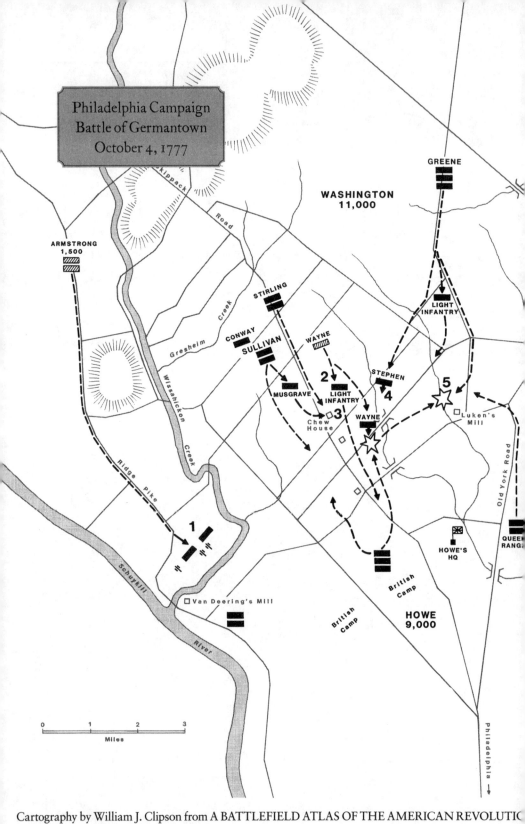

Philadelphia Campaign
Battle of Germantown
October 4, 1777

GREENE

WASHINGTON
11,000

ARMSTRONG
1,500

STIRLING

CONWAY
SULLIVAN

WAYNE

LIGHT
INFANTRY

MUSGRAVE

2

LIGHT
INFANTRY

STEPHEN

4

5

Chew
House

3

WAYNE

Luken's
Mill

Kippack Road

Greshelm Creek

Wissahickon Creek

Ridge Pike

Schuylkill

1

Van Deering's Mill

HOWE'S
HQ

QUEE
RANG

British
Camp

British
Camp

HOWE
9,000

Old York Road

River

Philadelphia →

0   1   2   3
Miles

Cartography by William J. Clipson from A BATTLEFIELD ATLAS OF THE AMERICAN REVOLUTIO
published by Savas Beatie, www.savasbeatie.com

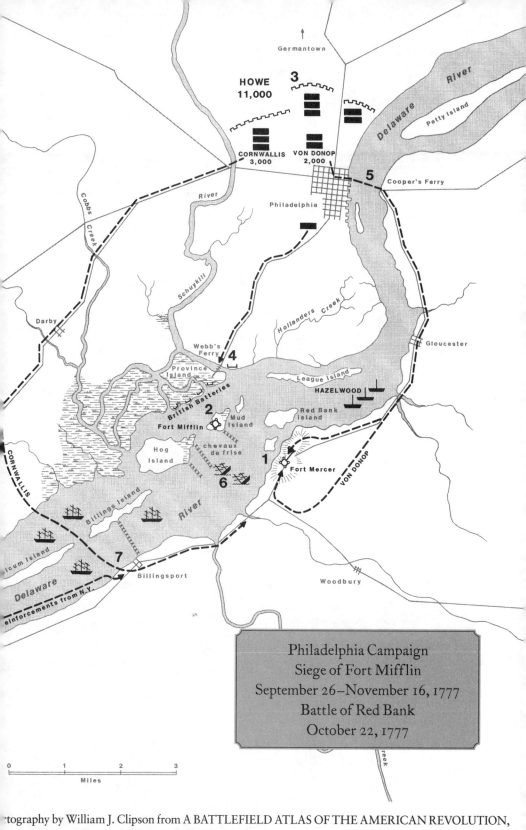

Germantown

HOWE
11,000

3

CORNWALLIS
3,000

VON DONOP
2,000

Delaware River

Petty Island

5

Cooper's Ferry

River

Philadelphia

Cobbs Creek

Schuylkill

Darby

Hollanders Creek

Webb's Ferry

4

Province Island

League Island

Gloucester

British Batteries

HAZELWOOD

2

Mud Island

Red Bank Island

Fort Mifflin

Hog Island

chevaux de frise

1

Fort Mercer

VON DONOP

6

CORNWALLIS

Billings Island

River

lcum Island

7

Billingsport

Woodbury

Delaware

einforcements from N.Y.

creek

Philadelphia Campaign
Siege of Fort Mifflin
September 26–November 16, 1777
Battle of Red Bank
October 22, 1777

0   1   2   3
Miles

tography by William J. Clipson from A BATTLEFIELD ATLAS OF THE AMERICAN REVOLUTION,
lished by Savas Beatie, www.savasbeatie.com

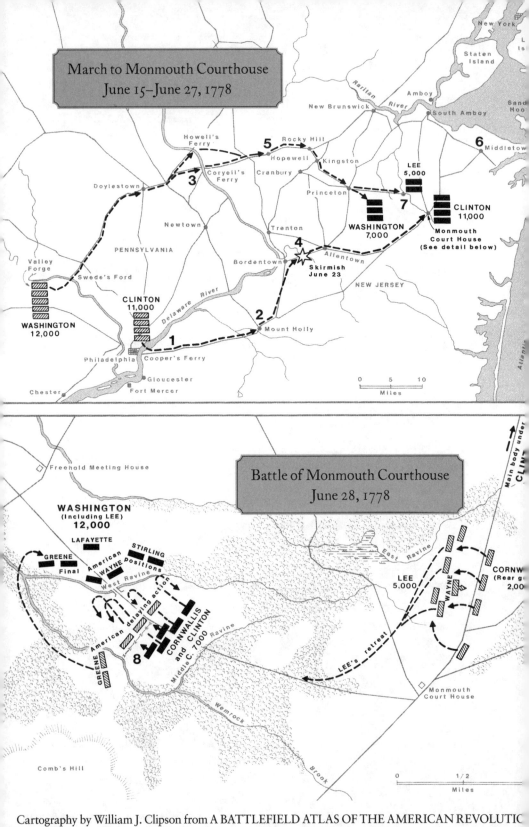

March to Monmouth Courthouse
June 15–June 27, 1778

Battle of Monmouth Courthouse
June 28, 1778

Cartography by William J. Clipson from A BATTLEFIELD ATLAS OF THE AMERICAN REVOLUTIC
published by Savas Beatie, www.savasbeatie.com

The Monmouth Campaign, June 1778: Tactical Draw, Political Victory

BY MARK EDWARD LENDER

News of the formal alliance between France and the rebellious American colonies reached the Continental Army at Valley Forge on May 3, 1778. For General George Washington, the army's hard-pressed commander in chief, the event was literally a matter of divine intervention. "The Almighty ruler of the Universe," he proclaimed, had raised "us up a powerful Friend among the Princes of the Earth to establish our liberty and Independence." He ordered a day of thanksgiving with a parade, cheers for Louis XVI, artillery salutes, and (no doubt to the soldiery's delight) a special issue of rum.[1] Word of the alliance was the best news Washington had received in months.

In occupied Philadelphia, news of the Franco-American alliance caused no rejoicing. In fact, early 1778 found British military fortunes problematic. Parliament had learned of the enemy alliance in late February and considered it tantamount to a declaration of war. This development, along with growing tensions with Spain and Holland, had raised the possibility of wider hostilities. Britain lacked the resources to fight everywhere, and the ministry understood that new operations in the American North were unlikely to be decisive. Thus Lord George Germain, the American secretary, ordered the new British commander in chief, Lieutenant General

Sir Henry Clinton (who had relieved Sir William Howe in May) to evacuate Philadelphia. The orders staggered British morale, but Clinton was to return his army to New York.

The British were not giving up. They planned to redeploy many of Clinton's men in a new effort in the American South—where they hoped for significant Loyalist support—and to bolster their garrisons in Florida and the valuable Caribbean sugar islands. They would also keep a worried eye on Europe. Thus, what had begun as a colonial rebellion had become part of a much broader struggle, all of which meant that Clinton could expect no significant reinforcements.

Clinton had intended to leave Philadelphia via the Delaware River. The Royal Navy, however, lacked the shipping to carry his troops and the throngs of frightened Tories who preferred flight to remaining in Philadelphia. Sir Henry therefore assigned the sick and wounded, military dependents, Loyalist civilians, and some Hessian regiments to the available ships; the rest of his army—some thirteen thousand men and camp followers—prepared for an overland march across New Jersey. As much as Clinton resented his orders to retreat, he planned to make the best of his trek. With any luck he would find a way to draw Washington into a showdown fight. After loading transports and moving advance units and equipment to a New Jersey bridgehead, Clinton's army completed its crossing on June 18. Shortly thereafter the transports dropped down the Delaware. In New Jersey, Clinton struck northeast. The stage for the Monmouth Campaign was set.

Background to Battle

While Clinton began his march, Washington was at Valley Forge ready to give chase. In fact, he was only too happy to leave the winter encampment behind as it held no fond memories. Valley Forge had been an ordeal. Logistical and fiscal failures, disease, and bouts of miserable weather had brought the army to the brink of collapse. Washington's reverses in combat in late 1777, including the loss of the de facto rebel capital of Philadelphia, had ignited a storm of criticism of his leadership. Indeed, there was a concerted effort among some in Congress—the so-called Conway Cabal—to curtail his authority as commander in chief, if not to replace him with Major General Horatio Gates, the victor at Saratoga.

Yet Valley Forge had also been a redemptive experience. Washington displayed considerable political finesse in outmaneuvering his critics; and the timely arrival of French arms, equipment, and other military aid had allowed the general to re-equip and reorganize his Continentals. The appointments of Jeremiah Wadsworth and Nathanael Greene as commissary and quartermaster generals, respectively, had vastly improved logistics operations. Moreover, the labors of Friedrich von Steuben as inspector general had retrained the regulars in a common disciplinary and tactical regimen. By June 1778 the result of all of these changes was an army better in almost every respect than the force that had straggled into Valley Forge in December 1777. How much better, however, and how it would do against Clinton's veterans remained to be seen.

Washington could only guess at British intentions. Before Clinton left Philadelphia the commander in chief had already dispatched General William Maxwell's New Jersey Brigade into New Jersey; now he hoped that Maxwell and state militia might slow Clinton enough for the Continentals to catch him. When the British actually crossed the Delaware, however, the rebel chief reacted cautiously. In May a council of war had agreed to adopt a defensive posture in any new campaign, reacting to enemy initiatives rather than boldly attacking. Yet on June 17 a second council was more contentious. Some officers, including Major Generals Charles Lee and Steuben, still unconvinced that the Continentals could handle the British regulars, urged continued caution. Other officers, including Greene, Lafayette, and Anthony Wayne, argued for bringing Clinton to battle. Washington decided on a middle ground; he would shadow the British, stay out of trouble, and hope for an opportunity to strike. His advance units left Valley Forge on the nineteenth and crossed into New Jersey on the twentieth. The campaign was on.

Washington's quarry was in no hurry. Clinton's soldiers plodded through "excessive heat" and torrential rains over sandy roads, all the while tormented by swarming mosquitoes. Their accordion-like baggage train, loaded with tons of supplies, occasionally stretched almost twelve miles long. The British columns moved on high alert as rebel detachments hovered on their flanks, destroying bridges, blocking roads, and searching for ambush opportunities. The threat increased when Washington sent Daniel Morgan's riflemen to support Maxwell and the militia. After skirmishing with the Americans at Crosswicks on June 23, Clinton arrived at Allentown on June 24. He had marched only forty miles in a week. But adverse weather and the Americans had little to do with Clinton's torpid advance. In fact, the British commander was deliberately taking his time, hoping against hope that Washington would come up and offer battle—and by June 24, intelligence reports had alerted Washington to Clinton's intentions.

At Allentown two routes lay open to Clinton. One tracked northeast through New Brunswick and on to Perth Amboy, where he could cross to British-held Staten Island. The other, southerly route led through the village of Monmouth Courthouse (also known as Freehold) and on to Sandy Hook. From there the Royal Navy could ferry the army to New York. Clinton elected to take the road to Sandy Hook. He feared that heading for New Brunswick would offer Washington a chance to hit his baggage train as it forded the Raritan River. Significantly, Clinton also hoped that easier terrain toward Freehold would favor him if Washington chose to fight. Thus on the morning of June 25 the British left Allentown for Monmouth Courthouse, where they arrived on the following day.

While Clinton moved deeper into New Jersey, Washington pondered his next move. By the twenty-fourth the Americans had reached Hopewell. Barely twenty miles now separated the armies. Learning of Clinton's move toward Freehold, Washington considered striking at least part of the retreating enemy. Another council of war, however, revealed little consensus among his generals. The hawks argued for hitting Clinton hard, although without precipitating a general engagement (that is, without committing the entire Continental Army). "If we suffer the enemy to pass through New Jersey without attacking," Greene warned, "I think we shall...regret it. People expect something from us and our strength demands it. I am by no means for rash measures," he concluded, "but we must preserve our reputation."[2] It was a political argument aimed at restoring popular faith in Washington and the army after the disappointments of 1777.

Other officers, however, supported the contrary views of Major General Charles Lee. A British veteran with considerable experience, Lee was the army's second-ranking officer. Competent early in the war, he had become critical of Washington during the defeats of late 1776. A British patrol had captured him in December, but Lee was exchanged and he rejoined the army only weeks before Clinton evacuated Philadelphia. He had little faith in Washington's regulars. Continentals, he warned, would prove no match for redcoat professionals. Lee argued for letting Clinton go, arguing that there was no need to risk the army. Wouldn't it be better, he asked, to await French intervention while preserving American strength? Lee insisted that a patriot victory in New Jersey would mean little, while a serious defeat could do irreversible harm. We should note that despite the pall cast over his career after Monmouth (more on that later), Lee's ideas had merit. Rebel spirits had soared at news of the French alliance and the British evacuation of Philadelphia, and Clinton wanted nothing more than to lure Washington into a showdown fight. He looked to pounce on any mistake the American general made, and Lee wanted to avoid just such an eventuality.

Beset by the council's conflicting opinions, Washington again chose a middle course. Agreeing to reinforce the advance troops shadowing Clinton, he dispatched Brigadier Charles Scott with 1,500 Virginians to support Maxwell, Morgan, and the militia. These reinforcements brought patriot strength near Clinton to some 3,500, and Washington wanted a major general in charge. When Lee refused the command—he considered it too small—a delighted Lafayette took the assignment. Eager hawks, however—notably Alexander Hamilton, Wayne, and

Greene—then forcefully argued for a still larger reinforcement. They prevailed, and Washington sent another 1,000 men under the fire-eating Wayne. Still, Washington was not rash; he warned Lafayette that hitting Clinton was "very desirable" but told the Frenchman not to exhaust his men in the scorching heat.[3] Thus the Hopewell council had resulted in a considerable movement toward the British, although Washington still remained cautious.

But not so the impetuous Lafayette. He became utterly reckless and planned to attack the royal troops on the morning of the twenty-sixth. He charged forward with inadequate supplies and poor intelligence of the enemy and moved well beyond supporting range of Washington's main army. Hamilton, serving as Lafayette's aide, feared a disaster. To everyone's relief, at the last minute Lafayette called off the assault, his men exhausted and his supplies nearly gone. Wisely, the commander in chief ordered Lafayette to Englishtown, eleven miles north. There he was to meet Lee, who, having reconsidered his initial reticence, now requested the forward command on the basis of its now considerable size. Washington had agreed, with the stipulation that Lee support Lafayette if the young Frenchman had already engaged. Lafayette almost had. Some of his units had come within a mile of Clinton's lines before he ordered them back. It had been a close call.

The Opening Rounds

The opposing armies had reached the eve of battle. On June 27, Washington's main body was at Cranbury, about four miles west of Lee's advanced corps of about 4,500 at Englishtown. Including militia, the Americans numbered some 13,000. Clinton had about as many. He had stayed in Freehold on the twenty-seventh, and if he hoped for Washington or one of the rebel generals to pick a fight, he was in luck.

Washington sought an engagement—but how? Late on June 27 he met with Lee and his chief subordinates. Everyone later agreed that the commander in chief wanted the vanguard—Lee's men—to advance early on the twenty-eighth. But Washington issued no specific orders on when, how, or even if to attack. Wayne later stated that he never heard "General Washington give any particular orders for the attack." Indeed, Washington was vague on exactly what he expected, and Lee reasonably concluded that his orders were discretionary and that he was to govern his conduct according to events. He had Washington's promise, however, to support Lee's advance with the main army.[4]

Lee moved early on Sunday, June 28, but his advance was hesitant. He had sent Colonel William Grayson with a "party of observation" toward Freehold, but even so intelligence on the British situation was conflicting. Lee knew that Clinton's baggage was already moving, but where was Clinton's main body? At around 7:30 a.m., as Lee and Wayne rode forward to reconnoiter and to catch up with Grayson, they heard firing ahead. But who was engaged?

It was not Grayson. The noise was from a sharp skirmish between state militia and the Queen's American Rangers, a crack Loyalist regiment. The rangers had come out to chase a rebel scouting party led by Steuben, who got cleanly away as the skirmishing flared. The rangers scattered the militia but backed off rather than confront another larger and strongly posted militia concentration. Thus the opening round of the battle was an all-American affair—patriot militia versus Tory rangers.

The end of the skirmish, however, revealed nothing of Clinton's dispositions. Lee hesitated to advance quickly, fearing a British attack would catch him in difficult terrain. Local militia officers warned of just such a risk. But after a wait with no solid information on British deployments, shortly before 9:00 a.m. an impatient Lee moved with Wayne in the lead.[5]

Battle was joined just after 10:00 a.m. Lee had spotted a redcoat column marching out of Freehold and thought it was a rear guard. Could he take it? He quickly came up with a plan: Wayne and supporting artillery would stay in position; he was to fix the enemy in place while Lee swung to the left to drop behind and encircle the redcoats. He would bag the lot without risking a major battle. The plan was reasonable, and Lee put his troops in motion.

With Lee moving, however, part of Wayne's command suddenly came under attack. While chasing some militia, the crack Sixteenth Light Dragoons spotted and made for the battalion of Colonel Richard Butler. Warned by the fleeing militia, Butler's men swung in line—just as Steuben had taught them—and fired a volley at the charging British. The dragoons broke off with several saddles emptied; first blood to the Continentals.

Butler's rebuff of the Sixteenth turned out to be the high point of the American morning. Lee had run into trouble. It turned out that the rebels had encountered more than a rear guard. Instead, they were facing Lord Cornwallis at the head of some six thousand men—with more coming. Clinton had spotted Lee's approach, and fearing an attack on his slow-moving baggage train or an effort to cut off his march to Sandy Hook, he ordered Cornwallis to counterattack.

As Cornwallis closed, Lee's battle fell apart. The British bore down on the American right in overwhelming strength, and as Lee considered a response, he was infuriated to find that his left had disappeared. Battalions under Brigadier Generals Charles Scott and William Maxwell had withdrawn. The brigadiers had misinterpreted the movements of other patriot units as a retreat, and they feared being cut off as the British advanced. With his left gone and Cornwallis threatening, Lee had no alternative but retreat—this time for real. Wayne wanted to stay and fight near Freehold, but the remaining Americans were vastly outnumbered and lacked any defensible position. As the British came on Lee conducted an orderly retrograde. Searching for ground to make a stand, Lee was at a loss until a Monmouth County militia officer pointed out Perrine's Hill. The hill was defensible terrain overlooking the bridge across Spotswood Middle Brook and a wide bog (the "West Morass"). Lee had crossed the bridge earlier during his advance toward Freehold, and he now directed his troops toward it with the intention of forming on the hill behind it.

Lee never made it. At about 1:00 p.m., still on the Freehold side of the bridge, Lee met Washington, who had come up ahead of the main army. The exhausted major general completely misread the situation. He honestly expected a compliment on his skillful retreat, which certainly had saved the Continental vanguard from probable annihilation. Instead, Washington curtly "desire[d] to know, sir," as Lee recalled, "the reason—whence arises this disorder and confusion?" "Confounded," Lee was momentarily at a loss for words, silenced less by the question itself than by Washington's tone. The commander in chief, as one of Lee's aides remembered, had displayed "considerable warmth." He was unmollified when Lee tried to explain the tactical situation; Washington insisted that Lee should have pushed his attack.[6] Whatever Washington's exact words, he clearly was annoyed to find Lee retreating. That a stand near Freehold would have been suicidal on Lee's part made no difference now; nothing Lee could have said in his defense would have mattered. Having in effect relieved Lee, Washington rode forward personally to assess the situation.

The Washington–Lee confrontation has become part of American folklore. Over the years various supposed witnesses to the incident dramatically embellished the story. Lafayette and Scott were classic examples. As old men, their accounts had Washington in a perfect fury. The Frenchman remembered the general calling Lee a "damned poltroon"; while Scott's version was astonishingly fanciful. Washington "swore on that day," the old brigadier famously insisted, "till the leaves shook on the trees, charming, delightfully. Never did I enjoy such swearing before or since. Sir, on that memorable day, he swore like an angel from Heaven."[7]

It's all nonsense. Neither man was remotely close enough to hear Washington or Lee. Scott was almost a mile away! No one made any such claim during Washington's lifetime, and even Lee never accused Washington of profanity. Lee's court-martial transcript told the tale: it reflected a blunt battlefield exchange between the two senior commanders of the

Continental Army—an occasion dramatic enough to need no embellishment after the fact.

In Desperate Battle

As Washington confronted Lee, the British advance continued. Lee's troops continued struggling west, covered by gallant Continental artillery that limbered up and withdrew with the enemy only yards behind them. By now Clinton had joined Cornwallis, and the British commander in chief bravely but recklessly led from the front. Washington quickly recognized the gravity of the British threat. Cooling off, he ordered Wayne and some nine hundred men into a "Point of Woods" to the right of the British approach, and he tasked Lee with organizing a holding action west of Wayne's position. Washington then rode back to meet the main army, which was still coming up. He and his officers worked feverishly to organize the regiments and batteries along Perrine's Hill—the very place to which Lee had been headed.

On the Freehold side of Spotswood Middle Brook, Lee formed behind a hedgerow directly in front of the British advance, some 850 yards west of Wayne's concealed men. The British had seen Lee taking position, but they had not seen Wayne scrambling into the woods. The redcoats paid a stiff price. Wayne's Continentals blasted the surprised First Guards at almost point-blank range as they marched by, heading for Lee. An instant response by the Guards and First Grenadiers—the pride of the British Army—and the charging Sixteenth Light Dragoons then overran Wayne in ferocious hand-to-hand fighting.

Under terrific pressure, Wayne's remnants pulled out and made for the bridge and the safety of Perrine's Hill. The rest of the British, now breaking into a rush, made for Lee at the hedgerow. Clinton led, swinging his sword and riding, as one of his junior officers recalled, "like a Newmarket jockey" and shouting for his men to forget formation and go flat-out for the rebels.[8] They did, and the fighting at the hedgerow was brutal but short. Continentals and redcoats exchanged fire only feet from each other and thrust bayonets through the fence and foliage. Lee ordered his men to fall back over the bridge only after dragoons and redcoats began to work around both of his flanks. It had been a gallant defense against an equally gallant assault.

The British made a final stab at the retreating Americans. As the last of Lee's men escaped, Lieutenant Colonel Henry Monckton led elements of the Second Grenadiers on a charge across the bridge while other grenadiers attempted to push across the bog and wade the stream. They were met by a withering barrage of rebel artillery fire. The Continentals had massed their largest artillery concentration of the war on Perrine's Hill, and the grenadiers didn't stand a chance as grapeshot and canister scythed them down. Monckton was mortally wounded, the highest-ranking British casualty of the day. It was over in a horrible minute, and the heaps of dead and wounded grenadiers marked the closest the British came to Washington's main line.

Monckton's defeat marked a lull in the action. The rebels had consolidated their position on Perrine's Hill while Clinton pulled back to the hedgerow Lee had recently defended. A British column that had tried to flank the American left sheltered in an orchard, stalled and pinned down by rebel artillery fire. Unknown to Clinton, a Continental detachment of infantry with four guns under Nathanael Greene was slowly working its way from Washington's right, aiming to get in position on Clinton's left. But it would be some time before Greene could engage. Meanwhile, both main armies got what rest they could. Troops on both sides had endured a brutally hot morning and early afternoon. Combat had raged in temperatures well above ninety degrees, and humidity held clouds of smoke in the air. Heat exhaustion proved as dangerous as enemy fire and likely accounted for more casualties.

It was now about 1:45 p.m., and for the moment the infantry battle was over—but not the artillery fight. While the exhausted infantry looked on, rival Continental and Royal Artillery batteries slugged it out in the longest continuous cannonade of the war. Rebel gun crews, re-equipped and reorganized at Valley Forge under the eye of Brigadier

General Henry Knox, the army's capable chief of artillery, proved as good as their veteran British opponents. The opposing gunners actually fought in line of sight. For all of the sound and fury, however, and for all of the hot metal flung through the torrid air, neither side inflicted much damage. Almost by some unstated mutual consent the fire lifted around 3:45 p.m., at which point Clinton decided to call it a day. Convinced Washington would not offer a decisive battle, and with his baggage train safely away, the royal commander considered it was time to pull out and head to Sandy Hook.

Washington had other plans. Now feeling safe from any attack, the patriot chief decided to risk some limited offensives before Clinton could withdraw. He sent two light infantry battalions to clear the redcoats from the orchard on the American left. These British were withdrawing anyway, but the patriot battalion under Colonel Joseph Cilley of New Hampshire forced them back in a sharp and skillful action. Wayne then sallied from Washington's center, hitting the grenadiers at the hedgerow and provoking a determined British counterattack. Supported by deadly artillery fire from Greene, who by now had occupied Combs Hill overlooking the British left, Wayne's command inflicted serious casualties in a brutal defensive stand on the grounds of a local parsonage. In both actions the rebels showed discipline and grit.

Clinton now disengaged. Late in the day Washington dispatched another probe, but it failed to make contact before nightfall. While the rebels slept on the field and expected renewed combat on Monday, Clinton saw no point. He skillfully slipped away in the dark—the Americans never heard him go—and he arrived at Sandy Hook two days later. On July 5, the Royal Navy began ferrying his units to safety in locations around New York, effectively ending the Monmouth Campaign.

The Aftermath

The morning of June 29 found the rebels jubilant. "It is Glorious for America," Colonel Israel Shreve wrote his wife, Polly. After tough fighting, the "Enemy was Drove off the Ground." In "all the actions hitherto," Colonel William Irvine exulted, "the Americans never took the field," but this time they had humbled "the pride of the British Tyrant." In near disbelief, another officer informed his wife that "Our little boys" had bested "their Gigantic Grenadiers."[9] Clinton, of course, scoffed at all of this, noting that in getting his army back to New York he had done what he had set out to do. But that failed to register with the ecstatic Americans.

For all of the rebel jubilation, Monmouth Courthouse had been a punishing battle. Washington officially tallied 69 American patriot dead, 161 wounded, and 141 missing. But post-battle losses from wounds, heat, and disease likely extended patriot casualties to something approaching 450–500 killed, wounded, and missing. Clinton's losses totaled well in excess of 300 killed (including those who died from the heat) and considerably more wounded. In addition, the British lost a fair number of prisoners and as many as a thousand deserters during the march from Philadelphia. Altogether it was a substantial loss.

The battle had demonstrated Continental mettle, and it also had shown Washington at his best. Posting Lee and Wayne forward to buy time had been correct, and Washington, along with Major General William Alexander (Lord Stirling) had capably organized an effective main line on Perrine's Hill. Sending Cilley and Wayne against specific targets showed initiative without risking a general engagement that could have endangered his still relatively weaker army. It was a deft tactical performance.

The general also made himself conspicuous during the fighting. Indeed, Washington's coolness as he rode the lines during the artillery barrage and then sent Cilley and Wayne forward was inspirational. According to Lafayette, the general's "nobility, grace, and presence of mind were never displayed to better advantage." "I do not think, for my part," remembered Dr. James McHenry, Washington's military secretary, "the general in one day displayed more military powers, or acquired more real reputation. He gave a new turn to the action.... He was always in danger—examining the enemies manoeuvres—exhorting the troops—and directing the operation of his plans, He unfolded surprising abilities, which produced uncommon effects."[10] In fact, McHenry and Lafayette spoke for many others who saw Monmouth as one of Washington's finest hours.

Monmouth also revealed, however, that the army still had some problems. The absence of American cavalry, as Lee's experience at the hedgerow and Wayne's in the "Point of Woods" painfully showed, left the army vulnerable to British horse. Serious command and control deficiencies remained. If Lee had lost touch with Scott and Maxwell, Washington was just as culpable in losing track of Lee's situation. Unaware of Lee's difficulties, the general was slow in bringing up the main army early on the twenty-eighth. Then there was the failure of Daniel Morgan to engage. Morgan had eight hundred men on the British left and was in a position to strike; he could hear the battle, but he never received clear orders. It was a genuine blunder, and a more experienced Continental staff would have handled command and control more effectively.

Yet for all of these problems, the Continentals had done well. Certainly many British thought so. "The Enemy were very troublesom[e]" at Monmouth, a junior officer conceded; the rebels had left his regiment "a good dale [sic] cut up." William Erskine, one of Clinton's ablest generals, reported the battle as "a handsome flogging. We had not receiv'd such an one in America."[11] Whatever it might have done better, the Continental Army had made its mark.

A Washington Spin

The Continentals had shown themselves to advantage at Monmouth, but their claims of victory were, at best, overstated. After all, as his orders demanded, Clinton had led his army safely back to New York—without the loss of a single wagon. But after the setbacks of 1777, Washington wanted, and politically needed, more than credit for a tactical draw. Thus Washington's loyalists set out to craft a victory narrative—a propaganda triumph for their chief. With the guns silent, the battle for popular perceptions of the fighting opened in earnest.

Washington took the initial step. On June 29, he sent Congress a brief account of the battle; he reported forcing "the Enemy from the Field" and promised further details. These followed on July 1 in the general's first detailed after-action report since the calamities of 1777. The communication was carefully understated, but it still proclaimed victory. Washington limned the course of the campaign, the ferocity of the fighting, the punishing heat, the gallantry of the troops, and Clinton's leaving the field.[12] The conclusion was unambiguous: Monmouth had been a triumph, and the revived Continental Army—and Washington as its commander—had passed the test of combat. The general had redeemed the disappointments of 1777.

Congressional reaction was all Washington could have hoped. John Hancock crowed that the battle had "discompos'd" and "Ruin'd" the British, while Connecticut's Titus Hosmer rejoiced at the supposedly disastrous state of the enemy. Henry Laurens, the president of Congress, who privately viewed the battle realistically—a "partial Victory gained over our Enemies"—was delighted at Washington's performance. Much of Congress believed Clinton had narrowly avoided John Burgoyne's fate, and on July 7 the delegates formally thanked Washington and his army for "gaining the important victory at Monmouth over the British grand army."[13] Few delegates doubted Monmouth had left the British reeling.

Washington's friends saw Monmouth as a final slap at the commander in chief's erstwhile critics. Elias Boudinot, the army's commissary general of prisoners, wrote Alexander Hamilton that "the General I allways revered & loved...has rose superior to himself. Every Lip dwells on his Praise for even his pretended friends (for none dare to acknowledge themselves his Enemies) are obliged to croak it forth."[14] So much for the Conway Cabal. Hamilton fully agreed. In fact, Hamilton and fellow Washington aide John Laurens (son of Henry Laurens) had worked hard to spin the Monmouth story favorably. After the battle, in which both young men had served gallantly, they had swung into action on behalf of their commander. Laurens wrote his influential father flattering Washington and casting aspersions on Lee's conduct. Hamilton did the same with anyone who would listen. "You know my way of thinking about our army," he told Boudinot, "and I am not about to flatter it. I assure you I never was pleased with them before this day."[15] The story was consistent: Washington had won the day and only Lee's morning retreat had prevented Clinton's complete destruction. The public got the message.

Dealing with Charles Lee was central to the Monmouth victory narrative. As a known critic of the commander in chief, Lee was unpopular with much of the officer corps, and his retreat on the twenty-eighth gave rise to considerable sniping from Washington's partisans. Hamilton and Laurens were hardly alone in this, and some rumors even implied disloyalty on Lee's part. Frankly, the attacks amounted to character assassination. Lee had fought well at Monmouth, and his fate had more to do with politics than the battlefield. Washington disliked his chief subordinate, but despite his curt battlefield exchange with Lee there is little indication that Washington envisioned any post-battle action against him. But Lee, offended at the circulating gossip, wanted Washington to squelch the insulting chatter. Rebuffed, Lee wrote two snarky letters to Washington insisting on a court-martial to clear himself of rumored misconduct. The commander in chief happily obliged.

Lee's trial was a travesty. He stood accused on three counts: disobeying orders in failing to attack on the morning of June 28 "agreeable to repeated instructions"; leading "an unnecessary, disorderly, and shameful retreat"; and disrespect toward the commander in chief in his letters after the battle. The first two charges were ridiculous, but Lee certainly had been disrespectful to Washington. That finished him. Lee had friends in the army, but most of the officer corps lined up solidly with the commanding general. "Under the circumstances," historian John Shy has noted, "an acquittal on the first two charges would have been a vote of no-confidence in Washington."[16] That was impossible; thus the guilty verdict on all counts was no surprise. However, the court did delete "shameful" from the second count, substituting "disorderly...in some few instances."[17] The court suspended Lee from the service for a year, and Washington forwarded the verdict to Congress, although the delegates were in no hurry to deal with the hot-button matter. The delay gave plenty of time for partisans of Washington and Lee to lobby for their favorites—and Lee had allies among Washington's old political critics, some of whom rallied to the major general's defense.

In fact, Lee's fate garnered a measure of public sympathy. In his *History of the American Revolution* (1789), historian David Ramsay recalled that "many were displeased." Ramsay, whose brother was wounded at Monmouth, was a Washington admirer, but he was skeptical of any argument that Lee should not have retreated on the twenty-eighth. Ramsay firmly believed Lee's orders had been discretionary and that circumstances at Monmouth had left him with no choice but to withdraw. And if Washington's orders had left any decision to engage up to Lee, then how could anyone accuse him of disobeying orders? To many, Ramsay concluded, it seemed that "a suspension from command, was not a sufficient punishment for his crimes, if really guilty. They therefore inferred a presumption of innocence from the lenient sentence of his judges." In fact, Ramsay's account reflected the private feelings of other patriots.[18]

Public sentiment was such that Congress could have brokered a compromise between Lee and Washington. Lee's allies cautioned him to remain calm and not to wage a personal battle with the commander in chief. In that case, as a matter of policy Congress would have to side with Washington; to discredit him would throw the Revolution into turmoil. That couldn't be allowed. But Lee, furious, caustically disparaged Washington's Monmouth performance and raged that he was a victim of army politics. "I am taught to think that equity is to be put out of the question," he wrote Aaron Burr (a wounded Monmouth veteran), "and the decision of the affair to be put entirely on the strength of party."[19] It was. On December 5, after months during which no one was sure how the delegates would decide, Congress resolved to sustain the guilty verdict. What choice was there? Could Congress risk the army's welfare to offer justice to one man? But the vote was not unanimous: Of the twenty-three delegates, seven believed Lee had been wronged.[20] Lee's disgrace virtually silenced any further public criticisms of the commander in chief. In the end, rather than accept his suspension, Lee resigned his commission in disgust.

What Kind of Victory?

In mid-August, at his new headquarters near the old White Plains battlefield, Washington took a few moments to wax philosophical on the Monmouth Campaign. "It is not a little pleasing," he wrote fellow Virginian Thomas Nelson, "nor less wonderful to contemplate, that after two long years...undergoing the strangest vicissitudes that perhaps ever attended any one contest since the creation," both armies had returned back to where they were in 1776. Now, however, the Continentals held the initiative while the British, "the offending party in the beginning," were on the defensive. "The hand of Providence has been so conspicuous in all this," he assured Nelson, "that he must be worse than an infidel that lacks faith, and more than wicked, that has not gratitude enough to acknowledge his obligations, but, it will be time enough for me to turn preacher, when my present appointment ceases."[21] Divine intervention aside, however, Washington had been essential to the turn of events. His fortitude, patience, careful planning, support for Steuben's training regimen, and political acumen had brought the army through the Valley Forge ordeal—and Monmouth was the payoff. The campaign demonstrated that the Continentals, if not fully equals of Clinton's professionals, were now the "respectable army" Washington had long wanted. They could fight, and their opponents grudgingly admitted as much.

Thus Monmouth stands out as one of the Revolution's critical campaigns. The Americans performed well in fighting the cream of Britain's professionals to a tactical draw. Measured strictly in terms of casualties, the rebels actually had the best of the fighting (although the British, usually attacking in the open, were at higher risk of getting hit).

Politically, however, Monmouth was a patriot triumph. The action provided a much-needed shot in the arm for rebel morale, seemingly reversing the misfortunes of 1777. And the battle restored the luster to Washington's reputation. Monmouth had indeed revealed a newly capable Continental Army, but it had also confirmed Washington as the Revolution's iconic "indispensable man"—and therein lay the campaign's greatest contribution to the rebel cause.

Further Reading

Lender, Mark Edward. *Cabal! The Plot Against General Washington*. Yardley, Pennsylvania: Westholme, 2019.

Lender, Mark Edward, and Garry Wheeler Stone. *Fatal Sunday: George Washington, the Monmouth Campaign, and the Politics of Battle*. Norman, Oklahoma: University of Oklahoma Press, 2016.

Lengel, Edward G. *General George Washington: A Military Life*. New York: Random House, 2005.

Martin, James Kirby, and Mark Edward Lender. *A Respectable Army, The Military Origins of the Republic, 1763–1789*. 3rd edition. Malden, Massachusetts: Wiley, 2015.

Bibliography

Adelberg, Michael S. *The American Revolution in Monmouth County: The Theatre of Spoil and Destruction*. Charleston, South Carolina: The History Press, 2010.

Bilby, Joseph G., and Katherine Bilby Jenkins. *Monmouth Court House: The Battle That Made the American Army*. Yardley, Pennsylvania: Westholme Publishing, 2010.

Lender, Mark Edward. "The Politics of Battle: Washington, the Army, and the Monmouth Campaign." In Edward G. Lengel, ed., *A Companion to George Washington*. Malden, Massachusetts: Wiley-Blackwell, 2012.

Lender, Mark Edward. "The Ever Controversial Charles Lee: A Review Essay." *Journal of Military History* 78, No. 4 (2014).

Lender, Mark Edward, and Garry Wheeler Stone. *Fatal Sunday: George Washington, the Monmouth Campaign, and the Politics of Battle.* Norman, Oklahoma: University of Oklahoma Press, 2016.

Lengel, Edward G. *General George Washington: A Military Life.* New York: Random House, 2005.

McBurney, Christian M. *George Washington's Nemesis: The Outrageous Treason and Unfair Court-Martial of Major General Charles Lee during the Revolutionary War.* El Dorado Hills, California: Savas Beatie, 2020.

Martin, David G. *The Philadelphia Campaign: June 1777–July 1778.* Conshohocken, Pennsylvania: Combined Books, 1993.

Mazzagetti, Dominick. *Charles Lee: Self before Country.* New Brunswick, New Jersey: Rutgers University Press, 2013.

Papas, Phillip. *Renegade Revolutionary: The Life of General Charles Lee.* New York: New York University Press, 2014.

Shy, John. "Charles Lee: The Soldier as Radical." In George Athan Billias, ed., *George Washington's Generals.* New York: William Morrow and Company, 1964.

Stryker, William Scudder. *The Battle of Monmouth.* Princeton: Princeton University Press, 1927.

About the Author

Mark Edward Lender has a Ph.D. in American History from Rutgers University. He is professor emeritus of history at Kean University, from which he retired as vice president for academic affairs in 2011. He is the author or coauthor of eleven books and many articles and reviews in early American social, military, and institutional history. His scholarship has won awards for writing and research, among them the *Society for Military History's Distinguished Book of the Year Award* (2017) and a

Distinguished Writing Award from the U.S. Army Historical Foundation. He was also a finalist for the 2017 George Washington Literary Prize. In 2018 he held a research fellowship at the Smith National Library at George Washington's Mount Vernon. Lender helped establish the Crossroads of the American Revolution National Heritage Area as their first vice president. Lender lives in Richmond, Virginia, with his wife, Rutgers University librarian emerita and author Penny Booth Page.

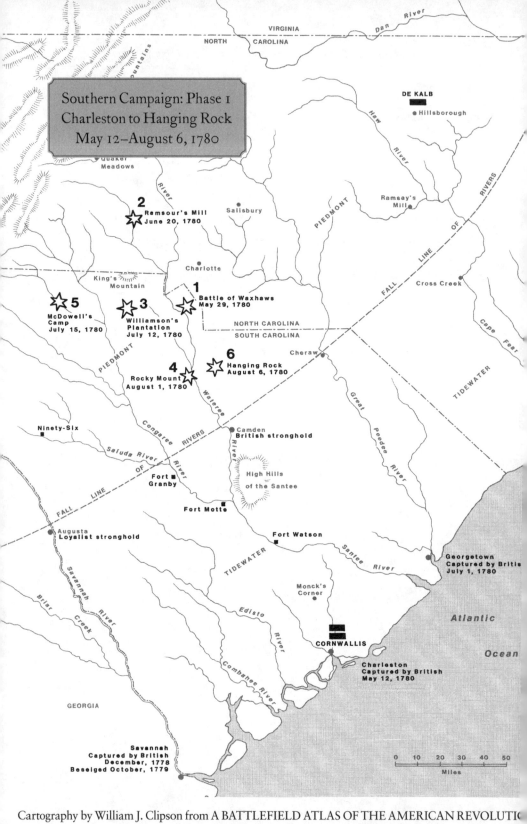

Southern Campaign: Phase 1
Charleston to Hanging Rock
May 12–August 6, 1780

VIRGINIA

NORTH CAROLINA

Dan River

Haw River

DE KALB

Hillsborough

Quaker Meadows

Mountains

River

Ramsour's Mill
June 20, 1780

2

Salisbury

PIEDMONT

Ramsay's Mill

FALL   LINE   OF   RIVERS

Charlotte

Cross Creek

King's Mountain

1   Battle of Waxhaws
May 29, 1780

5

McDowell's Camp
July 15, 1780

3

Williamson's Plantation
July 12, 1780

NORTH CAROLINA

SOUTH CAROLINA

Cape Fear

TIDEWATER

PIEDMONT

4

Rocky Mount
August 1, 1780

6

Hanging Rock
August 6, 1780

Cheraw

Wateree River

Great Peedee River

Ninety-Six

Congaree

RIVERS

River

Camden
British stronghold

Saluda River

FALL   LINE   OF   RIVERS

Fort Granby

High Hills
of the Santee

Fort Motte

Augusta
Loyalist stronghold

Fort Watson

Santee River

Georgetown
Captured by British
July 1, 1780

Savannah River

TIDEWATER

Monck's Corner

Atlantic

CORNWALLIS

Ocean

Briar Creek

Edisto River

Charleston
Captured by British
May 12, 1780

GEORGIA

Combahee River

Savannah
Captured by British
December, 1778
Beseiged October, 1779

0   10   20   30   40   50
Miles

Cartography by William J. Clipson from A BATTLEFIELD ATLAS OF THE AMERICAN REVOLUTIO
published by Savas Beatie, www.savasbeatie.com

Charleston to King's Mountain: The Southern Partisan Campaign

BY JOHN BUCHANAN

"We were a formidable flock of blue hen's chickens of the game blood...."[1]

That backwoods brag was written by Captain David Vance, a North Carolina rebel militia officer describing a battle he fought in—the pivotal militia victory at King's Mountain, South Carolina, on October 7, 1780.

The brag is amusing to twenty-first-century ears. But there is a ring of truth to it. The key word? Formidable. Disdained by low-country rice kings as a "pack of beggars,"[2] regarded by British officers as contemptible "crackers," the backcountry partisan militiamen of the Carolinas and Georgia were indeed formidable.[3]

The low-country rice kings, men of wealth and property, owners of big rice plantations and gangs of slaves, were largely responsible for the Revolution in the Carolinas and Georgia. But it was the "pack of beggars" in the backcountry who saved the rice kings' Revolution.

Both the Americans and the British faced a stalemate in the North after the drawn Battle of Monmouth, New Jersey, on June 28, 1778. But the British had been thinking of a southern offensive since 1776. Lord George Germain, who was King George III's minister in London in charge of the American war, believed that hordes of Americans loyal to Britain (Tories, or Loyalists) were in the majority in the southern backcountry and only awaited the appearance of British troops to rise and smite the rebels.

On May 12, 1780, the richest city in America, Charleston, South Carolina, with the only American army in the South, surrendered to a powerful expeditionary force of 8,500 British and German regulars led by General Sir Henry Clinton, commander in chief of British forces in America. The rebel rice kings, who had been in control since 1775, were stunned by the disaster, and some put property before honor and swore fealty to George III.

Shortly thereafter, British and provincial regulars began a march into the backcountry, which began about fifty miles west of Charleston and extended to the foothills of the Appalachian Mountains. They established forts along the Santee and Congaree Rivers to protect lines of communication and supply to their main bases at Camden in the mid-backcountry, Ninety Six in the far backcountry, and Augusta on the Savannah River in Georgia.

The backcountry was a newly settled land, with few roads, many rivers and streams but no bridges, lonely cabins here and there, and scattered settlements. Travel was a nightmare. The settlers matched their harsh land. A crude, hard people, "Root, Hog, or Die" prevailed in their struggle to survive; and they brought that mentality to war. Prominent among them were a pugnacious people called the Scotch-Irish. The Reverend Charles Woodmason's opinion of them matched that of many in America: "Ignorant, mean, worthless, beggarly Irish Presbyterians, the Scum of the Earth, and Refuse of Mankind."[4] But there is another view that is paramount. They were people who, in the blackest time for the cause, would bend but never break; they were accustomed to privation, travail their normal lot, and mercy to an enemy was never uppermost in their thoughts.

The backcountry was the key to controlling the Carolinas and Georgia. Why? Because the majority of the white population of those states lived in the backcountry, two-thirds to three-quarters in South Carolina alone. Lieutenant General Charles, 2nd Earl Cornwallis, drove home in clear language the significance of the backcountry: "The keeping possession of the Back Country is of the utmost importance. Indeed, the success of the war in the Southern District depends entirely upon it."[5]

In the beginning, British forces appeared to have secured the lands beyond Charleston and the low country. To cement their control before turning over command to Lord Cornwallis and returning to New York, Sir Henry Clinton appointed a British Army officer, thirty-six-year-old Major Patrick Ferguson, inspector of militia. His orders were to raise Tory militia to control the backcountry after most of the British Army had departed. Ferguson went at his mission with his usual zeal and soon had under his command between 1,100 and 1,300 Tory militia.

On June 30, 1780, Lord Cornwallis wrote to Sir Henry that the capitulation of the rebel post of Ninety Six in the far South Carolina backcountry and the "dispersion of a party of rebels assembled at an iron works on the northwest border of the province...put an end to all resistance in South Carolina." So sanguine was Cornwallis that in the same letter he expressed confidence that "with the forces at present under my command...I can leave South Carolina in security and march the beginning of September...into the back part of North Carolina, with the greatest probability of reducing that province to its duty."[6] Yet ten days before he wrote Sir Henry, his rosy picture had suffered its first major crack.

At Ramsour's Mill (modern Lincolnton), North Carolina, twenty miles north of the South Carolina border, about four hundred rebels attacked some one thousand Tories, many unarmed, on a ridge and drove them from the field of battle. The fight ended hand-to-hand, resembling an old-fashioned Pier 6 brawl between longshoremen and strikebreakers. After the battle, gunlocks were found embedded in the heads of some of the dead. It was a humiliating defeat for North Carolina Tories: the second time they had risen, and the second time they had been overwhelmingly defeated (the first defeat had come in 1776 at Moore's Creek Bridge near the coast, where Scottish Highlanders had been routed by rebel militia and cowed for the next four years). That fine small-unit combat commander, William Richardson Davie, described the result of Ramsour's Mill: "[I]n a few days that district of country lying between the [Catawba] River, the mountains," and the South Carolina line "was entirely cleared of the enemy."[7] It appeared that Lord Germain's theory of a backcountry teeming with the king's men was in question. Of course, it was early on; North Carolina had not yet felt the tread of British regulars, and matters seemed to be going very well in South Carolina, where strongpoints had been established and, according to official reports, resistance ended.

Were the Tories in the majority? In South Carolina, which was the main theater of war in the Southern Campaign, a perceptive Tory officer, Colonel Robert Gray, believed that there were even numbers of Tories and rebels in the far backcountry's Ninety Six district, while Tories prevailed in the mid-backcountry's Orangeburg district. Overall, however, he estimated Tory numbers in the state to be one-third of the population. A modern study has set the number of Tories in South Carolina at 22 percent.

Between Ramsour's Mill on June 20 and the Battle of Musgrove's Mill on August 19, 1780, there were by conservative count about eighteen actions between rebel militia and Tory militia or provincial regulars (the latter being Americans raised, outfitted, trained, disciplined, and armed in the manner of British regulars). Most of the encounters were skirmishes, but they bring home to us that the American Revolution against British rule was also a civil war—the first American civil war. The German word for civil war is Bruderkrieg—Brother's War. One small action reveals Bruderkrieg with a vengeance.

Tories had gathered at the home of a man named Stallions. A rebel militia commander, Colonel Thomas Brandon, attacked the house with about fifty men. Colonel Brandon took the larger party to the rear of the house to intercept Tories trying to escape. A Captain Love with sixteen men mounted an attack against the front. Fifteen-year-old Thomas Young, a rebel partisan serving under Captain Love, tells us what happened:

> Mrs. Stallions was a sister of Captain Love, and on the approach of her brother she ran out, and begged him not to

fire upon the house. He told her it was too late now, and that their only chance for safety was to surrender. She ran back to the house and sprang upon the doorstep, which was pretty high. At this moment the house was attacked in the rear by Col. Brandon's party, and Mrs. Stallions was killed by a ball shot through the opposite door.... After the fight Love and Stallions met and shed bitter tears. Stallions was dismissed on parole to bury his wife and arrange his affairs.[8]

The most important action before Musgrove's Mill was Huck's Defeat at Williamson's plantation. Captain Christian Huck, a Philadelphia Tory, commanded thirty-five British Legion dragoons, twenty mounted infantrymen of De Lancey's New York Volunteers—both units provincial regulars—and fifty to sixty mounted Tory militia. Huck burned the ironworks of William Hill, who not only made cannon and other ordnance but within a radius of fifty miles supplied farm tools for rebel and Tory farmers alike, ground their grain in his gristmill, and cut their logs in his sawmill. The rebels were enraged. Huck continued his raid of arson and destruction in rebel country in northwestern South Carolina. On July 11, 1780, he and his raiders swept onto Williamson's plantation, and at the house of Captain John McClure captured young James McClure and Edward Martin as they were melting pewter dishes to make bullets for rebel partisans. Captain Huck decreed that they would hang in the morning.

Either Mary McClure, daughter of Captain McClure, or Watt, a slave of the Bratton family, slipped away and rode hard through the night. Mary sought her father in the camp of the soon-to-be-famous rebel commander Colonel Thomas Sumter, and/or Watt looked for Colonel William Bratton. Perhaps both did. Whatever the details, Captain McClure and Colonel Bratton rallied their men, mounted, and headed for Williamson's plantation. In the wee hours, some 250 rebels reined in, dismounted, and crept forward.

Captain Huck was asleep in the Williamson house. His men were in tents between two rail fences. No patrols were out, no pickets posted.

Sentries were in the road in front of the house, but they failed to see or hear the rebels creeping up on them in the early hours before first light. Quiet orders were given and the rebel band split into two parties, approached from both sides, and took positions behind the rail fences.

At dawn the rebels opened fire from seventy-five paces. Captain Huck ran from the house and mounted his horse. Sixteen-year-old rebel militiaman James Potter Collins had dismounted and was advancing through a peach orchard when the provincial regulars "were soon mounted and paraded. This, I confess, was a very imposing sight, at least to me, for I had never seen a troop of British horse before, and thought they differed vastly from us—poor hunting shirt fellows. The leader drew his sword, mounted his horse, and began to storm and rave, and advanced on us…their leader called out, 'disperse you damned rebels, or we will put every man of you to the sword.' Our rifle balls began to whistle among them, and in a few minutes my Lord Hook was shot off his horse and fell at full length; his sword fell out of his hand as he fell and lay at some distance."[9]

An estimated thirty-five Tories were killed, twenty-nine wounded, and many captured. Huck's death and defeat had an important psychological effect. The rebel militia had soundly defeated Tory regulars, including dragoons of the hated and feared British Legion. Many men who had rebel sympathies but were unsure whether it was wise to challenge British strength began to flock to standards raised by militia leaders throughout the backcountry.

One of those leaders was Colonel Charles McDowell of North Carolina, and he set in motion a dramatic episode that would have far-reaching consequences.

McDowell was camped with followers on the north side of Smith's Ford on the Broad River. He sent out two scouts to seek targets of opportunity. They reported back that two hundred Tory militia were camped forty miles south of him at Musgrove's Mill on the Enoree River in South Carolina.

Meanwhile, a new American army was marching south under the command of Congress's darling, the hero of Saratoga, Major General Horatio Gates, who had neither the skill nor the stomach for combat command. On August 16, 1780, just north of Camden, South Carolina, Lord Cornwallis routed Gates's poorly deployed army. The survivors fled northward 180 miles to Hillsborough, North Carolina—Gates well ahead of them.

While Gates was being humiliated, in McDowell's camp three officers in their prime, Colonel Isaac Shelby (thirty years old) of North Carolina, Colonel Elijah Clarke (thirty-eight) of Georgia, and Colonel James Williams (forty) of South Carolina were putting together a strike force. Shelby, who would become the first governor of the future state of Kentucky, lived across the Appalachians on the cutting edge of the Cherokee frontier. He and his followers were known as the Overmountain Men. There was no overall commander, yet the three colonels worked smoothly together. On August 18, about two hundred "picked men well mounted" forded the Broad River "one hour before sundown" and set a torrid pace for Musgrove's Mill.[10] They did not know of Gates's disaster at Camden.

Shelby recalled that they traveled fast, mostly at a canter, and never stopped. At daylight the riflemen reined in on a timbered ridge about a mile and a half from the ford of the Enoree River at Musgrove's Mill. And there a surprise awaited them.

A friendly countryman who lived nearby appeared and told them that the 200 Tories had been joined by Lieutenant Colonel Alexander Innes, commanding provincial regulars and militia. The newcomers probably numbered 100 militia and 150 regulars. Fifty of the regulars were mounted South Carolina Royalists of dubious reliability. But the fifty New Jersey Volunteers and fifty from De Lancey's New York Brigade were high-quality troops. Fifteen North Carolina Tories were also there. Innes had marched in the night before, but he was not there to reinforce the militia stationed at Musgrove's Mill. He was on his way to join Major Patrick Ferguson, who was bivouacked fifty-five miles east of Musgrove's Mill. The arrival of rebels and Innes at about the same time was sheer coincidence.

The 200 rebels now faced a little over 400 of the enemy. But they could not withdraw. Their horses were blown from the pace set during the night and their riders fared little better. They quickly prepared for battle, but it would be defensive instead of offensive as they had originally intended. The only contemporary account states that the men spread out behind trees.

Two scouts were sent out to reconnoiter. During their return they ran into an enemy patrol. Firing ensued, a few Tories fell, and both scouting parties galloped for their comrades. Colonel Innes mustered his command and the two hundred Tories who had been at Musgrove's Mill and forded the river. The rebels sent out sixteen mounted riflemen to engage and draw the enemy to the main body on the ridge.

The rebel line stretched three hundred yards at the crest of the timbered ridge. Each colonel was with his command. Their horses had been picketed some three hundred yards behind under guard. Mounted rebels were deployed on either flank.

The Tories advanced in three columns, with provincial regulars in the middle and militia on their flanks. As was the custom then, their officers rode on horseback. The sixteen mounted rebels teased them forward. Yet it was not an ambush. There can be no doubt that Colonel Innes had at least an inkling of what awaited him on the ridgeline.

At 150 yards, the Tory force deployed from columns into line of battle and upon command delivered a volley. But their muskets were only accurate up to about eighty yards. If it was meant to frighten the rebels, the volley failed.

The Tories came on. The rebels were ordered to withhold fire until the enemy was about fifty yards away. The mounted rebels on the flanks fired at the Tories as they advanced. At some fifty yards, a volley erupted from the ridge. In the words of a rebel officer, "their ranks were thinned."[11]

Innes and his command fell back, reformed, and came on again. And again the long rifles cracked, and the toll they inflicted destroyed the

Tories' will to continue the fight. Colonel Innes was badly wounded, as were all but two of the regular officers. The Tory militia fled in disarray, and the provincial regulars' retreat was disorderly. All the while the rebels from front and flank kept firing, and then they came on in a wild, screaming charge that broke the Tories. Colonel Shelby recalled that "dead men lay thick on the ground over which our men pursued the enemy."[12] It was not until the Tories recrossed the Enoree that one of the two regular officers still on his feet was able to form a rear guard and establish control of the command.

The battle probably lasted about fifteen minutes. Rebel loss was minimal: four killed, nine wounded. Tory casualties were sixty-three killed, ninety wounded, and seventy-six taken prisoner. The rebels were elated. In the midst of strong Tory country they had routed provincial regulars. The colonels decided to mount up, push on, and attack the important British post of Ninety Six.

Readers will recall General Gates being badly defeated by Cornwallis at Camden. The victorious rebel colonels were ready to ride when a courier arrived who handed over a letter from Colonel McDowell informing them of Gates's disaster. All rebel detachments were advised to flee to safer parts. McDowell and his followers had left Smith's Ford and moved north to Gilbert Town (modern Rutherfordton), North Carolina. He would soon retreat further, over the Appalachians to Colonel Shelby's stomping grounds in what is now East Tennessee, but then was part of North Carolina.

The colonels turned their men and prisoners to the northwest and set out. To spare their tired horses, they occasionally dismounted and trotted alongside. Major Ferguson received news of Innes's defeat at seven o'clock that evening, just as he was about to march with the intention of engaging Thomas Sumter. Instead, he set out in pursuit of the rebel column. One of Ferguson's detachments pursued for about fifty miles until their horses broke down.

During their retreat, the colonels learned of another rebel defeat. On August 18, Thomas Sumter and his followers had been surprised and routed by Banastre Tarleton and his British Legion at Fishing Creek, South Carolina. The victors of Musgrove's Mill halted sixty miles northward and assessed their situation. In forty-eight hours they had completed two forced marches, neither slept nor rested, eaten peaches and raw corn plucked on the way, and defeated a superior force in a battle renowned for its ferocity. They were exhausted by the time they learned about Gates's debacle and the scattering of Sumter's force. Yet they were determined not to yield. Gates may have lost much of his army, but they had won their own fight, and they were not prepared to surrender the backcountry to the king's inspector of militia, Major Patrick Ferguson.

Colonel Shelby, thirty-five-year-old Colonel John Sevier (who, like Shelby, lived west of the Appalachians, and would become the first governor of the future state of Tennessee), thirty-five-year old Colonel William Campbell of Virginia, and Colonel McDowell began making plans. A courier service was established to keep everyone informed of Ferguson's movements. While this was going on, Ferguson and his force of some 1,000–1,100 militia, augmented by 70 provincial regulars (the American Volunteers), advanced into North Carolina to Gilbert Town. On or about September 10, 1780, he dispatched a released rebel prisoner with the following, famous verbal message to the leaders of the Over-mountain Men: "If they did not cease and desist from their opposition to the British arms, he would march his army over the mountains, hang their leaders, and lay their country waste with fire and sword."[13]

Colonel Shelby and his fellow Overmountain Men needed no further goad. On September 25, 1780, a multitude gathered where the Watauga River at Sycamore Shoals (modern Elizabethton, Tennessee) runs swiftly over the rocks. The group consisted of North Carolina Overmountain Men reinforced by Colonel Campbell's Virginia riflemen and Colonel McDowell's backcountry riders. McDowell himself had gone back over the mountains to spread the word that the Overmountain Men were coming and all good men should prepare to join them.

The following day, September 26, women, children, the aged, and fighting men left behind to protect the frontier from Cherokee raids gathered to see them off. Families prayed that they would see their men again but knew that when they returned there would be empty saddles among the ranks of horsemen. Befitting a time and community in which religion played a major role and the leaders of the expedition were Presbyterian elders, thirty-one-year-old Reverend Samuel Doak (of Ulster descent but Virginia-born) sent the men on their way with a sermon taken from the story of Gideon and the Midianites, ending it with a rousing cry, "The sword of the Lord and of Gideon." The riders responded with a ringing shout, "The sword of the Lord and of our Gideons."[14] Then, 1,040 strong, they rode out to catch Major Patrick Ferguson.

The Overmountain Men had trekked this route often as a matter of commuting. It was hard riding down steep, often dangerous, trails. From vantage points they would have seen ahead of them range after range of forested mountains, shimmering in a slight haze. Down those dark slopes, with the near constant sound of rushing mountain streams on first one flank and then the other, the long file of horsemen rode... tenacious in their resolve. Down through the foothills they went, into gentler country and on to their rendezvous at the McDowell's family farm at Quaker Meadows. They were eighteen miles from Gilbert Town and, they believed, Ferguson's camp.

They were welcomed warmly, and that same day joined by 350 North Carolina militia commanded by two experienced and able officers, Colonel Benjamin Cleveland, all 300 pounds of him, and Major Joseph Winston, a man of some education and formal manners.

In the meantime, Ferguson had begun withdrawing in a southerly direction while the Overmountain Men and their comrades were on the march from Sycamore Shoals. He had received some intelligence of the host crossing the mountains, sensed he was in danger, and sent word to Cornwallis that he would welcome reinforcements.

While the rebel host was marching south in search of their quarry, Ferguson issued an appeal to the men of North Carolina:

> Gentlemen: Unless you wish to be eat up by an inundation of barbarians, who have begun by murdering an unarmed son before his aged father, and afterwards lopped off his arms…I say, if you wish to be pinioned, robbed, and murdered, and see your wives and daughters, in four days, abused by the dregs of mankind—in short, if you wish or deserve to live, and bear the name of men, grasp your arms in a moment and run to camp. The Back Water men have crossed the mountains; McDowell, Hampton, Shelby, and Cleveland are at their head.… If you wish to be pissed upon by a set of mongrels, say so at once, and let your women turn their backs upon you and look out for real men to protect them.[15]

The results were much less than he hoped for, and one wonders if the language of his dramatic appeal frightened more than steeled his men. Did they really wish to confront barbarians lopping off people's arms? Which was more important, their limbs or their women's virtue? The allegiance of many was lukewarm regardless of which side they professed to be on, and some fit the description of a man who lived near King's Mountain, one Solomon Beason, "half-Whig, half-Loyalist, as occasion required."[16]

The rebels also had a problem. At Quaker Meadows there were five colonels but no commanding officer, and the colonels felt the need for one. Their men were seasoned fighters, but militia, a fractious lot, were prey to, as Colonel Shelby put it, "the little disorders and irregularities which began to prevail among our undisciplined troops."[17] They sent a message to General Gates in Hillsborough, asking that a senior officer be appointed to lead them. Shelby wrote that Colonel McDowell set out for Hillsborough with the request. Was this the colonels' way of getting rid of McDowell, the senior colonel among them? In two documents written after the war Colonel Shelby made clear that it was, claiming that Colonel McDowell was unpopular and lacked the energy to lead the expedition. In his absence Colonels Shelby, Sevier, Campbell, and Cleveland met and decided that waiting for a senior officer might allow Ferguson to escape. Their solution for command was for them to meet every day as a council and decide the direction for their army to take. Colonel Campbell, who commanded the largest regiment, was appointed officer of the day to carry out the councils' decisions. Then they marched on Gilbert Town.

Meanwhile, Ferguson kept withdrawing in the direction of Cornwallis's camp at Charlotte. The rebels were unsure of his exact location or destination but kept moving south, seeking intelligence of Ferguson's whereabouts. While they marched, other rebels rode in to join them. Thirty mounted Georgians from Colonel Elijah Clarke's band arrived around October 4. Major William Chronicle (only twenty-five years old) from the South Fork of the Catawba brought with him twenty South Fork Boys. Colonel James Williams rode in with his South Carolina men.

Thursday, October 5, was a low day. Horses were beginning to give out, men on foot were lagging, and discouragement appeared among some. The colonels acted quickly. Mounted men who felt they could not go farther were ordered to fall back and give their horses to footmen willing to push on. The colonels then chose either 700 or 910—sources differ—riders for a forced twenty-one-mile march.

After sunset on October 6, the column arrived at Cowpens, South Carolina, where cattle were grazed before being driven to downstate markets. About three months later another key battle of the Revolution would be fought there. A rebel spy, James Kerr, appeared with intelligence that Ferguson intended to be at King's Mountain that evening. The rebel host had just finished a long, tiring forced march, hard on men and horses alike, but the colonels decided they must not tarry. At nine o'clock that night, 910 picked men rode due east from Cowpens: 470 backcountry militia and 440 Overmountain Men. They were about thirty-three miles from the King's Mountain.

Major Patrick Ferguson and his force of about 1,125 had left their camp at four o'clock on the morning of October 6 and marched sixteen miles to King's Mountain. He sent two copies of a message to Lord Cornwallis that day, expressing contempt for his enemy yet claiming, incorrectly, that he was outnumbered and asking for reinforcements. One message never got through, and the other arrived too late.

Patrick Ferguson decided to make a stand atop King's Mountain. Tradition has it that Ferguson declared that "[h]e was on King's Mountain, he was king of that mountain, and God Almighty could not drive him from it."[18]

The pursuing rebel column rode through rain that varied from drizzle to downpour, lasting well into the next day. In the long run, rain was an ally, for the red earth of the Piedmont was too wet to raise telltale dust clouds over the horsemen. The riders would have wrapped hunting shirts around their gunlocks to try and keep them dry. In their rear around fifty footmen followed. Among Billy Chronicle's South Fork Boys was Enoch Gilmer, an intrepid and talented scout. He was sent ahead to gain intelligence. The column pushed on and crossed the Broad River at Cherokee Ford. They had come eighteen miles from Cowpens and were about fifteen miles from King's Mountain.

They caught up to the scout, Enoch Gilmer. A woman told him she had taken some chickens to Ferguson himself and said he was camped on a ridge between two streams, where deer hunters had camped in the autumn of the previous year. Major Billy Chronicle and Captain John Mattocks immediately identified the camp as theirs and said that Ferguson was camped on a spur of King's Mountain.

The colonels conferred and agreed on a simple plan. They would surround the mountain and attack. Since they commanded militia, who demanded the right of approval, they explained their plan and the men agreed. The long column pushed forward, the colonels deciding among themselves as they rode the positions each regiment would take around the mountain.

The rebels caught fourteen-year-old John Ponder riding hard with one of Ferguson's messages to Cornwallis. They asked the boy how Ferguson was dressed. He told them the major wore a checked shirt, or duster, over his bright red uniform coat. They were now so close that strict march discipline was in order, and the men divided into tight parallel columns, each a column of twos. Absolutely no talking, officers demanded, and the order was obeyed. Fractious militia they might be, but they were also veteran Indian or guerilla fighters who knew the value of silence at such a time.

The silent columns wended their way over broken, rain-soaked country. At three o'clock on Saturday afternoon, October 7, 1780, behind trees, they stopped, dismounted, secured their horses, and tied coats and blankets to their saddles. The horses of the rank and file were put in the charge of a few guards, but the officers would lead their men into battle on horseback.

Sixteen-year-old James Collins remembered, "[W]e were paraded and harangued...on the prospect before us. The sky was overcast and at times a light mist of rain was falling...." All cowards were invited to leave. No one moved, although young James later admitted that he would "willingly have been excused...but could not well swallow the appellation of coward."[19]

Swiftly, the grim host moved out to their assigned positions around King's Mountain, the wet leaves underfoot making no sounds.

King's is not really a mountain. It is part of a range of hills about sixteen miles long, extending from North Carolina into South Carolina. The ridge, roughly shaped like a human foot, is about six hundred yards long at its crest, and in width ranges from about sixty yards at the southwest heel of the foot to some two hundred yards at the northwest ball of the foot. The crest was then clear of trees and undergrowth. The sides of the ridge were—then as now—heavily wooded, steep, and rocky; terrain made to order for irregulars experienced in guerilla and Indian fighting. Ferguson was camped at the ball of the foot.

Once the battle commenced, no one on the rebel side was in overall command. Fifteen-year-old militiaman Thomas Young recalled that "the orders were at the firing of the first gun for every man to raise a whoop, rush forward, and fight his way as best he could."[20] Young's fellow teenager James Collins remembered "every man throwing four or five balls in his mouth to prevent thirst, also to be in readiness to reload."[21]

The shrill, drawn-out war cries of the Overmountain Men resounded clearly on the crest. Ferguson's deputy, Captain Abraham de Peyster, had heard those bloodcurdling cries during the carnage at Musgrove's Mill. He said to his chief, "This is ominous. These are the damned yelling boys."[22] Up they went, weaving through the trees, leaping over boulders, and firing when they had a target. An explosion of firing, smoke, and wild yells erupted around King's Mountain.

Ferguson ordered his seventy provincial regulars to form, fix bayonets, and charge Campbell's Virginians. Cold steel would win the day. The American Volunteers responded with vigor. The Virginians turned and fled back down the slope. A Tory officer, Lieutenant Anthony Allaire, caught up with a rebel captain and "killed him with one blow of my sword."[23] But then the Volunteers were recalled by blasts from Ferguson's silver whistle to meet the threat from Shelby, who was attacking up the opposite side. Campbell's men rallied, reloaded their rifles, and returned to the fight. That was the pattern of the Battle of King's Mountain. Three times the Overmountain Men at the heel of the ridge were chased down the mountainside. Three times they returned. All the while their rifles took a deadly toll.

On the slope leading to the ball of the ridge, a South Fork Boy, sixteen-year-old Robert Henry, lay on his back with a dead Tory militiaman on top of him. As young Robert had cocked his rifle, the charging Tory's bayonet ran along the barrel "through my hand and into my thigh; my antagonist and I both fell." Robert had fired and "the load must have passed through his bladder and cut a main artery, as he bled profusely."[24]

A Tory officer, Captain Alexander Chesney, implied that they could have successfully defended King's Mountain "had it not been covered with wood which sheltered the Americans and enabled them to fight in their favorite manner... from behind trees and other cover."[25]

Another Tory, Drury Mathis, fell badly wounded in the third charge against Campbell's Virginia mountaineers. He played possum and watched. To him, "those bold, brave riflemen appeared like so many devils from the infernal regions... as they darted like enraged lions up the mountain... the most powerful looking men he ever beheld; not overburdened with fat, but tall, raw-boned and sinewy, with long matted hair—such men as were never before seen in the Carolinas." Mathis recovered and lived to old age, but "used stoutly to swear that he never desired to see King's Mountain again."[26]

The Overmountain men and Virginians reached the crest and drove forward. At about the same time, the backcountry men, also forced to fall back before fixed bayonets but urged forward again by their officers, came on and poured onto the crest.

The end was near, but Ferguson refused to acknowledge it. Mounted on a white charger, he rode hither and thither, trying to rally his men. At twenty to thirty yards the two sides blazed away at each other. White flags began to appear among the Tories. Ferguson charged at them, slashed at them with his sword, and blew blasts on his silver whistle to rally his troops. Near Colonel Sevier's regiment, several rifles leveled and fired. Major Patrick Ferguson was shot from his horse and may have been dead before he hit the ground. He had been hit at least seven times, wrote young James Collins, and "both of his arms were broken, and his hat and clothing were literally shot to pieces."[27] His personal belongings were looted and he was stripped naked. Some rebels may have urinated on his corpse. Captain de Peyster assumed command and raised the white flag.

But the killing did not stop. Their blood up, the undisciplined rebels kept firing. The colonels, especially Shelby and Campbell, placed themselves in danger to finally stop the slaughter.

Twenty-eight rebels were killed, including Colonel James Williams, who was mortally wounded leading his men into battle; Major Billy Chronicle, dead on the field at the head of his South Fork boys; and thirteen officers of Campbell's Virginians. Sixty-two rebels were wounded.

But dead Tories lay in heaps: 157 dead, 163 too badly wounded to be moved. Of Ferguson's 70 provincial regulars, the American Volunteers, 50 were killed or wounded. The prisoners forced to endure a march of terror northward numbered 698.

The Tories never recovered from the disaster. Thereafter the rebel militia maintained the initiative. John Harris Cruger, commanding at Ninety Six, reported that "the whole district had determined to submit as soon as the Rebels should enter it."[28] Cornwallis, his left flank in the air after King's Mountain and fearing unnecessarily that hordes of rebels were descending on him, abandoned his plan to invade North Carolina and withdrew from Charlotte to winter quarters in Winnsboro, South Carolina.

Now let us be clear: The backcountry partisan militia stymied the British pacification effort. The events in our narrative, plus the efforts of Thomas Sumter and other backcountry militia commanders, demoralized and defeated the Tory militia, upon which the British depended to control the South after the regulars moved on. But they could not drive the British Army from South Carolina and Georgia. That awaited the brilliant campaign waged by Nathanael Greene from December 3, 1780, when he took command of the southern army, to December 14, 1782, when Greene and his ragged, unpaid, malaria-ridden Continentals entered Charleston as the British evacuated the citadel of the rice kings. But Greene's campaign would not have been possible if the partisan militia hadn't bought the time necessary for his appearance on the scene. They truly changed the course of the war.

Cornwallis was driven to Yorktown and surrender by the backcountry rising in the Carolina and Georgia backcountry, coupled with His Lordship's Pyrrhic victory over Greene at Guilford Courthouse that crippled his army. Nobody has put it better than Sir Henry Clinton, who wrote some two hundred years ago that King's Mountain "unhappily proved the first link in a chain of evils that followed each other in regular succession until they at last ended in the total loss of America."[29]

We began our tale with part of a backwoods brag by Captain David Vance, celebrating the victory he and his comrades won at King's Mountain. Let's finish it: "We were a formidable flock of blue hen's chickens of the game blood. Our equals were scarce, and our superiors hard to find."

Further Reading

Buchanan, John. *The Road to Guilford Courthouse: The American Revolution in the Carolinas.* New York: John Wiley & Sons, 1997.

Buchanan, John. *The Road to Charleston: Nathanael Greene and the American Revolution.* Charlottesville, Virginia: University of Virginia Press, 2019.

Edgar, Walter. *Partisans and Redcoats: The Southern Conflict That Turned the Tide of the American Revolution.* New York: William Morrow, 2001.

Lambert, Robert Stansbury. *South Carolina Loyalists in the American Revolution.* Columbia, South Carolina: University of South Carolina Press, 1987.

About the Author

John Buchanan was born in Glens Falls, NY, and raised in Upstate New York and Ohio. After army service from 1951–1954, he went to St. Lawrence University and graduated in 1958 with Highest Honors in History. He was a high school history teacher, an archivist at Cornell University, and in 1966 joined the staff of the Metropolitan Museum of Art in New York City as museum archivist. He later became chief registrar of the museum in charge of art packing, transportation, security in transit, and fine arts insurance. For twenty-two years he traveled with art exhibitions in the U.S. and worldwide, including Tutankhamen, Treasures of the Vatican, India, Chinese Bronzes, Treasures of Early Irish Art, and many others. He retired in 1993 and began a new career as historian and writer. In addition to his books on the Revolution, his *Jackson's Way: Andrew Jackson and the People of the Western Waters*, appeared in 2001. He has also published short stories in *Ellery Queen Mystery Magazine* and a Cold War novel, *The Rise of Stefan Gregorovic*. Visit his website at https://www.jackbuchanan.net/.

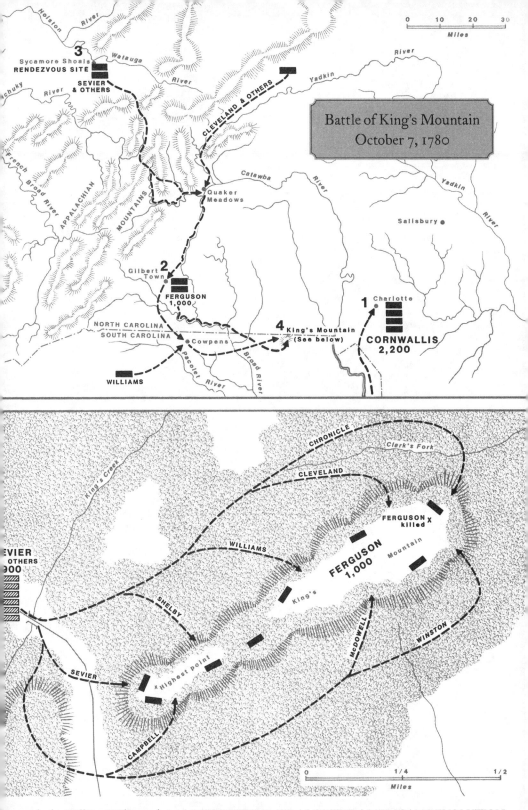

Battle of King's Mountain
October 7, 1780

0 10 20 30
Miles

Holston River
Watauga River
Yadkin River
River

3
Sycamore Shoals
RENDEZVOUS SITE
SEVIER & OTHERS

CLEVELAND & OTHERS

French Broad River
Nolichucky River

APPALACHIAN MOUNTAINS

Quaker Meadows

Catawba River

Salisbury

Yadkin River

River

2
Gilbert Town
FERGUSON 1,000

1
Charlotte
CORNWALLIS 2,200

NORTH CAROLINA
SOUTH CAROLINA

Cowpens

Pacolet River

Broad River

4
King's Mountain
(See below)

WILLIAMS

CHRONICLE
Clark's Fork
CLEVELAND

FERGUSON killed X

King's Creek

SEVIER & OTHERS
900

WILLIAMS

FERGUSON 1,000

Mountain

SHELBY

King's

McDOWELL

WINSTON

SEVIER

x Highest point

CAMPBELL

0   1/4   1/2
Miles

...tography by William J. Clipson from A BATTLEFIELD ATLAS OF THE AMERICAN REVOLUTION,
...lished by Savas Beatie, www.savasbeatie.com

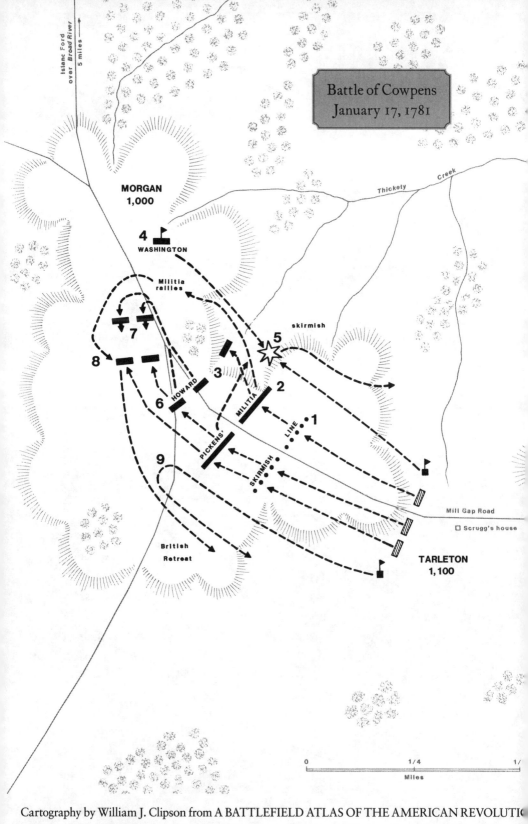

Battle of Cowpens
January 17, 1781

MORGAN
1,000

Islanc Ford over Broad River 5 miles

Thickety Creek

4 WASHINGTON

Militia rallies

skirmish

7

8

5

3

2

6 HOWARD

1

MILITIA LINE

9

PICKENS'

SKIRMISH

Mill Gap Road

☐ Scrugg's house

British Retreat

TARLETON
1,100

0   1/4   1/
Miles

Cartography by William J. Clipson from A BATTLEFIELD ATLAS OF THE AMERICAN REVOLUTIO
published by Savas Beatie, www.savasbeatie.com

From Cowpens to Guilford Courthouse

BY JOHN R. MAASS

The salient American victory at King's Mountain, South Carolina, in October 1780 was a significant setback for British plans to invade North Carolina that fall, especially with the loss of a thousand Loyalist troops captured and killed. The patriots' autumn victory also served to boost the sagging morale of pro-independence southerners and reduced attacks and depredations by their Tory neighbors. In the wake of the crushing defeat the American army had suffered at Camden, South Carolina, less than two months earlier, it was a remarkable reversal of fortune. Decades later, Thomas Jefferson remembered the battle—fought while he was the governor of Virginia—as the "turn of the tide of success which terminated the Revolutionary War."

The hilltop defeat in the distant Carolina backcountry put the British commander in the South in a difficult spot. With Major Patrick Ferguson's column wiped out, forty-one-year-old Lieutenant General Charles Cornwallis, the British commander in chief in the South, prudently withdrew his now-weakened force from Charlotte, North Carolina, sixty-five miles south to Winnsboro, South Carolina, which he called a "healthy spot, well situated to protect the greatest part of the northern frontier, and to assist [the posts at] Camden and Ninety-Six" in the

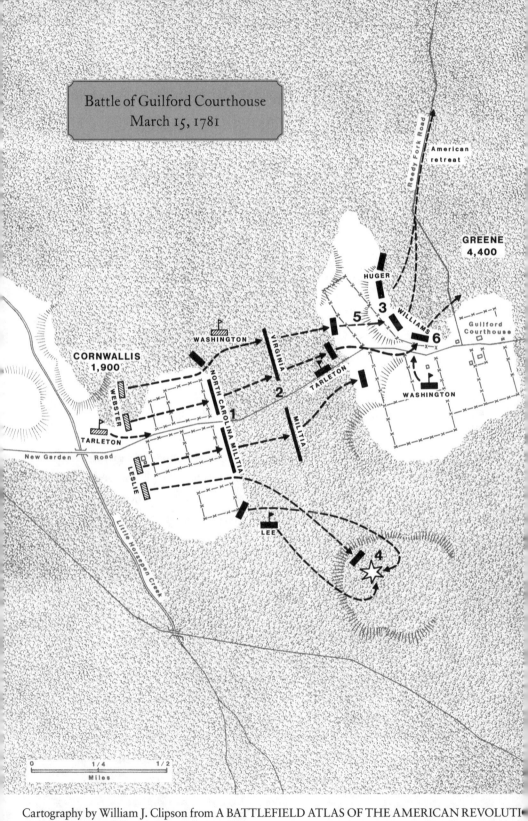

Battle of Guilford Courthouse
March 15, 1781

American retreat

Ready Fork Road

GREENE
4,400

HUGER

3

5

WILLIAMS

6

Guilford
Courthouse

CORNWALLIS
1,900

WASHINGTON

VIRGINIA

NORTH CAROLINA MILITIA

2

TARLETON

WEBSTER

1

WASHINGTON

TARLETON

MILITIA

New Garden   Road

LESLIE

Little Horsepen Creek

LEE

4

0   1/4   1/2
Miles

Cartography by William J. Clipson from A BATTLEFIELD ATLAS OF THE AMERICAN REVOLUTION
published by Savas Beatie, www.savasbeatie.com

backcountry. By October 30 his footsore troops had encamped at Winns-boro, and they remained refitting and receiving reinforcements until mid-January 1781. Troops led by Major General Alexander Leslie joined him there, having arrived from the Chesapeake Bay region, where Leslie's forces had been engaged in raiding rebel depots and tobacco warehouses in the Virginia Tidewater.

Meanwhile, North Carolina state officials and Major General Hora-tio Gates, commander of the Continental Army's Southern Department, made strenuous efforts to raise more troops and reequip the army at Hillsborough, Salisbury, and Charlotte to oppose an imminent invasion. That fall, the Continental Congress at Philadelphia made two significant military appointments for the Southern Department. On October 25, Colonel Daniel Morgan, a tough French and Indian War veteran, a Vir-ginia Continental officer, and a key figure in the American victory at Saratoga in 1777, received a brigadier general's commission to command light troops in the Carolinas. After Saratoga he had quit the army over a dispute regarding the command of the light forces, but after Gates's defeat at Camden in August he again made himself available for active service. More important, several days earlier Congress formally appointed thirty-eight-year-old Major General Nathanael Greene as Gates's replace-ment in command of the Southern Department, after consulting General Washington. Greene, a native Rhode Islander in continuous service to the American cause since before the 1775–1776 Siege of Boston, was arguably Washington's closest subordinate officer and had been the army's former quartermaster general. "You will…proceed without delay to the Southern army, now in North Carolina, and take the command accordingly," Washington ordered Greene, who had only recently assumed the assign-ment as the garrison commander at West Point, New York.

Greene made an exhausting journey south, during which he con-sulted with Congress, financiers, and the governors and assemblies of Maryland and Virginia, attempting to procure food, men, money, and weapons with which to wage war in the Carolinas. Riding with a small staff through Annapolis, Richmond, Petersburg, and Hillsborough, he finally arrived at the American army's squalid camps in Charlotte on the afternoon of December 2, 1780, and relieved the unfortunate Gates. Greene was soon shocked at the miserable condition of the army. "The Difficulty of carrying on the war in this Department is much greater than my imagination had extended to," he realized after assuming command, and described the troops as "the Shadow of an Army in the midst of Distress." Greene reported in detail to Governor Jefferson in Virginia about the army's dreadful condition:

> I find the troops...in a most wretched condition, destitute of every thing necessary either for the comfort or convenience of soldiers. It is impossible that men can render any service...whilst they are starving with cold and hunger. Your [Virginia] troops may be literally said to be naked and I shall be obliged to send a considerable number of them away into some secure place and warm quarters until they can be furnished with clothing. It will answer no good purpose to send men here in such a condition, for they are nothing but added weight upon the army, and altogether incapable of aiding in its operations.... The life of a soldier in its best state is subject to innumerable hardships, but when they are aggravated by a want of provisions [and] clothing, his condition becomes intolerable, nor can men long contend with such complicated difficulties and distress—deaths, desertion and the hospital must soon swallow up an army under such circumstances.

Despite his frequent plaintive letters to southern state officials, the Continental Congress, and military officers throughout the coming years, Greene was forced to fight the grueling war in the South with too few men, scanty supplies, and little additional support through to the war's conclusion in 1783.

Gathering all the troops he could find in North Carolina, including about one thousand veteran Continentals from Maryland and Delaware, Greene faced a difficult situation. In part to solve the precarious logistical problems in supplying his ragged, hungry men, who were often surviving "hand to mouth," he decided to split his small force. He sent Morgan's mounted light troops, called a "flying army," southwest of Charlotte across the Catawba River. In this strategy, Morgan was to gather back-country militiamen under prominent officers Thomas Sumter, William L. Davidson, and Elijah Clarke; protect exposed patriots in the distant backcountry; and "annoy" the enemy in upcountry South Carolina, especially around their fortified post at Ninety Six, a key Loyalist stronghold. Meanwhile Greene moved the rest of his soldiers southeast to Cheraw, to a "camp of repose" on Hick's Creek, a small tributary of South Carolina's Pee Dee River (called the Yadkin River in North Carolina). Greene also hoped his unexpected advance into South Carolina would be perceived by disheartened patriots as an offensive move and buoy their flagging spirits. Should Cornwallis advance from Winnsboro, the two patriot forces could reunite in North Carolina, although the British could also attack each part of Greene's army separately—a grave danger that Greene would be hard-pressed to oppose, since his two elements would be about 120 miles apart.

To counter Morgan's threat to his west, Lord Cornwallis directed about 1,200 men in a mixed force of cavalry, artillery, and infantry, led by Lieutenant Colonel Banastre Tarleton, to bring the rebels to battle while the rest of the British troops, wagons, and artillery would simultaneously march into North Carolina. Only twenty-six years old, Tarleton had already established himself and his British Legion of green-coated, American Loyalist dragoons and infantry as a hard-hitting, often ruthless force that took few prisoners. Referred to by patriots as "Bloody Ban," he relied on surprise, impetuosity, and daring to rout patriot forces and ruthlessly pursue them after British victories, such as the 1780 Battles of Lenud's Ferry and Waxhaws in May and Camden in August. To chase Morgan, his Legion was augmented by the redcoats of the First Battalion of the Seventy-First Highland Regiment, the Seventh Regiment of Foot (Royal Fusiliers), part of the Seventeenth Light Dragoons, two three-pounder field artillery pieces, and a contingent of light infantry.

Lord Cornwallis started to move the main body of Crown forces from Winnsboro toward Charlotte, while by January 12 Tarleton rapidly advanced to find Morgan to the west, in cold, wet weather. Fearful of being caught between the two British columns on the west side of the Catawba River, Morgan began marching north away from his encampment at Grindal Shoals on the Pacolet River and Tarleton's rapidly marching column, which had crossed the Enoree and Tyger Rivers. Several miles south of the rain-swollen Broad River, in a large open pasture area called the Cowpens in South Carolina, the American general decided to make a stand with the troops he had on hand on the evening of January 16, 1781. Morgan's command of about 1,900 men included Maryland and Delaware Continentals: experienced regulars in five companies that formed the core of his small army, led by Lieutenant Colonel John Eager Howard, a talented young officer from Baltimore. These soldiers were augmented by Lieutenant Colonel William Washington's Continental Light Dragoons, reinforced by state cavalrymen of Virginia and the Carolinas. Morgan was also joined there by hundreds of militiamen from Virginia, North and South Carolina, and Georgia—many of whom were veterans and some of whom had seen action at King's Mountain three months earlier. The tall, dour Colonel Andrew Pickens of South Carolina, which provided most of Morgan's militia, was in overall command of that state's troops.

General Morgan, an officer who had seen extensive combat at the battles of Quebec, Saratoga, and Monmouth, deployed his gathering troops to take advantage of their strengths. He knew well the unreliability of militia soldiers when facing disciplined British regular troops in battle and was aware of many instances during the war in which inexperienced militiamen panicked and fled the battlefield when assaulted by onrushing redcoats or Hessians with fixed bayonets. Morgan was certainly aware of the recent disastrous experience American forces suffered among the tall pines and humid air at the Battle of Camden, where General Gates posted jittery militia from Virginia and North Carolina on the left and center of his main battle line, largely unsupported by the veteran Continental units posted on his right. Pressed and unnerved by a vigorous early-morning British bayonet charge at the beginning of the engagement, the frightened militia fled the battlefield, many tossing away their muskets without having fired a single shot.

Morgan was not going to imitate Gates's faulty disposition of his regiments at Camden. At Cowpens, the gritty American general deployed his troops in three parallel lines, posted with a ravine on the right and a creek on the left, making both flanks secure. He placed about one hundred Georgia and South Carolina militia skirmishers and riflemen in his advanced first line and ordered them to each fire two shots at the enemy as they advanced, then fall back in an orderly manner to a second line, where South Carolina militiamen commanded by Colonel Pickens were posted about 150 yards away in the predawn darkness. These second-line troops would also fall back after firing several volleys at the oncoming foe, and reform behind a third line of redoubtable Continental infantry on higher ground 150 yards distant, bayonets fixed, supported by Colonel Washington's dragoons posted and concealed in the rear. The first two lines would thus blunt and bloody the enemy attack, and the plan allowed the militia to fall back intentionally, without exessive risk. When facing Tarleton, however, nothing was guaranteed.

Morgan's innovative deployment of his men was completed by nightfall, after which the troops readied their weapons, ate what food they had, and huddled around campfires in the damp night. Additional militia continued to arrive the night before the battle and that morning, eager to come to blows with Tarleton. In the mist Morgan mingled among groups of his soldiers, confidently explaining his plan, reassuring and shoring up the morale of his men.

On the cold, early morning of January 17, Tarleton advanced north on the Green River Road leading to Morgan's position. The young colonel must have concluded that he now had Morgan pinned against the flooded Broad River in a trap. Eager to get at the rebels who had eluded him for days, Tarleton hurriedly deployed his winded forces with the leather-helmeted Legion dragoons on his left and the Seventh

Regiment's redcoats, the Legion infantry, the light infantry companies, and finally the Seventeenth Light Dragoons on his right flank. The Seventy-First Regiment was in reserve, posted behind the British left; the artillery deployed on the road in the middle of the field, gunners at the ready to fire a salvo.

Tarleton began his attack immediately, perhaps before all of his soldiers were ready. The militia marksmen on the first line fired at the oncoming foe as soon as they were visible, particularly targeting officers. As planned, these expert riflemen scurried back to the second position as the British kept coming. Pickens's militia on the second line fired off two volleys, then retreated behind Howard's Continental infantry to the American left rear. "The whole of Colonel Picken's Command then kept up a Fire by Regiments retreating agreeable to their Orders," Morgan wrote. While these men were regrouping, however, they were struck by a bold charge from the Seventeenth Light Dragoons, numbering about forty sabers. Scattered and bloodied by this mounted attack, Pickens's soldiers were relieved to see Colonel Washington's dragoons courageously charge the British dragoons in a sudden assault, which threw the surprised enemy horsemen back with losses.

Meanwhile, on the American right and center, the infantry of both armies slugged it out as the battle lines drew very close. Tarleton ordered an attack from his left, so the Seventy-First Foot moved forward to assault the right of Morgan's line, with the British Legion Dragoons nearby to sweep around the flank and get in the American rear. To counter this menacing threat, Howard quickly ordered a company of Virginia light infantry on the far end of the line to refuse their right, in order to protect the American flank. Due to a misunderstanding and the confusion of battle, the company retreated instead of wheeling in place to the rear. Seeing this mistaken retrograde maneuver, other soldiers nearby also began to retire, assuming a general retreat had been ordered. As third-line soldiers began to move back, they were met by Morgan, who designated a new position for his hard-pressed troops. Seeing what appeared to be a rout, the excited British troops began a disorderly pursuit of Morgan's force, many of them breaking ranks to rush forward.

But the day was not lost for the Americans, who had retired in good order and had no intention of giving up the fight. Once they reached the new position, Morgan's men halted, turned about, and fired a staggering, close-range volley into the approaching enemy. Stunned, the British retreated in confusion. The Americans then made a determined bayonet charge into the ranks of the reeling Highlanders of the Seventy-First, "which was done with such Address that they fled with the utmost Precipitation," Morgan reported. Meanwhile, Washington's cavalry arrived and hit the redcoats' left and rear. Pickens advanced on the patriot left flank as well with his hundreds of reformed militiamen, now encouraged by the success of Howard's charge. Soon the British line was overwhelmed in a double envelopment, forcing almost all of Tarleton's troops to surrender, including their two artillery pieces.

Tarleton left the field with just a few dozen dragoons, but as he rode off, he glimpsed Washington approaching at the head of his galloping column. Turning back, Tarleton rode at Washington with a few other officers and, in a brief swirling encounter, the two fought hand-to-hand until the former withdrew. Washington's life was spared in this brawl by a nearby servant who wounded an attacking Legion officer intent on killing Washington. Tarleton "was Persued 24 miles," Morgan reported, "but owing to our having taken a wrong Trail at first, we never could overtake him" on his ride to rejoin Cornwallis.

For the patriots, the battle was an unqualified success. "The Troops I had the Honor to command," Morgan reported proudly to General Greene, "have been so fortunate as to obtain a compleat Victory over a Detachment from the British Army commanded by Lt Colonel Tarlton." Although rejoicing in triumph, Morgan and his men could ill afford to linger on the bloody field for long, with Cornwallis nearby to the east and hundreds of prisoners to hurry off to Salisbury. The American force lost about 150 killed and wounded that morning compared to Tarleton's casualties of around 900, most of whom were prisoners.

Morgan marched north from Cowpens on January 18, headed for the Catawba River in North Carolina by way of Gilbert Town and Ramsour's Mill. He was chased by Cornwallis and the main British Army of 2,400 soldiers, intent on following the patriots into North Carolina. At Ramsour's Mill in late January, Cornwallis destroyed most of his army's excess baggage to facilitate a more rapid pursuit of the American forces, who were already ahead crossing the Catawba River at Sherrald's (Sherrill's) Ford, thirty miles north of Charlotte. Several bodies of militia also began to gather to defend numerous other fords on the river ahead of the British advance, which Morgan hoped to delay or block. Unfortunately for Morgan, there were too many fords and not enough soldiers to guard them. Cornwallis forced a crossing of the cold Catawba under fire at Cowan's Ford, seventeen miles downriver from Sherrald's Ford, on February 1, pushing aside hundreds of North Carolina militia defenders under Brigadier General William Lee Davidson. The British troops flanked the militia and forced them to fall back; Davidson was mortally wounded during the fight.

With the enemy host now on the same side of the Catawba as Morgan's troops, it was too dangerous for the Americans to remain nearby. General Greene had joined Morgan on January 30 at the flooded Catawba River fords, having ordered the rest of the army at Cheraw, led by Brigadier General Isaac Huger, to join Morgan's troops at Salisbury, on the Yadkin River. But with the British now across the river, Greene ordered a concentration at Guilford Courthouse instead as he knew he was too weak to face Cornwallis's pursuing army in battle. The British pushed Morgan's men out of Salisbury, where the rebels crossed the Yadkin at Trading Ford but prevented the British from doing so by taking all the local boats with them.

With all his troops now assembled at Guilford Courthouse, a tiny crossroads hamlet, Greene conferred with his senior officers to assess the army's situation. He decided to retreat northeast through the Carolina Piedmont toward Virginia, where he hoped to be resupplied and reinforced with militia and newly raised, tolerably equipped Continentals. But he had to outrun the enemy first.

Using a ruse, Greene selected a small corps of light troops and cavalry, all under Colonel Otho Holland Williams, to lure Cornwallis into chasing the detachment north to Dix's Ferry on the Dan River, a wide stream flowing along the Virginia border that the patriots sought to put between their army and the quick-marching enemy. Greene's main body, however, would march instead northeast from Guilford Courthouse, hurrying to cross the Dan at Irwin's and Boyd's Ferries, both downstream from Dix's. Once assured that Greene had crossed the Dan, the light corps would also head to the lower fords, cross the river, and prevent Cornwallis's troops from crossing.

The British took the bait and gave chase, closely following the light troops and dragoons beginning on February 10, in what later came to be called "the Race to the Dan." Williams's detachment, which included the cavalries of Washington and Lieutenant Colonel Henry "Lighthorse" Harry Lee, parried the dogged British pursuers constantly during this period and were often just a hundred yards away during the chase, with little time for rest or proper meals. "On the road," an impressed Colonel Tarleton later recalled, "many skirmishes took place between the British and the American light troops, without great loss to either party, or any impediment to the progress of the main body." Although it was a close-run affair, Cornwallis reached the lower fords on the rain-swollen river on February 14. But he was too late to catch Greene's footsore soldiers, including Williams's light corps, who had finished crossing by boat earlier that evening. Unable to catch the rebels at the fords, Cornwallis withdrew his men south to Hillsborough two days later. Safe on the north side of the river near Halifax, Colonel Williams deemed the march one of Greene's "most masterly and fortunate maneuvers" and said, "[T]he propriety of the retreat...has not been exceeded by any military maneuver practiced this war."

Greene spent several days north of the Dan resting his troops and beginning to receive reinforcements. Going forward, however, he would have to do without Morgan, whose broken health necessitated his leaving the army at Boyd's Ferry and retiring to his home near Berryville, Virginia. Greene's forces soon returned to North Carolina for several weeks to watch and cautiously shadow Cornwallis's tired army, which was now quite far from its base of supplies and was joined by few ardent Carolina Loyalists willing to fight. Tarleton noted that many nearby inhabitants "rode into the British camp, to talk over the proclamation, inquire the news of the day, and take a view of the King's troops," but few took up arms.

The two belligerents maneuvered between Hillsborough and Guilford Courthouse, fifty miles to the west, and they fought several sharp skirmishes, including "Pyle's Defeat" on February 24 and the Battle of Weitzel's Mill on Reedy Fork Creek on March 6. Afterwards, Greene moved his troops to the north side of the creek in a defensive position while Cornwallis brought his command west to the Deep River Friends (Quaker) Meeting House on March 13, where he hoped to obtain supplies from the British post at Wilmington.

Greene followed Cornwallis as far as Guilford Courthouse, twelve miles away. His army numbered approximately 4,400 men, as over the previous few days he had been reinforced by hundreds of militia soldiers, Virginia riflemen, and about 400 Continentals. Although he intended to advance and attack the British at Deep River, his cavalry scouts advised him early on the morning of March 15 that the British had broken camp and were on the move to attack him.

Upon receipt of this intelligence, Greene took up a defensive position that morning around Guilford Courthouse with his reinforced army, consisting of Maryland, Virginia, and Delaware Continental infantry and cavalry and North Carolina and Virginia militia. On the advice of Morgan, Greene placed his army in three lines as at Cowpens. In advance he deployed the North Carolinians, over a third of whom were draftees, supported on both flanks by more seasoned Continental and militia dragoons led by Colonel Washington and "Lighthorse" Harry Lee, who had arrived in the southern theater shortly after Greene. The American second line consisted of Virginia militia troops led by Brigadier Generals Edward Stevens and Robert Lawson, some of whom had seen prior combat experience. In his third and rearmost line by the small courthouse, along Reedy Fork Road, stood most of Greene's Continental infantry, Maryland and Virginia regulars, on high ground above a sluggish creek, supported by two pieces of field artillery.

The British, hungry, tired, and on the march since 4:00 a.m., approached Greene's army from the New Garden Quaker Meeting House eight miles to the southwest. Tarleton's cavalry led the British column, followed by the foot regiments and artillery. American cavalry under Lee sparred with Tarleton's horsemen in a series of early-morning sharp skirmishes along the Great Salisbury (also called New Garden) Road leading to the courthouse, then fell back to the rebel lines with their fighting blood up.

The first line of the American army was on a wooded ridge overlooking muddy, stubbled farm fields the enemy would have to cross, and consisted for the most part of largely untested North Carolina militia companies behind a split rail fence at the forest's edge. To bolster this line, veteran riflemen and Continental dragoons secured each flank. Imitating Morgan on the night before the Battle of Cowpens, the mounted Greene inspired his men by telling them to fire two volleys. They could fall back through the brushy woods to the second line of two Virginia militia brigades once the British regulars closed in.

Lord Cornwallis was on the offensive, and he wasted little time preparing for the attack. Once he reached a small farmstead belonging to the Hoskin family that straddled the New Garden Road, he deployed his army of 1,900 men on either side of the road. On the army's right the troops were led by General Leslie, who had joined Cornwallis in South Carolina with reinforcements just after Cowpens. Leslie now commanded the Second Battalion of the Seventy-First Regiment; the Regiment von Bose, a Hessian battalion; and two battalions of the elite Guards, men drawn for American service from all three British Guards regiments in London and commanded by Brigadier General Charles O'Hara, a popular officer. On the left side of the road, Lieutenant Colonel James Webster commanded the red-coated troops, with the Twenty-Third Foot (Royal Welch Fusiliers) posted immediately north of the road and next to them the Thirty-Third

Foot, both very experienced regiments. Behind them were the tall grenadiers and nimble light infantry of the Guards—the elite companies of the British regiments—along with a company of rifle-bearing Hessian light infantry called Jaegers. The commanding general placed several cannons of the Royal Artillery in the road with Tarleton's Legion behind them, ready to exploit anticipated success.

Artillery on both sides opened the contest, firing from the sandy road by about 1:00 p.m. After thirty minutes of this exchange, Cornwallis sent his troops forward to attack the rebel militia. When the redcoats advanced uphill to about one hundred yards from the militia line, the Carolinians let loose "a most galling and effective fire," wrote one British officer, many of them resting their weapons on the top fence rail for better accuracy. The bloodied redcoat regiments and one Hessian battalion paused to regroup after suffering fearful casualties but returned the rebel fire and charged ahead with bayonets fixed. It is unclear how many of the Carolinians fired a second or even a third volley of musketry, but soon all retreated through the woods, some in a state of panic, "scattered in every direction," one of them later recalled. Colonel Lee later recalled with disdain that he "joined in the attempt to rally the fugitives, threatening to fall upon them with his cavalry. All was vain, so thoroughly confounded were these unhappy men, that, throwing away arms, knapsacks, and even canteens, they rushed like a torrent headlong through the woods." Later, a frustrated Greene would tell Congress that the Carolinians

> waited the attack until the enemy got within about one hundred forty yards, when part of them began a fire, but a considerable part left the ground without firing at all; some fired once, and some twice, and none more, except a part of a battalion of General [Thomas] Eaton's brigade. The general and field officers did all they could to induce the men to stand their ground, but neither the advantages of position nor any other consideration could induce them to stay. They left the ground and many of them threw away their arms.

The Crown forces, though bloodied, pressed forward toward the Virginians in the forest and brush several hundred yards away.

The thickly wooded terrain, however, disrupted tight British unit alignments so that their assault on the waiting Virginians was disjointed and "of almost infinite diversity," according to a British Army witness. The fighting in the late-winter forest was confusing, made more so by the dense blue smoke of the musket fire. Still, "the Virginia militia gave the enemy a warm reception and kept up a heavy fire for a long time," boasted Greene, who could hear from the courthouse area the roar of the shooting. Eventually Cornwallis's men pressed the Virginians back with bayonet charges and superior discipline, but they suffered heavy casualties in their advance. A British soldier declared that "the second line of the enemy made a braver and stouter resistance than the first. Posted in the woods, and covering themselves with trees, they kept up for a considerable time a galling fire, which did great execution." Although some of the Virginia militiamen fled in panic, almost five hundred men from the first and second lines did regroup around the courthouse to the rear of Greene's third line.

Meanwhile, on the far right of Cornwallis's line, a separate battle began to develop away from the main scene of action. British and Hessian troops, including a detachment of Tarleton's feared dragoons, pushed Virginia riflemen under Colonel William Campbell and Colonel Lee's mixed legion of cavalry and infantry south through the woods, away from the American left flank. Many of Greene's soldiers in this part of the field were killed or suffered saber wounds from slashing British cavalrymen, but Cornwallis's troops were hard-hit too. A rebel rifleman recalled years later that he "received two wounds at the battle at Guilford[,] wounds...occasioned by a ball having been shot in his right leg and by a blow from a British Light horse man's sword on the left hand."

At one point in the fighting, near the second American line, gun smoke and dense brush obscured the landscape to such an extent that Lord Cornwallis was almost captured. Luckily for him, a British sergeant of the Twenty-Third Regiment grabbed the bridle of the general's mount and brought him to safety. "I then mentioned to him, that if his lordship pursued in the same direction, he would in a few moments have been surrounded by the enemy, and perhaps cut to pieces or captured," wrote the redcoat ranker.

Finally, about ninety minutes after the fluid battle opened, tired British troops approached Greene's third line, which to that point had been unengaged in the fight. Initially the First Maryland and Second Virginia Regiments soundly repulsed a British attack from Webster's troops on the rebel right, but on the rebel left the inexperienced Second Maryland broke and fled almost instantly when attacked close to the New Garden Road by General O'Hara's Second Battalion of Guards, which also captured two American six-pounder cannons close to the courthouse as they surged forward. O'Hara's successful attack put his men in the rear of the steadfast First Maryland, which, once warned of the danger, faced about and gave "some well directed fires" in close combat. Joining the attack on the British Guards was Colonel Washington's Continental Light Dragoons, which charged straight into the Guards' ranks with about eighty mounted men, who then made a second pass through the enemy troop formation, slashing and firing. In this confused action, the First Maryland was able to recapture some prisoners, and the bitter fighting was hand-to-hand. Several blasts of cannon fire from the nearby British lines soon checked the danger from Washington's cavalry.

All of the British regiments were now up to the third line, and Greene had engaged in heavy fighting, including in the ignominious rout of the Second Maryland. He concluded that a withdrawal from the field was now prudent. At about 3:30 p.m., his forces withdrew from the field in good order and made their way north on the Reedy Fork Road to Speedwell Ironworks on Troublesome Creek, the army's predesignated rallying point. British forces initially pursued but were checked by Virginia Continentals as rain began to fall on the dead and wounded left on the field. It was "one of the most hazardous, as well as severe battles that occurred during the war," wrote Tarleton. Greene, taking some solace in the disappointing result of the "long, obstinate, and bloody" contest, wrote to Congress that the British "have met with a defeat in a victory," while Major St. George Tucker of the Virginia militia concluded that "Cornwallis undoubtedly gained a dear bought victory." American losses were 79 killed, 184 wounded, and 1,046 missing, most of the latter being militiamen who fled the field and did not return to the ranks. Greene's army lost four guns to the redcoats as well. Cornwallis lost 93 killed, 413 wounded, and 26 missing, a staggering casualty rate of about 25 percent. His army held the bloody field, but at great cost. "Another such victory would ruin the British Army," quipped Charles James Fox, a prominent member of the British Parliament who opposed the war.

Although much of Greene's militia had left the army for home during the retreat to Speedwell Ironworks, he still had a force of which the British had to be wary. Given Cornwallis's losses, the British commander knew he had won only a Pyrrhic victory. He left about seventy of his severely wounded soldiers among the Quakers at the New Garden Meeting House and began to march his men south "by easy marches" to Cross Creek. He brought his worn-down troops to Wilmington on the lower Cape Fear River on April 7.

As Cornwallis marched south along the Cape Fear River toward the coast, Greene followed him part of the way to Ramsay's Mill on the Deep River. Cornwallis managed to avoid a battle against Greene's command and reached Wilmington in a few days. Greene then decided to move his army into South Carolina with 1,200 Continentals and several hundred militia rather than chase the enemy to Wilmington. He explained his plan to General Washington from North Carolina:

> I am determined to bring the war immediately into South Carolina. The enemy will be obliged to follow us or give up their posts in that state. If the former takes place it will draw the war out of [North Carolina] and give it an opportunity to raise its proportion of men. If they leave their posts to fall

they must lose more there than they can gain here. If we continue in this state the enemy will hold their positions in both.
All things considered I think the movement is warranted by
the soundest reasons both political and military. The maneuver will be critical and dangerous.

Greene was risking leaving the enemy in the rear once he entered
South Carolina. He explained to a staff officer that by moving south the
"enemy now have almost entire command of the supplies of the state and
by going there we shall be able to share it with them at least." By April
19, Greene's army was just north of Camden.

Cornwallis elected not to follow Greene south, but rather to march
north to Virginia and the Chesapeake Bay region. He reported to his
superior Lieutenant General Sir Henry Clinton in New York:

Until Virginia is in a manner subdued, our hold of the Carolinas must be difficult, if not precarious. The rivers of Virginia
are advantageous to an invading Army, but North Carolina
is, of all the provinces in America, the most difficult to attack,
(unless material assistance could be got from the inhabitants,
the contrary of which I have sufficiently experienced) on
account of the great extent of the numberless rivers and
creeks, & the total want of interior navigation.

His troops were made ready to renew their southern campaigns of
long marches and bloody battles and left Wilmington on April 25, bound
for Virginia. Six months later most of them were killed, wounded, or made
prisoners at Yorktown when Cornwallis surrendered his weary soldiers to
Washington's army, which was allied with French troops and naval assets.

In the Carolinas, Greene managed to keep his army together through
logistical difficulties, financial challenges, and three major battles until
the British finally evacuated their posts in the South in 1783. Always
pithy with his words, the Rhode Island general neatly summed up much

of the American military experience in the Revolutionary War in the South: "We fight, get beat, rise, and fight again."

Further Reading

Babits, Lawrence E. *A Devil of a Whipping: The Battle of Cowpens.* Chapel Hill, North Carolina: University of North Carolina Press, 1988.

Babits, Lawrence E., and Joshua L. Howard. *Long, Obstinate, and Bloody: The Battle of Guilford Courthouse.* Chapel Hill, North Carolina: University of North Carolina Press, 2013.

Buchanan, John. *The Road to Guilford Courthouse: The American Revolution in the Carolinas.* New York: Wiley & Sons, 1999.

Maass, John R. *The Battle of Guilford Courthouse: A Most Desperate Engagement.* Charleston, South Carolina: The History Press, 2020.

O'Shaughnessy, Andrew J. *The Men Who Lost America: British Leadership, the American Revolution, and the Fate of the Empire.* New Haven, Connecticut: Yale University Press, 2013.

About the Author

John R. Maass is a programs and education staff member of the new National Museum of the U.S. Army at Fort Belvoir, Virginia. He received a B.A. in history from Washington and Lee University and a Ph.D. in early American history at Ohio State University. He is the author of several books and numerous articles on early U.S. military history, including *North Carolina and the French and Indian War: The Spreading Flames of War* (2013); *Defending a New Nation, 1783–1811* (2013); *The Road to Yorktown: Jefferson, Lafayette and the British Invasion of Virginia* (2015); *George Washington's Virginia* (2017); and *The Battle of Guilford Courthouse: A Most Desperate Engagement* (2020). He lives near Mount Vernon, Virginia.

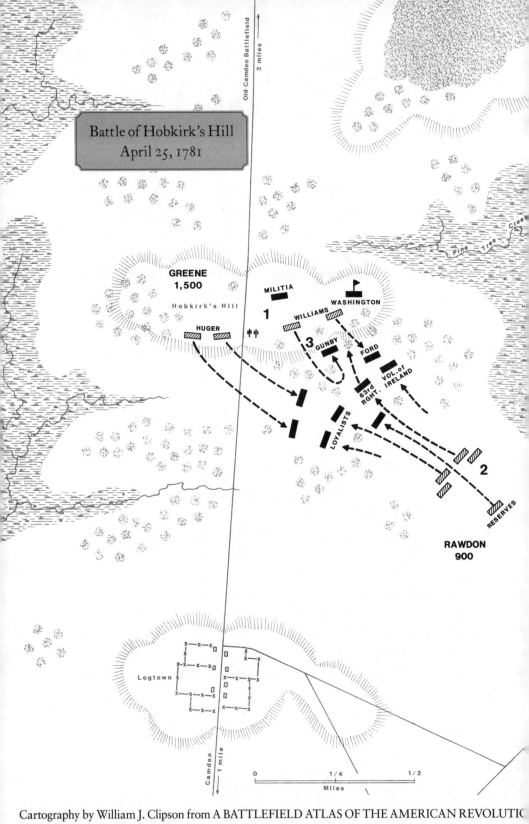

Battle of Hobkirk's Hill
April 25, 1781

Old Camden Battlefield

3 miles

Pine Tree Creek

GREENE
1,500

Hobkirk's Hill

MILITIA

WASHINGTON

HUGER

WILLIAMS

1

3 GUNBY

FORD

VOL. of
IRELAND

63rd
RGHT.

LOYALISTS

2

RESERVES

RAWDON
900

Logtown

Camden

1 mile

0   1/4   1/2
Miles

Cartography by William J. Clipson from A BATTLEFIELD ATLAS OF THE AMERICAN REVOLUTIO
published by Savas Beatie, www.savasbeatie.com

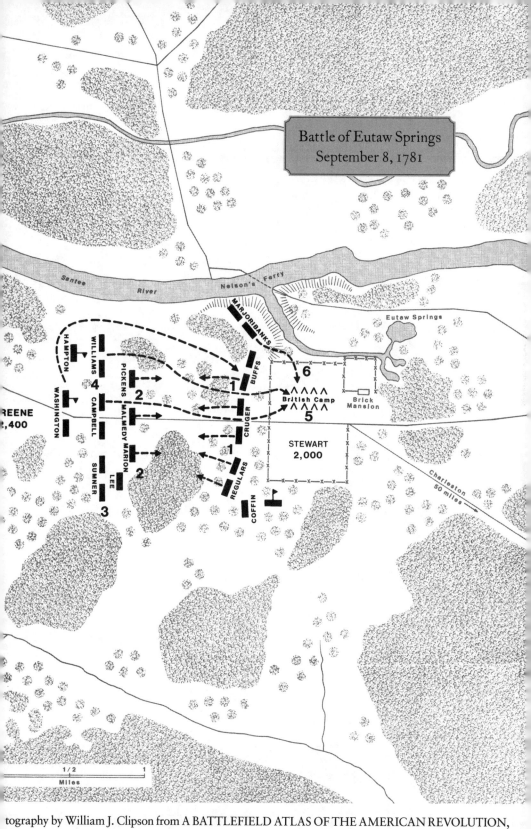

Battle of Eutaw Springs
September 8, 1781

Santee River

Nelson's Ferry

MARJORIBANKS

Eutaw Springs

HAMPTON

WILLIAMS

PICKENS

BUFFS

6

GREENE
2,400

WASHINGTON

CAMPBELL

MALMEDY MARION

4

2

1

British Camp

Brick Mansion

CRUGER

5

SUMNER

LEE

1

2

STEWART
2,000

REGULARS

3

COFFIN

Charleston
50 miles

1/2   1
Miles

tography by William J. Clipson from A BATTLEFIELD ATLAS OF THE AMERICAN REVOLUTION,
lished by Savas Beatie, www.savasbeatie.com

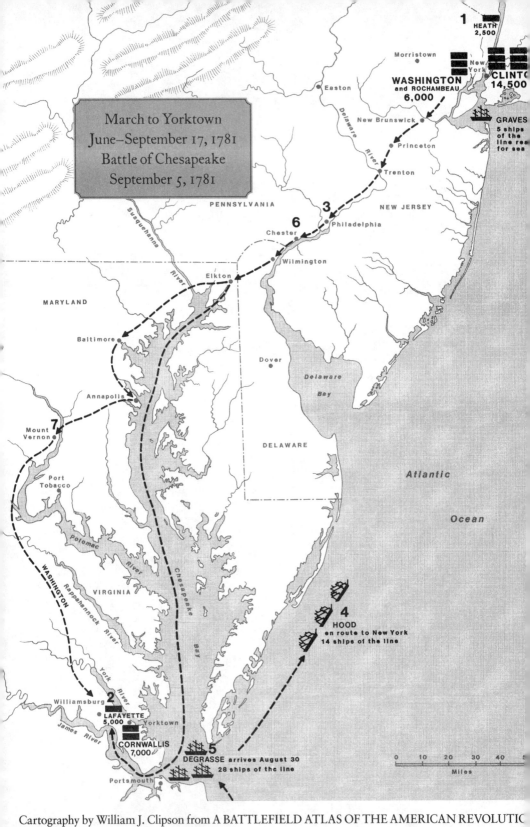

March to Yorktown
June–September 17, 1781
Battle of Chesapeake
September 5, 1781

1 HEATH 2,500

Morristown

WASHINGTON and ROCHAMBEAU 6,000

New York

CLINTO 14,500

GRAVES 5 ships of the line rea for sea

Easton

New Brunswick

Princeton

Trenton

PENNSYLVANIA

NEW JERSEY

3 Philadelphia

6 Chester

Wilmington

Elkton

Susquehanna River

MARYLAND

Baltimore

Dover

Delaware Bay

Annapolis

7 Mount Vernon

DELAWARE

Atlantic

Port Tobacco

Ocean

Potomac River

VIRGINIA

Chesapeake Bay

Rappahannock River

WASHINGTON

4 HOOD en route to New York 14 ships of the line

Williamsburg

York River

2 LAFAYETTE 5,000

Yorktown

James River

CORNWALLIS 7,000

5 DEGRASSE arrives August 30 28 ships of the line

Portsmouth

0 10 20 30 40
Miles

Cartography by William J. Clipson from A BATTLEFIELD ATLAS OF THE AMERICAN REVOLUTIO
published by Savas Beatie, www.savasbeatie.com

En Avant to Victory: The Allied March to Yorktown, June–October 1781

BY ROBERT A. SELIG

As the winter of 1780–1781 turned into spring, the Continental Army, plagued by lingering discontent that erupted in open mutiny in early January, barely maintained its strength. George Washington had written despairingly on April 9 to Lieutenant Colonel John Laurens, who was about to depart for France to once again plead for assistance from King Louis XVI: "We are at the end of our tether, and...now or never our deliverance must come."[1] If the grueling struggle for independence was to end in victory, the campaign of 1781 would preferably end, as far as Washington was concerned, in the conquest of New York City.

The ardently desired victory was indeed won in the fall of 1781: not along the banks of the Hudson, however, but in Washington's home state of Virginia. In late September, six months after he had laid bare his innermost fears to Laurens, American and French soldiers and sailors cast an impenetrable siege ring around British forces at Yorktown. Surrounded on water and on land, Charles Lord Cornwallis ordered his men to lay down their arms in the early afternoon of October 19, 1781. A perfectly executed naval campaign, close Franco-American land–sea coordination, and a great deal of good luck turned 1781 into an annus mirabilis, a wonderful, miraculous year.

The victory at Yorktown not only assured American independence but also brought the nation together on a human level, as New Englanders and Southerners got to know each other while fighting for a common cause. For over a hundred days, thousands of soldiers marched, rode, and sailed from Newport, Rhode Island; and Newburgh, New York to Yorktown, encountering fellow Americans and cultures far from their own homes. The march to victory became a crucial step in the development of an American identity in the cauldron of the war and the diversity of Revolutionary America.

Personal encounters with their French brothers in arms dispelled decades-old prejudices, making Americans realize who they were by recognizing who they were not. Until 1780, Americans had viewed their French allies with suspicion and sometimes contempt. Personal encounters changed that perception. William Channing of Newport, Rhode Island, wrote of the French on August 6, 1780, that "Neither Officers nor men are the effeminite [sic] Beings we were heretofore taught to believe them. They are as large & as likely men as can be produced by any nation."[2] Colonel John Fontaine of Virginia wrote on October 26, 1781, that "the French are very different from the ideas formerly inculcated in us of a people living on frogs and coarse vegetables."[3]

Washington had once been opposed to bringing French ground troops to the United States. By the winter of 1779–1780, however, American and French leaders both decided they had no choice but to send a strong force across the ocean to rescue the Revolution. On March 1, 1780, King Louis XVI of France promoted Jean-Baptiste Donatien de Vimeur, comte de Rochambeau, to lieutenant general and put him in charge of a mission code-named "Expédition particulière." On May 2, a convoy of thirty-two transports and cargo ships protected by seven ships of the line, four frigates, four flutes, a cutter, and a schooner left Brest for the United States. Besides their crews of about 7,000 sailors, the French ships carried the Bourbonnois, Soissonnois, Saintonge, and Royal Deux-Ponts regiments of infantry of about 1,000 men each; a reinforced battalion of the Auxonne Regiment of Artillery with a strength of about 450; the 600-man strong Lauzun's Legion; and a pioneer detachment: altogether, about 450 officers and 5,300 men.

Around 10:30 a.m. on July 11, the French fleet under the command of Charles-Henri-Louis d'Arsac, chevalier de Ternay, sailed into Newport Harbor. After more than seventy days on the ocean, about 800 soldiers and some 1,500 sailors were afflicted with scurvy, and hundreds of them died over the next few weeks. Rochambeau anyway had arrived too late in the season to embark on a campaign in 1780. On September 22, he met with Washington in Hartford, Connecticut, where they decided to wait until the following spring before finalizing campaign plans. On November 1, Rochambeau's infantry entered winter quarters in Newport, while the hussars of Lauzun's Legion and their horses were sent to Lebanon, Connecticut.

Several months later, from May 21 to May 23, 1781, the generals met in Wethersfield to discuss their plans. On May 22, Washington summarized their decisions in his diary:

> That the French Land force (except 200 Men) should March as soon as the Squadron could Sail [from Newport] for Boston—to the North [i.e. Hudson] River—and there, in conjunction with the American, to commence an operation against New York (which in the present reduced State of the Garrison it was thought would fall, unless relieved)…or to extend our views to the Southward as circumstances and a Naval superiority might render more necessary and eligible.

In view of "the insurmountable difficulty and expence of Land transportation—the waste of Men in long Marches (especially where there is a disinclination to the service—objections to the climate &ca)," an attack on New York remained preferable to any other objective for 1781.[4]

On May 28, Rochambeau informed Admiral François Joseph Paul, comte de Grasse, the commanding officer of French naval forces in the West Indies, that Washington had "asked for the march of the French forces to the North River to threaten, and maybe attack New York in cooperation with his army in order to create a diversion for the southern states." Asking for de Grasse's cooperation, Rochambeau continued:

> There are two points at which an offensive can be made against the enemy: Chesapeak and New York. The southwesterly winds and the state of defense in Virginia will probably make you prefer the Chesapeak Bay, and it will be there where we think you may be able to render the greatest service, whereas you will need only two days to come from there to New York. In any case it is essential that you send, well in advance, a frigate to inform de Barras where you are to come and also General Washington.[5]

This letter has often been cited as evidence that the Yorktown Campaign had been planned at Wethersfield, but the facts do not bear out this interpretation. Washington had had no intelligence from Virginia since May 5, when Marie-Joseph Paul Yves Roch Gilbert du Motier, marquis de La Fayette, informed him that Cornwallis had left Wilmington, North Carolina, on April 25. On May 20, Cornwallis was in Petersburg, a fact not known in New Windsor until June 4. No one could predict where Cornwallis would be in September, and as long as he remained far inland, de Grasse's fleet would be of little help, no matter when or with how many ships he entered the Chesapeake.

Conversely, Rochambeau had no idea where de Grasse was on May 28 when he wrote his letter. Only when the frigate *Le Sagittaire* sailed into Boston on June 10, almost three weeks after the Wethersfield Conference, did Rochambeau learn through a letter de Grasse had written on the high seas on March 29 that he had sailed from Brest on March

22 with 20 ships of the line, 3 frigates, and 156 transports and would be in Saint-Domingue by the end of June. If all went well, he could be in American waters by July 15, and therefore would need to be appraised of campaign plans. On July 16, de Grasse entered the port of Cap Français in Saint-Domingue, today's Cap Haitien in Haiti. Until then he had been completely in the dark about Franco-American plans; it was only on July 16 that he read Rochambeau's letter of May 28.

By then, the Franco-American armies had been outside New York City for ten days already. Assuming that de Grasse would appear off the coast sometime in late July, the Continental Army had left winter quarters at Newburgh on June 21 and marched along the Hudson to Philipsburg. On June 10, French forces had emerged from winter quarters in Newport as well and sailed up the Providence River. That same day Rochambeau told de Grasse:

> I do not need to hide from you, Monsieur, that these people here are at the end of their rope, that Washington does not have half the troupes that he counted on having, and that I believe, though he covers himself about that, that he currently has not 6,000 men, that M. de la Fayette has not 1,000 men regular troops and militias to defend Virginia, and...that is therefore of the utmost importance that you take on board as many troops as you can, that 4 or 5 thousand men would not be too many.[6]

On June 18, the Bourbonnois Regiment of Infantry set out from Providence for New York. Marching one day apart and one regiment at a time, Rochambeau's forces encountered their allies at White Plains on July 6. "In beholding this army," Jean-Francois-Louis, comte de Clermont-Crèvecœur, "was struck, not by its smart appearance, but by its destitution: the men were without uniforms and covered with rags; most of them were barefoot. They were of all sizes, down to children who could not have been over fourteen."[7] To Baron Ludwig von Closen he wrote, "It was really painful to see these brave men, almost naked with only some trousers and little linen jackets, most of them without stockings, but would you believe it? Very cheerful and healthy in appearance."[8] What a difference to the French line, which was "well lined up, of an equal height, well dressed."[9]

On July 21, Washington and Rochambeau set out for a three-day reconnaissance of British fortifications around New York City. Impressed by enemy preparations, Washington decided that he lacked the resources to successfully conduct a siege. Between his roughly 6,100 Continental Army troops and the almost 5,000 troops Rochambeau had brought to Westchester County, the combined armies were still smaller than the 12,500-man British garrison in New York. The few thousand militia Washington was hoping for would not make a difference. De Grasse had written that he might be outside New York City by July 15, but there was no sign of him. All that Washington could do was wait. On July 26, his private secretary Jonathan Trumbull Jr. wrote in his diary: "The Genl is exceedingly anxious & finds himself in a most perplexing & ridiculous scituation, not being able to determine on any fixed plan of operation, from the incertainty of his expectations & prospects."[10]

Two weeks later, on August 11, the frigate *Concord* arrived in Newport with a letter by de Grasse dated July 28. When it was opened at Rochambeau's headquarters at the John Odell House in Greenburgh around noon on Tuesday, August 14, it completely changed Washington's plans. De Grasse was on his way from Saint-Domingue "to render himself in all diligence to the Chesapeake Bay, the place which seems to have been indicated to me by you, M. le comte [de Rochambeau], and by [Messieurs] Washington, [Ambassador Anne-César] de la Luzerne, and [Admiral Jacques-Melchior Saint-Laurent, comte] de Barras as the surest place to carry out the good which you propose."[11]

Though Washington had planned on a siege of New York City, he quickly shifted gears. "Matters having now come to a crisis and a decisive plan to be determined on, I was obliged, from the shortness of Count de

Grasse's promised stay on this Coast [and] the apparent disinclination in their Naval Officers to force the harbour of New York…to give up all idea of attacking New York." Rochambeau had pointed out that French ships of the line had a draught of twenty-seven feet compared to the Royal Navy's twenty-two feet and could not sail into New York Harbor. Washington wrote that he had instead decided "to remove the French Troops and a detachment from the American Army to the Head of Elk to be transported to Virginia for the purpose of co-operating with the force from the West Indies against the Troops in that State."[12] De Grasse had made the decision for Washington.

Once the decision to deploy to Virginia had been made, Washington sent a letter to Lafayette on August 15 , instructing him to "immediately take such position as will best enable you to prevent [Cornwallis's] retreat thro' North Carolina."[13] If Lafayette could keep Cornwallis bottled up in Yorktown; if de Grasse's fleet appeared in time to complete the siege ring on water; and if the allied armies could get to Yorktown before de Grasse sailed back to the West Indies, then Cornwallis might just be caught and Britain's last operational field army captured. There was no time to lose.

De Grasse had informed Washington that he would remain in American waters until October 15. That left Washington sixty-two days, from August 14 to October 15, to move his forces to Yorktown, besiege Cornwallis, and force him to surrender. But first he had to get there—at 1.2 to 1.5 miles per hour, ten to twelve miles per day. That was the speed of the oxen pulling the wagons. The distance from Philipsburg to Yorktown was almost five hundred miles. With a few days of rest, and delays crossing the Delaware, Susquehanna, and Potomac Rivers, Washington could hope to arrive outside Yorktown within fifty days, around October 7–8. Unless de Grasse could be convinced to extend his stay, that left barely a week to force the surrender of Lord Cornwallis.

For months, Washington, Rochambeau, and de Grasse had exchanged letters not knowing where the recipient was, when he would receive the missive, when he would reply, and whether the issues raised would still be valid when the response arrived. The same holds true for Washington's letter to Lafayette. On August 15 he did not know that by digging in at Yorktown and Gloucester since August 2, Cornwallis had done exactly what the Americans would have wanted him to do.

On the morning of August 18, Rochambeau's French forces, almost 300 officers and 4,400 men, broke camp and began their march to Virginia. Since Washington had to leave around 3,500 men under General William Heath outside New York City to keep watch on Sir Henry Clinton's 12,500 British soldiers, the Continental Army that crossed the Hudson River in the days after August 18 was only about 2,400 officers and men strong. Marching on three parallel routes across New Jersey, the Americans reached Trenton less than two weeks later, on August 31. On September 2 they paraded before the Continental Congress in Philadelphia; over the next two days French forces marched through the city as well.

As the allied armies continued toward the Delaware state line, Rochambeau and his aides-de-camp took a staff ride down the Delaware River guided by artillery captain Mauduit du Plessis. Approaching the landing site at Marcus Hook in the mid-afternoon of September 5, Baron Closen "discerned in the distance General Washington, standing on the shore and waving his hat and a white handkerchief joyfully. There was good reason for this; for he informed us as we disembarked that M. de Grasse had arrived in Chesapeake Bay with 28 ships of the line and 3,000 troops."[14] What he did not know was that just about then the British and French fleets had begun firing at each other in the waters off the Chesapeake.

On August 5, de Grasse had raised anchor with his 28 ships of the line and 4 frigates at Cap Français for the "most perfectly executed naval campaign of the age of sail."[15] Besides their crews and almost 3,000 soldiers drawn from regular line infantry regiments supplementing the ship garrisons, his vessels carried the soldiers of the infantry regiments Gâtinais, Agenais, and Touraine; 100 artillery men from the Metz Artillery with their guns; and 100 hussars: altogether, some 3,300 men under Claude-Anne de Rouvroy, marquis de Saint-Simon-Montbléru. Along the way de Grasse dispatched a frigate to Havana to pick up 1.2 million livres for Rochambeau.

On August 17, *L'Aigrette* rejoined de Grasse's fleet as it emerged from the channel between Cuba and the Bahamas. The admiral had chosen that rarely used route in a successful bid to avoid detection by Admiral Samuel Hood. Aware that de Grasse had departed for the American mainland, Admiral George Brydges Rodney had ordered Hood to take the British fleet to New York by way of the Chesapeake and Delaware Bays. Hood sailed from Antigua on August 10, and though he had a longer route and departed five days after de Grasse, his fourteen copper-sheathed ships outsailed the French fleet and arrived off the Chesapeake on August 25. Sighting no French vessels, Hood sailed on to New York, arriving on August 31.

Along the way Hood missed the eight ships of the line, four frigates, and eighteen transports of Admiral de Barras, who had taken his squadron with the siege artillery out of Newport on August 23 and was on his way to Virginia. On August 31, Barras's fleet was just south of New York City, but far out on the Atlantic to avoid detection. Upon arrival in New York City, Admiral Thomas Graves added Hood's fourteen vessels to his own, and on August 31 he hurried back to Virginia. For the second time in a week, the British and French fleets missed each other in the vastness of the Atlantic between New York and the Chesapeake.

The ship crews assisting in the landing of St. Simon's troops had not yet returned when the lookouts aboard *L'Aigrette* reported sighting Graves's fleet of two 98-gun vessels, twelve 74s, one 70, four 64s, a 50-gun ship, six frigates, and a fire ship. Sailing at full speed, around six knots, or seven miles per hour, they were making straight for the entrance of the ten-mile-wide bay. *L'Aigrette* hurried back to alert de Grasse. There was not much he could do. Not only were wind and tide against him, but he had to leave 90 officers and about 1,900 crew members behind.

De Grasse's 104-gun flagship and three 80s, seventeen 74s, and three 64s were slow in forming a line of battle: the *Ville-de-Paris*, the eleventh ship in line, did not clear the bay until almost 1:00 p.m. Rather than order "close action" and head straight for the disorganized French fleet, at around 2:15 p.m. Graves gave orders to get into "line ahead" formation. Following the admiralty's fighting instruction, which demanded that battle be waged in close formation with each ship engaging her opponent, Graves wanted to bring his vessels into a roughly parallel position with the French fleet. This meant that his ships, sailing west-southwest, had to turn almost 180 degrees to change course to east-southeast and head back out to sea. The maneuver not only took one and a half hours to perform, it also reversed the order of his ships: his best and fastest ships, which had been in the lead, now found themselves at the rear of the column while three badly leaking 74s under Sir Francis Drake formed the new lead division.

The maneuver gave de Grasse time to clear the bay. The two fleets were arranged like the sides of a funnel when Graves raised the flag for "close action". It was exactly 3:46 p.m. At 4:15 p.m. the Royal Navy commenced firing, but confusion reigned aboard the British fleet. In a memorandum compiled the day after the battle, Hood claimed that Graves did not lower the ensign signaling "line ahead" as the standard for "close action" went up. Claiming they did not know which signal to follow, Hood's division stayed "line ahead." To remedy the situation, Graves had sent a frigate to order Hood to attack, but it was too late. Seven ships, including Hood's *Barfleur*, never caught up. When battle commenced, de Grasse had five more ships with 1,794 cannons compared to Graves's 1,410 British guns, sailing in closer formation than the Royal Navy. De Grasse's best vessels, forming the vanguard of his fleet, fired broadside after broadside into Sir Francis Drake's ships, the worst in Graves's fleet.

By 6:30 p.m. it was getting too dark to continue the fight, and Graves ordered his ships to disengage. The Royal Navy had suffered 336 casualties. The 74-gun ships *Ajax*, *Shrewsbury*, and *Terrible* were almost un-sailable; the *Terrible* had to be burned at sea a few days later.

The *Montague*, also a 74, was in danger of losing her masts. The *Intrepid*, struck by sixty-five cannon balls in the first volley alone, had to leave the fleet with a broken rudder. On the French side, the *Diademe* and the *Pluto*, both 74s, and the *Reflechi* and the *Caton*, both 64s, needed repairs. About 240 French sailors were casualties of the battle.

For the next few days, the fleets drifted southward until de Grasse decided on September 10 to return to the Chesapeake. Tactically the battle was a draw, but strategically it was a huge French victory. After eighteen days on the Atlantic, Barras had slipped into the bay on September 10; the next day de Grasse joined him there. By drawing the Royal Navy away from the Chesapeake, he had opened the way for Barras to safely bring in the siege guns. With the addition of Barras's vessels, de Grasse now had thirty-six ships of the line. Graves, with only eighteen, decided on September 13 to return to New York City, where he arrived on September 20. The naval superiority Washington had hoped for had been achieved; the siege ring on water was established. Things were looking grim for Cornwallis, and Graves knew it.

As the two fleets drifted southward, Washington and his army reached Head of Elk on September 6. On September 7, the First French Brigade joined them, and the Second Brigade arrived on September 8. Once the rearguard had arrived the two armies were ready for the last leg of the journey. But there was grumbling in the ranks. The Continental Army wanted to get paid, and it was. "This day," September 8, remembered Major William Popham, "will be famous in the annals of History for being the first in which the Troops of the United States received one month's Pay in Specie."[16] For many a Continental soldier this was indeed the first, and only, time he was ever paid with silver. Washington had borrowed the funds from Rochambeau, who paid his troops and for his supplies in specie. The approximately twenty million livres in gold and silver his army spent had a huge economic impact by nearly doubling the amount of specie circulating in the United States.

While his troops were embarking, Washington rode on to Mt. Vernon, which he had not seen since early in 1775. Following their visit from September 9–12, Washington and Rochambeau continued their journey to Williamsburg. In the morning of September 12, Trumbull recorded that "between Colchester and Dumphries meet letters giving an account of an action between the two Fleets, & that the French were gone out from the Bay in pursuit of the English. The event not known. Much agitated." With all of 130 miles to go, the outcome of the campaign once again hung in the balance. The next day they heard "Rumors of the return of the French Fleet, with some advantage, which relieved our fears."[17]

Hurrying on, Washington reached Williamsburg on September 14. "About 6 o'clock this afternoon," a witness wrote, "we were agreeably alarmed with intelligence that his Excellency Gen. Washington being within one mile of our camp. The troops immediately paraded and with inexpressible joy renewed and saluted that great good General.... The joy that appeared in everyone's face requires an abler pen than mine to describe at his arrival in camp."[18] Only now did Washington learn of the fortunate outcome of the Battle of the Capes.

Washington and Rochambeau had arrived, but where were their troops? On September 11 most of the Continental Army and about 1,200 men from Rochambeau's forces set sail from Head of Elk. The remainder of the French forces, close to 3,500 officers and men, as well as the First and Second New York Regiments with about 800 officers and men and the 350-man strong Rhode Island Regiment, marched on to Baltimore. Taken aback by the poor quality of the boats assembled at Fell's Point, Charles-Joseph-Hyacinthe du Houx, baron de Vioménil, Rochambeau's second-in-command, decided to march overland to Yorktown and left Baltimore on September 17. Later that day Vioménil learned that de Grasse had sent transports to Annapolis to take his troops to Virginia.

In the early evening of September 21, the men set sail for College Landing, where they arrived on September 24. Two days later they were joined by their comrades who had embarked at Head of Elk. News of de Grasse's hurried departure on September 5 to meet a British fleet had reached the flotilla as it put into Annapolis in the evening of September 12. Here they anxiously waited for the outcome of the battle. If Graves emerged victorious, the guns of the Royal Navy would be waiting at New Point Comfort for the dozens of small boats carrying the allied forces. When news of de Grasse's safe return to the Chesapeake Bay reached Annapolis in the evening of September 14, the troops reboarded and debarked at College Landing twelve days later, on September 26.

That same day the last link of the siege ring around Cornwallis fell into place. On September 14, Lauzun's three hundred hussars rode out of Baltimore for Yorktown. At Fredericksburg four days later, they received orders to change their route and ride to Gloucester Courthouse opposite Yorktown, where Brigadier General George Weedon's Virginia militia was unable to stop the depredations of Colonel John Simcoe's Queen's Rangers. The hussars joined Weedon on September 24, reinforcing the siege ring on the left bank of the York River, which became stronger still when the Legion's infantry arrived there three days later.

In the morning of September 28, the allied armies set out for Yorktown in three columns. The Continental Army, almost 6,000 strong now that Lafayette's division had been added to Washington's corps, formed the right flank of the siege forces. About 3,300 militia brought American forces to a little over 9,000 men. The Bourbonnois Regiment, part of Rochambeau's almost 5,000-strong corps, marched in the center, and the Agenois Regiment, part of St. Simon's 3,500-strong division, formed the left column. Taking the most direct road from Williamsburg, the Agenois was the first to make contact with the British at around 3:30 p.m. The following day, allied forces established a preliminary siege ring around Cornwallis, who abandoned his outer defensive works on September 30, thus allowing allied forces to approach even closer.

Fearing that Cornwallis might transport his approximately 7,100 men across the York River and break through the siege lines in Gloucester,

Washington strengthened allied forces on October 1 with 800 infantry-men detached from the ship garrisons of de Grasse's fleet. On October 2, General Gabriel de Choisy, who had taken command in Gloucester, felt strong enough to move closer to the British positions. Shortly before noon on October 3, Lauzun's 300 hussars pushed an equal number of Lieutenant Colonel Banastre Tarleton's dragoons of the British Legion back behind their earthworks in the largest cavalry engagement of the War of Independence. There the 1,000-man British garrison stayed for the remainder of the siege. Cornwallis's last escape route was closed off. During the night of October 6, allied soldiers began digging the trenches for the first parallel, or siege line, at a distance of 500 to 600 yards from British works. As they dug through the night, they were safe from British fire. When Cornwallis became aware of their activities the next morning his artillery opened up on the besiegers.

His guns would soon be silenced. On October 6, the oxen of the recently arrived American wagon train began to pull the first guns of the siege artillery from Barras's vessels at Jamestown Landing and into their emplacements before Yorktown. Around 4:00 p.m. on October 9, the Continental standard was hoisted over the Grand American Battery on the far right of the trenches closest to the York River. As Washington put the fuse to the touchhole of a thirty-six-pound cannon, the discharge became the signal for a furious artillery barrage that erupted along the siege line.

During the almost 200 hours of artillery bombardment from October 9 to the afternoon of October 17, when Cornwallis asked for a cease-fire, allied batteries fired almost 15,500 solid balls and shells of all calibers into Yorktown, some 80 rounds per hour. Thirteen-year-old John Hudson remembered that "between the flashes from the guns and from the fuses of the shells, it was rendered light enough for us to attend to all necessary work during any portion of night."[19] Dr. James Thacher of the light infantry recollected mortar shells crossing the lines "like fiery meteors with blazing tails, most beautifully brilliant."[20] On October 11 one of those "fiery meteors" was launched from a French battery of twelve-inch mortars firing "red-hot balls." "At 9 o'clock in the evening" one of them set fire "to the Charon, a ship of 44, anchored off York, as well as to 2 transports. The fire was superb to see; all the sky was reddened by it."[21]

That same evening work began on the second parallel, closer to British positions. But the trench line could not be completed as long as redoubts no. 9 and 10, located 400 yards in advance of the British inner defenses on the extreme right of the siege line, were still in British hands. Attacked by men wielding sabers and bayonets, both redoubts fell in less than thirty minutes on the evening of October 14. Four hundred French grenadiers of the Royal Deux-Ponts and the Gatinais regiments, led by William de Deux-Ponts, took no. 9, defended by 3 officers and 160 men; while 400 American light infantrymen under Alexander Hamilton captured the smaller no. 10, defended by 45 British troops.

Count Wilhelm von Schwerin of the Grenadier Company of the Royal Deux-Ponts took part in the assault:

> At 8 o'clock at night we approached the redoubts, always hidden behind our entrenchments. At 8 1/4 we were ordered to march in attack step up to the enemy redoubt and ascend it in an assault, our colonel-en-second at the head. There was a very lively fire from all sides for about 1/4 of an hour, after which the enemy offered to surrender. The garrison of the fort consisted of 160 men, of which we took no more than 40 prisoners without counting the dead; the others saved themselves as best they could. On our side we lost 80 men killed or wounded.[22]

When Count Rechteren went to see the carnage "at daybreak, [he] saw the entrenchments which presented a shocking scene, for dead bodies stripped naked lay strewn all about."[23]

On September 16, a sortie at daybreak under Lieutenant Colonel Robert Abercrombie with 600 light infantrymen served only to uphold

British honor. Around 1:00 p.m. the next day, Cornwallis asked for a truce to negotiate surrender terms. Conditions had deteriorated rapidly within Yorktown. Hessian Jager captain Johann Ewald penned this harrowing description of a British hospital: "These unfortunates died like flies from want, and the amputated arms and legs lay around in every corner and were eaten by the dogs."[24] Walking along the beach at Gloucester Point in the evening of October 21, Lieutenant Joachim du Perron of the garrison of Le Languedoc "found at our feet several dead bodies that stank horribly and we learned that some large tents, that we saw along the shore, concealed 1,500 of the sick; so many of them died that there was no time to bury them, and they simply threw the dead out of the tents as they expired."[25]

Shortly after 10:00 a.m. on October 19, 1781, Colonel Elias Dayton wrote in a letter to his son, "The drums are now beginning to beat for parade. I must now break off and hast to receive, a haughty cruel, unjust but now crest fallen foe."[26] As stipulated in Article 3 of the instrument of surrender, the garrison "at 2 o'clock precisely" was to "march out to a place to be appointed in front of the posts...with Shouldered Arms, Colors cased and Drums beating a British or German March."

Led by General Charles O'Hara, the faces of the 3,300 officers and men still fit for duty filing out of Yorktown reflected a "mortification and unfeigned sorrow [which] will never fade from my memory," wrote Captain Lieutenant Samuel Graham. Many were "sullen and cross" and angry enough to try and smash their flintlocks.[27] A considerable number appeared to be "in liquor," as the *Pennsylvania Packet* reported on November 13, 1781. All the while, their drummers were beating any number of tunes "as if they did not care how."[28] Over on the Gloucester side, George Gibson of Mercer's Grenadiers watched "the british stack their arms at Cornwallis's defeat he saw Tarletons Core dismount & some of them cried."[29] During the thirty-day siege, 156 British soldiers had been killed, 326 wounded, and 70 were missing. French casualties amounted to 60 killed and 194 wounded, and the Americans lost 28 killed and 107 wounded. The "ragged Continentals" and their French allies had won a stunning victory as the annus mira-bilis ended "in a most glorious day."[30]

Success at Yorktown had depended on many factors. By selecting Rochambeau to command the "Expédition particulière," Louis XVI had made an exceedingly good choice. Washington and Rochambeau respected each other and worked well together. Washington was sorely aware of his need for French naval support. Only France had the naval assets to establish the temporary naval superiority needed to build a siege ring on water around British forces. De Barras could have refused to serve under de Grasse since he had once been his commanding officer, but willingly accepted his temporary subordinate role for the greater good. All of the vessels carrying the correspondence between New York and the West Indies reached their destinations. No storm dispersed de Grasse's fleet on the way to Virginia, and while it did not end in a French victory, the Battle of the Capes achieved its purpose. French assistance on sea and even more so on land tipped the scales in favor of the Franco-American alliance outside Yorktown.

More than anything else, however, that success was due to Washington's skillful and determined leadership. For years Washington had hoped to take New York City, the center of Britain's military and political power, and to wipe away the stain of his greatest military humiliation. Yet on August 14, when he read de Grasse's letter informing him that the French fleet was sailing for the Chesapeake, he did not hesitate for a moment to abandon his dream of taking New York City. It took all of four days of planning, and the allied armies were on their way to his home state of Virginia and the victory which for all practical purposes sealed American independence.

About the Author

Robert A. Selig is a historical consultant who received his Ph.D. in history from the Universität Würzburg in Germany in 1988. He published a number of books on the American War of Independence such as *Hussars in Lebanon! A Connecticut Town and Lauzun's Legion during the American Revolution, 1780–1781* (Lebanon, 2004) and a translation of *A Treatise on Partisan Warfare by Johann von Ewald. Introduction and Annotation by Robert A. Selig and David Curtis Skaggs* (Westport, 1991). He is a specialist on the role of French forces under the Comte de Rochambeau during the American Revolutionary War and serves as project historian to the National Park Service for the Washington-Rochambeau Revolutionary Route National Historic Trail Project. He also serves as project historian for the American Battlefield Protection Program. He has been a regular contributor to popular history magazines such as the *William and Mary Quarterly, Eighteenth-Century Studies*, the *Yearbook of the Society for German-American Studies, Journal of Caribbean History, American Heritage, Naval History, Military History Quarterly, Colonial Williamsburg*, and chapters in various books and anthologies.

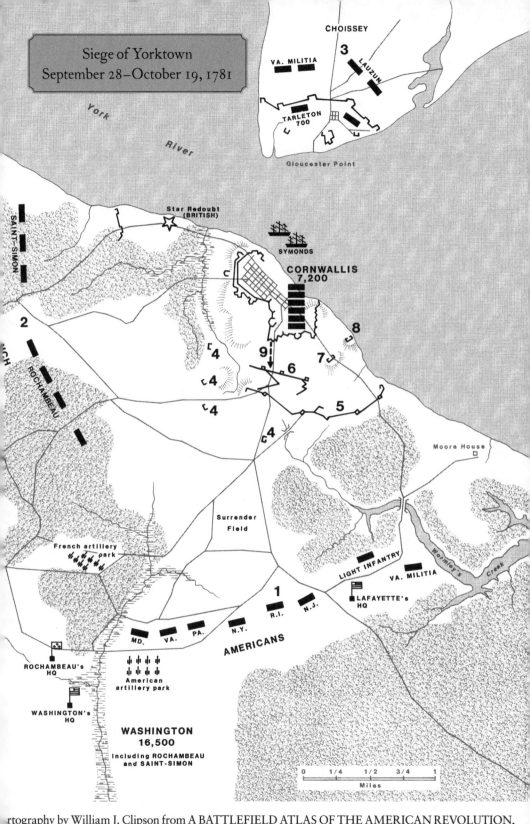

Siege of Yorktown
September 28–October 19, 1781

CHOISSEY

VA. MILITIA

3

LAUZUN

TARLETON
700

Gloucester Point

York

River

Star Redoubt
(BRITISH)

SAINT-SIMON

SYMONDS

CORNWALLIS
7,200

2

ROCHAMBEAU

4

4

9

6

8

7

4

5

4

Moore House

Surrender
Field

Wormley's

Creek

French artillery
park

LIGHT INFANTRY

VA. MILITIA

1

R.I.

N.J.

LAFAYETTE'S
HQ

MD.

VA.

PA.

N.Y.

AMERICANS

ROCHAMBEAU's
HQ

American
artillery park

WASHINGTON's
HQ

WASHINGTON
16,500

including ROCHAMBEAU
and SAINT-SIMON

0   1/4   1/2   3/4   1
Miles

rtography by William J. Clipson from A BATTLEFIELD ATLAS OF THE AMERICAN REVOLUTION,
blished by Savas Beatie, www.savasbeatie.com

Publisher's Note

Why *The 10 Key Campaigns of the American Revolution?* There are other fine books that explain the battles and skirmishes of the American War for Independence from 1774 to 1783. This volume is a collection of narratives from some of today's most respected experts in the field, focusing on the momentous actions that forged what became the most powerful nation in modern history. Launched by the ideals of the Age of Enlightenment, the American War for Independence from Britain set in motion a model of democratic republican government. The American Revolution was a world war. Societies and other nations would transform from ancient and medieval aristocracies to the precepts of self-governance. The founding principles were a reflection of both their era and the vision of men who recognized that society changes, that government would have to adjust to change, and that only the collective peoples of a nation should decide how that change would benefit the population.

The ten key campaigns of the American Revolution were the military nexuses of this global transformation. This book is a primer for those who want to begin their understanding of the Revolution, an introduction for those who know about some of the battles but would like to know more, and a collection of new insights for scholars and historians who are just looking for a more robust understanding of this momentous time in world history. We are truly blessed to have had the time and attention from Edward G. Lengel and his colleagues in this endeavor.

One key feature of this book is the suggested further readings and resources about this topic of import to all readers: Americans, new immigrants, and readers from other countries. We invite you to support all the authors in this book by reading the books they have recommended. A more complete list of recommended titles can be found at the *Journal of the American Revolution*'s website at allthingsliberty.com, under the "Books" tab.

Special Mention: We are grateful to the partnership and support of Ted Savas, publisher of Savas Beatie (savasbeatie.com). The maps in this volume are from Savas Beatie's *A Battlefield Atlas of the American Revolution* by Craig L. Symonds, with cartography by William J. Clipson. Savas Beatie also publishes books from the Emerging Revolutionary War Series. As its mission states, the Emerging Revolutionary War Era group "offers engaging perspectives on the Revolutionary War era" at emergingrevolutionarywar.org.

We encourage all to visit and support America's Revolutionary War sites and museums. There are some excellent podcasts, conferences and American Revolutionary War round tables that offer stories, author talks, and demonstrations. There are heritage organizations that will help citizens learn more about their ancestors, offer educational programs for all ages, benefit communities, and support civic organizations and historic preservation. You can ask your local reference librarian to help you find resources. Here are a few recommended resources:

Recommended Websites
1. boston1775.blogspot.com
2. revolutionarywar.us
3. allthingsliberty.com
4. amrevmuseum.org
5. mountvernon.org
6. battlefields.org
7. tencrucialdays.org

Podcasts

1. *Ben Franklin's World*
2. *The American Revolution Podcast*
3. *American Military History Podcast*
4. *Dispatches, The Podcast of the Journal of the American Revolution*

Heritage Organizations

1. Society of the Cincinnati
2. Daughters of the American Revolution
3. Children of the American Revolution
4. Sons of the Revolution
5. Sons of the American Revolution
6. Sons and Daughters of the United States Middle Passage

Notes

Let It Begin Here

1. Thomas Gage Papers, 1754–1783, William Clements Library, Ann Arbor, Michigan: University of Michigan.
2. John Parker, disposition dated Lexington, April 25, 1775, in Peter Force, ed., *American Archives*, Series 4, Volume II, 491.
3. Ibid; Major John Pitcairn to Lieutenant General Thomas Gage, letter report dated Boston, April 26, 1775, Thomas Gage Papers.
4. Entries June 14–17, 1775, *Journals of the Continental Congress, 1774–1789*, edited from the original records in the Library of Congress, vol. 2 (Washington, D.C.: Government Printing Office, 1904), 89–96.

The Fourteenth Colony: The Quebec Campaign

1. *Journals of the Continental Congress*, vol. 2 (Washington, D.C.: Government Printing Office, 1905), online edition, http://memory.loc.gov/ammem/amlaw/lwjclink.html, 109–10.
2. "Philip Schuyler to Continental Congress, September 19, 1775," in Peter Force, ed., *American Archives*, Series 4, 3: 738.
3. "George Washington to Benedict Arnold, September 15, 1775" and "Address to the Inhabitants of Canada, September 14, 1775," in W. W. Abbot, ed., *Papers of George Washington* (Charlottesville, Virginia: University of Virginia Press, 1985), 1: 455, 462.
4. "George Morison Journal, November 4, 1775," in Kenneth Roberts, ed., *March to Quebec: Journals of the Members of Arnold's Expedition* (New York: Doubleday, 1938), 571.

All London Was Afloat

1. Daniel McCurtin, "Journal of the Times at the Siege of Boston Since Our Arrival at Cambridge Near Boston," in Thomas Balch, ed., *Papers*

Relating to the Maryland Line during the Revolution (Philadelphia, 1857), 127.

2. Tryon to Lord George Germain, July 8, 1776. Colonial Office, Class 5, Volume 1107, folio 372, Great Britain, the National Archives (hereafter cited as TNA).

3. Ambrose Serle, *The American Journal of Ambrose Serle,* ed. by Edward H. Tatum Jr. (San Marino, California: the Huntington Library, 1940), 40. The term "Tory Hunting" was indeed used occasionally by American troops as shown in this letter from November 13, 1776: "Last night I went tory hunting with a party of 50 men, but the birds had flown before we arrived...." *Pennsylvania Journal and Weekly Advertiser,* November 20, 1776.

4. Winslow to Dr. John Jeffries, c. 1781. Winslow Family Papers, Vol. 2, No. 40, University of New Brunswick Archives.

5. Letter of Lieutenant Loftus Cliffe, Forty-Sixth Regiment of Foot, New York, September 21, 1776. Loftus Cliffe Papers, No. 3, University of Michigan, William L. Clements Library.

6. The Journals of Lt. Col. Stephen Kemble, 1773–1789. Collections of the New-York Historical Society for 1883, printed for the society (1884), 81.

7. *New-York Gazette* and the *Weekly Mercury,* August 5, 1776.

8. Washington to Hancock, New York, July 10, 1776. Papers of the Continental Congress, M247, Reel 166, Item 152, Vol. 2, 189–93, National Archives and Records Administration (hereafter cited as NARA).

9. Serle, *The American Journal,* 71.

10. Asa Stone to Benjamin Stone, Camp in Greenwich, August 24, 1776. Miscellaneous Manuscript No. 13237, New York State Library.

11. Some Hessian troops were armed with rifles. Known as Jaegers (Hunters), these marksmen served on both horse and foot, wearing a distinctive green uniform.

12. British General Orders, New Utrecht, August 25, 1776. Orderly Book of Lieutenant John Peebles, Fourth Battalion Grenadiers, GD 21/492/2, Scottish Record Office.

13. Captain William Dansey to his mother, Long Island, September 3, 1776. William Dansey Letters, Historical Society of Delaware.

14. "Extract of a Letter from an Officer in Col. Atlee's Battalion of Pennsylvania, August 27," *Virginia Gazette,* September 14, 1776.

15. Pension Application of Isaac Pier, September 26, 1832. Collection M-804, Pension and Bounty Land Application Files, No. S1082, Isaac Pier, New Jersey, NARA.

16. Pension Application of James Karr, October 12, 1833. M-804, Pension and Bounty Land Application Files, No. S2673, James Karr, Pennsylvania, NARA.

17. Brodhead to unknown recipient, camp near Kingsbridge, September 5, 1776. Lloyd W. Smith Collection, No. 2952, Morristown National Historical Park Library.

18. Pension Application of Matthias Riker, November 12, 1832. Collection M-804, Pension and Bounty Land Application Files, No. S11294, Matthias Riker, New Jersey/New York, NARA.

19. *Virginia Gazette* (Williamsburg), September 21, 1776.

20. Unpublished Diary of Thompson Forster, Staff Surgeon of His Majesty's Detached Hospital in North America, transcribed in 1938 from the original in the possession of Robert Ethelstone Thompson Forster, 89–91.

21. Memorial of Richard Vanberbugh to the Lords of the Treasury, c-1781. Audit Office, Class 13, Vol. 67, folios 386–387, TNA.

22. Colonel Johann August von Loos to Frederick Christian Arnold, freiherr von Jungkenn, Long Island, August 31, 1776. Henry J. Retzer and Don Londahl-Smidt, ed., "The New York-New Jersey Campaign, 1776–1777, Letters from the von Jungkenn Papers," *Journal of the Johannes Schwalm Historical Association* 5, no. 4 (1996), 75.

23. Sir Henry Clinton, *The American Rebellion: Sir Henry Clinton's Narrative of His Campaigns, 1775–1782, with an Appendix of Original Documents,* William B. Willcox, ed. (New Haven, Connecticut: Yale University Press, 1954), 43.

24. Bernhard Uhlendorf, ed., *Revolution in America: Confidential Letters and Journals 1776–1784 of Adjutant General Major Baurmeister of the Hessian Forces* (New Brunswick, New Jersey: Rutgers University Press, 1957), 39.

25. Howe to Lord George Germain, Newtown, Long Island, September 3, 1776. Colonial Office, Class 5, Vol. 93, 515–21, TNA.

26. Grant to Richard Rigby, Long Island, September 2, 1776. James Grant Papers of Ballindalloch Castle, Scotland; Library of Congress Microcopy, Reel 28, Container/Box 29 MFilP/GD494/1/Box 29.

27. Continental Army Council of War, Long Island, August 29, 1776. George Washington Papers, Series 4, General Correspondence,

1697–1799, MSS 44693, Reel 038, Library of Congress (hereafter cited as LOC).

28. Pension Application of George Owrey, May 21, 1833. M-804, Pension and Bounty Land Application Files, No. S17613, George Owrey, Pennsylvania, NARA.

29. *Continental Journal* and *Weekly Advertiser* (Boston), September 19, 1776.

30. Pension Application of John Ely, November 26, 1832. M-804, Pension and Bounty Land Application Files, No. S3329, John Ely, Connecticut, NARA.

31. *New-York Gazette* and the *Weekly Mercury*, September 2, 1776.

32. The muster rolls of the Second Battalion, Royal Highland Emigrants show September 3, 1776, to be they date of enlistment of these men. The case of Robert William Walker, planter of Maryland, undated. Audit Office, Class 13, Vol. 40, folios 234–236, TNA.

33. Serle, *The American Journal,* 100–101.

34. Scott to Washington, New York, August 31, 1776. George Washington Papers, Series 4, General Correspondence, 1697–1799, MSS 44693, Reel 038, LOC.

35. Letter of Captain Francis, Lord Rawdon. Great Britain, Historical Manuscripts Commission, Report on the Manuscripts of the late Reginald Rawdon Hastings Esq. Francis Bickley, ed. (London: H.M. Stationery Office, 1928), III, 179–80, as quoted in William P. Cumming and Hugh Rankin, *The Fate of a Nation: The American Revolution through Contemporary Eyes* (London: Phaidon Press, 1975), 110–11.

36. Resolve of Congress, signed by John Hancock, September 10, 1776. George Washington Papers, Series 4, General Correspondence, 1697–1799, MSS 44693, Reel 038, LOC.

37. Serle, *The American Journal,* 47–48.

38. Henry Knox to Lucy Knox, Camp near White Plains, November 10, 1776. Henry Knox Papers, Vol. 3, No. 83, Massachusetts Historical Society.

39. "[I] saw Gen. George Washington in tears, walking the porch & conversed with him." Pension Application of Lawrence Everhart, April 7, 1834. Collection M-804, Pension and Bounty Land Application Files, No. S25068, Lawrence Everhart, Maryland, NARA.

The Times That Try Men's Souls:
The Crossing and the Ten Crucial Days

1.   Colonel John Chester to Colonel Samuel Blachley Webb, Wethersfield, January 17, 1777, from original in "Webb" MSS, Henry Johnston, *Yale and Her Honor Roll in the American Revolution* (New York: 1888), 61–62.
2.   David Avery, *The Lord Is to Be Praised for the Triumphs of His Power* (Norwich, Connecticut: 1778), 24.
3.   Johann Ewald, *Diary of the American War: A Hessian Journal* (New Haven, Connecticut: Yale University Press, 1979), 49–50.
4.   *The Pennsylvania Packet*, December 6, 1781, 3.

Gentleman John Burgoyne's Great Gamble:
Ticonderoga to Saratoga

1.   Quoted in A. J. O'Shaughnessy, *The Men Who Lost America: British Leadership, the American Revolution, and the Fate of the Empire* (New Haven, Connecticut: Yale University Press, 2013), 87. See also the author's incisive essay on Burgoyne, 123–64.
2.   J. K. Martin, *Benedict Arnold, Revolutionary Hero: An American Warrior Reconsidered* (New York: New York University Press, 1997), 246–92.
3.   John Burgoyne to Henry Clinton, July 7, 1776, and Burgoyne to Clinton, November 7, 1776, in D. R. Cubbison, ed., *Burgoyne and the Saratoga Campaign: His Papers* (Norman, Oklahoma: Arthur H. Clark Co., 2012), 151, 158–60.
4.   Ibid., 160–161.
5.   "Thoughts for Conducting the War," February 28, 1777, ibid., 178–86. See also "Memorandum & Observations Related to the Service in Canada, submitted to Lord George Germain," Burgoyne's Commentary on Guy Carleton's Thoughts for German, ibid., 169–78.
6.   James Kirby Martin, "The Northern Theater: Setting the Stage for Victory," in J. K Martin and D. L. Preston, eds., *Theaters of the American Revolution: Northern, Middle, Southern, Western, Naval* (Yardley, Pennsylvania: Westholme Publishers, 2017), 28–29; O'Shaughnessy, *Men Who Lost America*, 144–47; Cubbison, *Burgoyne*, 46–51.
7.   British generals traveling in great style was fairly common in the class-based realities of the era. Certainly, General Howe represents an

excellent example with all of his baggage plus his well-known consort, Mrs. Joshua, Elizabeth Loring. See O'Shaughnessy, *Men Who Lost America*, 96–98, 147–49. Chronicler Horace Walpole was the commentator who called Burgoyne "General Swagger."

8. "Manifesto Issued by Lieut. Genl. Burgoyne," June 24, 1777, in Cubbison, ed., *Burgoyne*, 201–3.

9. Phillips quoted in Hoffman Nickerson, *The Turning Point of the Revolution, or Burgoyne in America*, 2 vols. (Port Washington, New York: Kennikat Press, 1967), 144. Reprint of original 1928 edition.

10. B. M. Venter, *The Battle of Hubbardton: The Rear Guard Action That Saved America* (Acadia, South Carolina: The History Press, 2015).

11. John Burgoyne to George Germain (Private), July 11, 1777, in K. G. Davies, ed., *Documents of the American Revolution, 1770–1783* (21 vols., Shannon: Irish Academic Press, 1972–1981), 14: 142.

12. F. E. Grizzard et al., eds., "Benedict Arnold to George Washington, July 27, 1777," in. F. E. Grizzard, *The Papers of George Washington, Revolutionary War Series* (Charlottesville, Virginia: University Press of Virginia), 10: 433–35.

13. John Burgoyne to George Germain, July 30, 1777, and Burgoyne to Germain (Private), July 30, 1777, in Davies, ed., *Documents of the American Revolution*, 14: 153–55.

14. M. L. Brown, ed., *Baroness von Riedesel and the American Revolution: Journal and Correspondence of a Tour of Duty, 1776–1783* (Chapel Hill, North Carolina: University of North Carolina Press, 1965), 55–56.

15. John Burgoyne to George Germain (Private), August 20, 1777, in Davies, ed., *Documents of the American Revolution*, 14: 164.

16. J. T. Glatthaar and J. K. Martin, *Forgotten Allies: The Oneida Indians and the American Revolution* (New York: Hill and Wang, 2006), 124–87.

17. John Burgoyne to George Germain, October 20, 1777, in Davies, ed., *Documents of the American Revolution*, 14: 231.

The Monmouth Campaign, June 1778: Tactical Draw, Political Victory

1. General Orders, 5 May 1778, PGWde, RWS, 15:38–39; Bloomfield, Diary, 134; Washington to the President of Congress, 4 May 1778, and General Orders, 5 May 1778, PGWde, RWS, 15:39.

2. Nathanael Greene to GW, 24 June 1778, in Richard K. Showman, Robert E. McCarthy, and Margaret Cobb, eds., *The Papers of Nathanael Greene*, 13 vols. (Chapel Hill: University of North Carolina Press, 1980–2005), 2: 447.

3. GW to Lafayette, 26 June 1778, PGWde, RWS, 15:552–53.

4. Testimony of Charles Scott and Anthony Wayne, in Charles Lee, defendant, Proceedings of a General Court Martial. Held at Brunswick, in the State of New Jersey, by Order of His Excellency Gen. Washington...for the Trial of Major-General Lee. July 4, 1778. Major-General Lord Stirling, President [hereafter PLCM] (New York: privately printed, 1864), 5–8.

5. For a full timeline of the campaign and battle, see Lender and Stone, *Fatal Sunday*, 441–50.

6. Testimony of Lee and Lieutenant Colonel John Brooks, PLCM, 169, 215, 218–19.

7. Lafayette and Scott are quoted in Lender and Stone, *Fatal Sunday,* 290. For a full discussion of the Washington–Lee encounter, see ibid., 288–91.

8. William Hale to his father, 14 July 1778, in W. H. Wilkin, ed., *Some British Soldiers in America* (London: Hugh Rees, 1914), 263.

9. Israel Shreve to Polly Shreve, 2 July 1778, Ferdinand J. Dreer Collection, Soldiers of the American Revolution Series, Box 4, Sr. 52:2, Vol. 4, Historical Society of Pennsylvania, Philadelphia; William Irvine to John Davis, 30 June 1778, Pennsylvania Magazine of History and Biography 2 (1878): 148; Persifor Frazer to Polly Frazer, 30 June 1778, Persifor Frazer, *Persifor Frazer: A Memoir Compiled Principally from His Own Papers* (Philadelphia, privately printed, 1907), 183.

10. Marie Joseph Paul Yves Roch Gilbert Du Motier, Marquis de Lafayette, in Stanley J. Idzerda et al., eds., *Lafayette in the Age of the American Revolution: Selected Letters and Papers, 1776–1790,* 5 vols. (Ithaca, New York: Cornell University Press, 1979), 2: 11; James McHenry, "The Battle of Monmouth," *Magazine of American History* 3 (1879): 356.

11. Loftus Cliffe to unknown, 5 July 1778, Loftus Cliffe Papers, William L. Clements Library, University of Michigan; Erskine's remark is related in Henry Laurens to Lachlan McIntosh, 23 August 1778, LDC, 10:494.

12. GW to Henry Laurens, 29 June 1778, PGWde, RWS, 15:587; GW to Henry Laurens, 1 July 1778, ibid., 16:2–26.

13. John Hancock to Dorothy Hancock, 1 July 1778, LDC, 10:216–17; Titus Hosmer to Richard Law, and Hosmer to Thomas Mumford, 6 July 1778, ibid., 10:226–27. For similar letters, see also Elias Boudinot to

Hannah Boudinot, 7 July 1778; John Mathews to Thomas Bee, 7 July 1778; Thomas McKean to William Atlee, 7 July 1778; ibid., 10: 232, 234–35, 237; Samuel Adams to John Adams, 25 October 1778, in *The Writings of Samuel Adams*, ed. by Harry Alonzo Cushing, 4 vols. (New York: G. P. Putnam's Sons, 1907), 4:79; John Banister to Theodorick Bland, 6 July 1778, *The Bland Papers: Being a Selection from the Manuscripts of Colonel Theodorick Bland, Jr.; To Which Are Prefixed an Introduction, and a Memoir of Colonel Bland.*, ed. by Charles Campbell, 2 vols. (Petersburg, Virginia: Edmund & Julian C. Ruffin, 1840–42), 1:96; Henry Laurens to John Laurens, 6 July 1778, LDC, 10:229; 7 July 1778, *Journals of the Continental Congress, 1774–1789*, ed. by Worthington C. Ford et al., 34 vols. (Washington, D.C.: U.S. Government Printing Office, 1904–1937), 11:673; General Orders, 11 July 1778, PGWde, RWS, 16:51.

14. Elias Boudinot to Alexander Hamilton, 8 July 1778, LDC, 10:238.
15. Alexander Hamilton to Elias Boudinot, 5 July 1778, *The Papers of Alexander Hamilton*, ed. by Harold C. Syrett and Jacob E. Cooke, 27 vols. (New York: Columbia University Press, 1961–1987), 1:513.
16. John Shy, "Charles Lee: The Soldier as Radical," in George Athan Billias, ed., *George Washington's Generals* (New York: William Morrow and Company, 1964), 45.
17. PLCM, 4.
18. David Ramsay, *The History of the American Revolution* (Philadelphia, Pennsylvania: R. Aitken & Son, 1789), 85–86; Henry Laurens to Rawlins Lowndes, 18 August 1778, LDC, 10:478; Gouverneur Morris to George Washington, 26 October 1778, ibid., 11:127; Henry Laurens to Rawlins Lowndes, 7 December 1778, ibid., 11:297.
19. Charles Lee to Benjamin Rush, 13 August 1778, *The Lee Papers, 1754–1811*, 4 vols., Collections of the New-York Historical Society (New York: New-York Historical Society, 1871–74), 3:299; Charles Lee to Aaron Burr, October 1778, ibid., 3:238.
20. Lender and Stone, *Fatal Sunday*, 400.
21. George Washington to Thomas Nelson, 20 August 1778, PGWde, RWS, 16:340.

Charleston to King's Mountain:
The Southern Partisan Campaign

1. David Vance, *Narrative of the Battle of King's Mountain* (Greensboro, North Carolina: D. Schenck, 1891), 28.
2. Charles Woodmason, *The Carolina Backcountry on the Eve of the Revolution: The Journal and Other Writings of Charles Woodmason, Anglican Itinerant,* ed. by Richard J. Hooker (Chapel Hill, North Carolina: University of North Carolina Press, 1953), 273.
3. Archibald Campbell, *Journal of [...] Archibald Campbell, Esquire, Lieut. Colo of His Majesty's 71ˢᵗ Regiment, 1778,* ed. Colin Campbell (Darien, Georiga: Ashantilly Press, 1981), 45–46.
4. Woodmason, *The Carolina Back Country,* 60–61.
5. Cornwallis to John Harris Cruger, August 5, 1780, in *The Cornwallis Papers [...]* , 6 vols., ed. by Ian Saberton (Uckfield, U.K.: 2010), 1:256.
6. Cornwallis to Clinton, June 30, 1780, in Benjamin Franklin Stevens, *The Campaign in Virginia, 1781: An Exact Reprint of Six Rare Pamphlets on the Clinton-Cornwallis Controversy,* 2 vols. (London, 1882), 1: 223.
7. William Richardson Davie, *The Revolutionary War Sketches of William R. Davie,* ed. Blackwell P. Robinson (Raleigh: North Carolina Division of Archives & History, 1976), 8.
8. Thomas Young, "Memoir of Major Thomas Young, a Revolutionary Patriot of South Carolina," *Orion* 3 (October 1843), 85-86.
9. James Collins, *Autobiography of a Revolutionary Soldier, in Sixty Years in the Nueces Valley, 1870–1939* (San Antonio: Naylor Printing Company, 1930), 239.
10. Isaac Shelby, "Kings Mountain, Letters of Colonel Isaac Shelby," ed. by J. G. Roulhac Hamilton, *Journal of Southern History,* 4:3 (August 1938), 371.
11. Samuel Hammond's Account, in William T. Graves, *Backcountry Revolutionary: James Williams (1740–1780) [...]* (Lugoff, South Carolina: Woodward Corporation, 2012), 104.
12. Shelby, "Letters," 372.
13. Lyman C. Draper, *King's Mountain and Its Heroes [...]* (Cincinnati, Ohio: P. G. Thomson, 1881), 169.
14. Draper, *King's Mountain,* 176.
15. Pat Ferguson, speech, November 11, 1780, quoted in Draper, *King's Mountain,* 204.
16. Draper, *King's Mountain,* 230.

17. Ibid., 564
18. Ibid., 511.
19. Collins, *Autobiography*, 259–60.
20. Young, *Memoir*, 86.
21. Collins, *Autobiography*, 260–61.
22. Henry Lumpkin, *From Savannah to Yorktown: The American Revolution in the South* (New York: Paragon House, 1981), 100.
23. Allaire, letter, February 24, 1781, in Draper, *King's Mountain*, 517.
24. Henry's Account, in Vance, *Narrative*, 35.
25. Alexander Chesney, *Journal of Capt. Alexander Chesney*, ed. by Bobby Gilmer Moss (Blacksburg, South Carolina: Scotia-Hibernia Press, 2002), 31.
26. Draper, *King's Mountain*, 313.
27. Collins, *Autobiography*, 26.
28. Cruger's opinion is in Lord Rawdon to Clinton, October 29, 1780, in Charles Cornwallis, *Correspondence of Charles, First Marquis Cornwallis*, 3 vols., ed. Charles Ross (London: John Murray, 1859), 1:63.
29. Henry Clinton, *American Rebellion* […], ed. by William B. Willcox (New Haven, Connecticut: Yale University Press, 1954), 226.

En Avant to Victory: The Allied March to Yorktown, June–October 1781

1. John C. Fitzpatrick, ed., *The Writings of George Washington*, 39 vols., (Washington, D.C.: Government Printing Office, 1937), 21:439.
2. Ezra Stiles, *The Literary Diary of Ezra Stiles*, vol. 2 (New York: Charles Scribner's Sons 190), 459.
3. William P. Palmer et. al., eds., *Calendar of Virginia State Papers and other Manuscripts from April 1, 1781, to December 31, 1781*, vol. 2. (Richmond, Virginia: James E. Goode, 1881), 567.
4. George Washington, *The Diaries of George Washington, 1748–1799*, ed. by John C. Fitzpatrick, 3 vols., (Boston and New York: Houghton Mifflin Co., 1925), 2:217–18.
5. J. Henry Doniol, *Histoire de la participation de la France a l'Établissement des États-Unis d'Amérique,* 5 vols. (Paris: Imprimerie Nationale, 1886–1892), 5:475.
6. Doniol, *Histoire*, 5:487; the English translation quoted here in Washington, *Writings*, 22:206n91.

7. Clermont-Crèvecœur, Journal, in Rice and Brown, *American Campaigns*, 1:33.
8. Evelyn Acomb, ed., *The Revolutionary Journal of Baron Ludwig von Closen, 1780–1783* (Chapel Hill, North Carolina: University of North Carolina Press, 1958), 89.
9. Journal de l'Armée aux ordres de Monsieur de Comte de Rochambeau pendant les campagnes de 1780, 1781, 1782, 1783 dans l'Amérique septentrionale, fol. 74., Bibliothèque Nationale, Nouvelle Acquisitions Françaises, 17691, Paris, France.
10. Jonathan Trumbull, *The Trumbull Papers*, vol. 2, in Collections of the Massachusetts Historical Society, Fifth Series vol. 10, (Boston: The Society, 1888), 256–57.
11. Doniol, *Histoire*, 5:521.
12. Washington, *Diaries*, 2:254.
13. Washington, *Writings*, 22:501–502.
14. Acomb, *The Revolutionary Journal*, 123.
15. Jonathan R. Dull, *The French Navy and American Independence: A Study of Arms and Diplomacy, 1774–1787* (Princeton, New Jersey: Princeton University Press, 1975), 239.
16. Popham to Gov. Clinton of New York, 8 September 1781, quoted in Henry P. Johnston, *The Yorktown Campaign and the Surrender of Cornwallis, 1781* (New York, 1881), 173.
17. "Minutes of Occurrences respecting the Seige and Capture of York in Virginia, extracted from the Journal of Colonel Jonathan Trumbull, Secretary to the General, 1781," Proceedings of the Massachusetts Historical Society, vol. 14 (1875–1876), 331–338, 333.
18. John Van Court, Ensign John Van Court Journal, Society of the Cincinnati, Washington, D.C.
19. *Cist's Advertiser* (Cincinnati) vol. 3, no. 5, February 11, 1846.
20. James Thacher, *Military Journal of the American Revolution* (Hartford, Connecticut: 1862), 284.
21. Acomb, *The Revolutionary Journal*, 146–47.
22. Robert A. Selig, "Eyewitness to Yorktown," *Military History* (February 2003), 58–64, 60.
23. Jane A. Baum, Hans-Peter Baum, Jesko Graf zu Dohna, eds., *Die Abenteuer des Grafen Friedrich Reinhard von Rechteren-Limpurg im Mittelmeer und im Amerikanischen Unabhängigkeitskrieg 1770 bis 1782/The Adventures of Friedrich Reinhard Count of Rechteren-Limpurg in the Mediterranean and the American War of*

Independence 1770–1782 (bi-lingual), Mainfränkische Hefte 115 (Würzburg, 2016), 109.

24. Johann Ewald, *Diary of the American War: A Hessian Journal*, trans. and ed. by Joseph P. Tustin (New Haven and London: Yale University Press, 1979), 341.

25. Joachim du Perron, Comte de Revel, *Journal Particulier d'une Campagne aux Indes Occidentales (1781-1782)* (Paris: Chez Henri Charles-Lavauzelle, 1898), 172.

26. "'The Drumbeats to Arms.…' Two Letters from Yorktown and a Missing Map," *The Princeton University Library Chronicle* 31, no. 3 (1970), 209–13, 213.

27. "Traditions of the American War of Independence," *Museum of Foreign Literature, Science and Art* 26 (Philadelphia, Pennsylvania: 1835), 91–97.

28. *Pennsylvania Packet* (Philadelphia), November 13, 1781.

29. Revolutionary War Pension and Bounty Land Application Files, Collection M-804, Record Group 15, No. W 8852, National Archives and Records Administration, Washington, D.C.

30. Thacher, Military Journal, 288.

Index